LibreOffice Draw 4.3

A catalogue record for this book is available from the Hong Kong Public Libraries.

Published by Samurai Media Limited.

Email: info@samuraimedia.org

ISBN 978-988-14435-5-7

Contents

Preface

Who is this book for?

Anyone who wants to get up to speed quickly with LibreOffice Draw will find this guide valuable. You may be new to drawing software, or you may be familiar with another program.

What is in this book?

This book introduces the main features of LibreOffice Draw. Draw is a vector graphics drawing tool, although it can also perform some operations on raster graphics (pixels) such as photographs. Using Draw, you can quickly create a wide variety of graphical images.

A few examples of the drawing functions are: layer management, snap functions and grid-point system, dimensions and measurement display, connectors for making organization charts, 3D functions that enable small three-dimensional drawings to be created (with texture and lighting effects), drawing and page-style integration, and Bézier curves.

The *Draw Guide* is not a course book to be worked through from beginning to end. Rather, it is a reference work in which you can browse for guidance on particular topics.

Where to get more help?

This guide, the other LibreOffice user guides, the built-in Help system, and user support systems assume that you are familiar with your computer and basic functions such as starting a program, opening and saving files.

Help system

LibreOffice comes with an extensive Help system. This is your first line of support for using LibreOffice.

To display the full Help system, press *F1* or go to **Help > LibreOffice Help** on the main menu bar. In addition, you can choose whether to activate *Tips*, *Extended tips*, and the *Help Agent* by going to **Tools > Options > LibreOffice > General** on the main menu bar.

If *Tips* are enabled, place the mouse pointer over any of the icons to see a small box (tooltip) with a brief explanation of the icon function. For a more detailed explanation, select **Help > What's This?** On the main menu bar and hold the pointer over the icon.

Free online support

The LibreOffice community not only develops software, but provides free, volunteer-based support. See Table 1 and this web page: http://www.libreoffice.org/get-help/

Users can get comprehensive online support from the community through mailing lists and the Ask LibreOffice website, http://ask.libreoffice.org/en/questions/. Other websites run by users also offer free tips and tutorials.

This forum provides community support for LibreOffice: http://en.libreofficeforum.org/.

This site provides support for LibreOffice and other programs: https://forum.openoffice.org/en/forum/.

Paid support and training

Alternatively, you can pay for support services. Service contracts can be purchased from a vendor or consulting firm specializing in LibreOffice.

Table 1: Free support for LibreOffice users

Free LibreOffice support	
Ask LibreOffice	Questions and answers from the LibreOffice community http://ask.libreoffice.org/en/questions/
Documentation	User guides, how-tos, and other documentation. http://www.libreoffice.org/get-help/documentation/ https://wiki.documentfoundation.org/Documentation/Publications
FAQs	Answers to frequently asked questions http://wiki.documentfoundation.org/Faq
Mailing lists	Free community support is provided by a network of experienced users http://www.libreoffice.org/get-help/mailing-lists/
International support	The LibreOffice website in your language. http://www.libreoffice.org/international-sites/ International mailing lists http://wiki.documentfoundation.org/Local_Mailing_Lists
Accessibility options	Information about available accessibility options. http://www.libreoffice.org/get-help/accessibility/

What you see may be different

Illustrations

LibreOffice runs on Windows, Linux, and Mac OS X operating systems, each of which has several versions and can be customized by users (fonts, colors, themes, window managers). The illustrations in this guide were taken from a variety of computers and operating systems. Therefore, some illustrations will not look exactly like what you see on your computer display.

Also, some of the dialogs may be differ because of the settings selected in LibreOffice. You can either use dialogs from your computer system (default) or dialogs provided by LibreOffice. To change to using LibreOffice dialogs:

1) On Linux and Windows operating systems, go to **Tools > Options > LibreOffice > General** on the main menu bar to open the dialog for general options.

2) On a Mac operating system, go to **LibreOffice > Preferences > General** on the main menu bar to open the dialog for general options.

3) Select *Use LibreOffice dialogs* in *Open/Save dialogs* to display the LibreOffice dialogs on your computer display.

4) Click **OK** to save your settings and close the dialog.

Icons

The icons used to illustrate some of the many tools available in LibreOffice may differ from the ones used in this guide. The icons in this guide have been taken from a LibreOffice installation that has been set to display the Galaxy set of icons.

If you wish, you can change your LibreOffice software package to display Galaxy icons as follows:

1) On Linux and Windows operating systems, go to **Tools > Options > LibreOffice > View** on the main menu bar to open the dialog for view options.

2) On a Mac operating system, go to **LibreOffice > Preferences > View** on the main menu bar to open the dialog for view options.

3) In *User interface > Icon size and style* select *Galaxy* from the options available in the drop down list.

4) Click **OK** to save your settings and close the dialog.

Note	Some Linux operating systems, for example Ubuntu, include LibreOffice as part of the installation and may not include the Galaxy icon set. You should be able to download the Galaxy icons from the software repository for your Linux operating system.

Using LibreOffice on a Mac

Some keystrokes and menu items are different on a Mac from those used in Windows and Linux. The table below gives some common substitutions for the instructions in this chapter. For a more detailed list, see the application Help.

Windows or Linux	Mac equivalent	Effect
Tools > Options menu selection	**LibreOffice > Preferences**	Access setup options
Right-click	*Control+click* and/or *right-click* depending on computer setup	Open a context menu
Ctrl (Control)	⌘ *(Command)*	Used with other keys
F5	*Shift+⌘+F5*	Open the Navigator
F11	*⌘+T*	Open the Styles and Formatting window

What are all these things called?

The terms used in LibreOffice for most parts of the *user interface* (the parts of the program you see and use, in contrast to the behind-the-scenes code that actually makes it work) are the same as for most other programs.

A *dialog* is a special type of window. Its purpose is to inform you of something, or request input from you, or both. It provides controls for you to use to specify how to carry out an action. The technical names for common controls are shown in Figure 1. In most cases we do not use the technical terms in this book, but it is useful to know them because the Help and other sources of information often use them.

1) Tabbed page (not strictly speaking a control).

2) Radio buttons (only one can be selected at a time).

3) Checkbox (more than one can be selected at a time).

4) Spin box (click the up and down arrows to change the number shown in the text box next to it, or type in the text box).

5) Thumbnail or preview.

6) Drop-down list from which to select an item.

7) Push buttons.

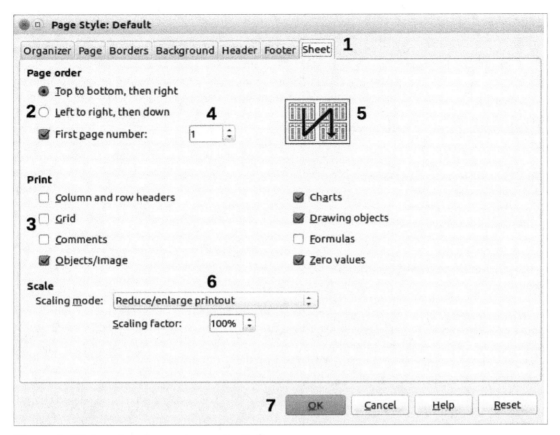

Figure 1: Dialog showing common controls

In most cases, you can interact only with the dialog (not the document itself) as long as the dialog remains open. When you close the dialog after use (usually, clicking **OK** or another button saves your changes and closes the dialog), then you can again work with your document.

Some dialogs can be left open as you work, so you can switch back and forth between the dialog and your document. An example of this type is the Find & Replace dialog.

Who wrote this book?

This book was written by volunteers from the LibreOffice community. Profits from sales of the printed edition will be used to benefit the community.

Acknowledgements

This book is adapted and updated from *OpenOffice.org 3.3 Draw Guide*. The contributors to that book are:

Agnes Belzunce   Daniel Carrera   Martin Fox
Thomas Hackert   Regina Henschel   Peter Hillier-Brook
Jared Kobos   Hazel Russman   Gary Schnabl
Bernd Schukat   Wolfgang Uhlig   Jean Hollis Weber
Claire Wood   Linda Worthington

Frequently asked questions

How is LibreOffice licensed?
> LibreOffice is distributed under the Open Source Initiative (OSI) approved Mozilla Public License (MPL). The MPL license is available from http://www.mozilla.org/MPL/2.0/.

May I distribute LibreOffice to anyone?
> Yes.

How many computers may I install it on?
> As many as you like.

May I sell it?
> Yes.

May I use LibreOffice in my business?
> Yes.

Is LibreOffice available in my language?
> LibreOffice has been translated (localized) into over 40 languages, so your language probably is supported. Additionally, there are over 70 *spelling*, *hyphenation*, and *thesaurus* dictionaries available for languages, and dialects that do not have a localized program interface. The dictionaries are available from the LibreOffice website at: www.libreoffice.org.

How can you make it for free?
> LibreOffice is developed and maintained by volunteers and has the backing of several organizations.

How can I contribute to LibreOffice?
> You can help with the development and user support of LibreOffice in many ways, and you do not need to be a programmer. For example, you can help with producing and maintaining written user documentation, producing video tutorials, and other user support services. To start, check out this webpage: http://www.documentfoundation.org/contribution/

May I distribute the PDF of this book, or print and sell copies?
> Yes, as long as you meet the requirements of one of the licenses in the copyright statement at the beginning of this book. You do not have to request special permission. In addition, we request that you share with the project some of the profits you make from sales of books, in consideration of all the work we have put into producing them.

What's new in LibreOffice 4.3?

The LibreOffice 4.3 Release Notes (changes from version 4.2) are here: https://wiki.documentfoundation.org/ReleaseNotes/4.3

You may also want to read the LibreOffice 4.2 Release Notes (changes from version 4.1) here: https://wiki.documentfoundation.org/ReleaseNotes/4.2.

Chapter 1
Introducing Draw

Introduction

Draw is a vector graphics drawing tool, although it can also perform some operations on raster graphics (pixels) such as photographs. Using Draw, you can quickly create a wide variety of graphical images.

Vector graphics store and display a picture as simple geometric elements such as lines, circles, and polygons rather than as a collection of pixels (picture elements or points on the screen). This permits simpler storage and supports precise scaling of the picture elements.

Draw is fully integrated into the LibreOffice suite and this simplifies exchanging graphics with all components of the suite. For example, if you create an image in Draw, reusing it in a Writer document is as simple as copying and pasting the image. You can also work with drawings directly from within Writer or Impress using a subset of the functions and tools from Draw.

The functionality of LibreOffice Draw is extensive and, even though it was not designed to rival high-end graphics applications, it possesses significantly more functionality than the drawing tools that are generally integrated with most office productivity suites.

A few examples of the drawing functions are: layer management, magnetic grid-point system, dimensions and measurement display, connectors for making organization charts, 3D functions that enable small three-dimensional drawings to be created (with texture and lighting effects), drawing and page-style integration, and Bézier curves.

This *Draw Guide* is not a course book to be worked through from beginning to end. Rather, it is a reference work in which you can browse for guidance on particular topics.

This document describes only the functions associated with Draw. Some concepts, such as file management or the way the LibreOffice environment works, are mentioned only briefly; they are covered in more detail in the *Getting Started Guide*.

Draw workplace

The main components of the Draw interface are shown in Figure 2.

Note	The maximum size of a drawing page in LibreOffice Draw is limited by your computer setup and the page size that you can set and use in your printer.

Workspace

The large area in the center of the window is where you make the drawings and is called the Workspace. You can surround this drawing area with toolbars and information areas. The number and position of the visible tools vary with the task in hand and user preferences. Therefore your setup may look different. For example, some users put the main Drawing toolbar on the left-hand side of the Workspace and not in the default position at the bottom of the Workspace, as shown in Figure 2.

By default, the Workspace consists of three layers (*Layout*, *Controls* and *Dimension Lines*) and the tabs for these default layers appear in the bottom left corner of the Workspace. The default layers cannot be deleted or renamed, but you can add layers as and when necessary. For more information on layers, see *Chapter 11 Advanced Draw Techniques*.

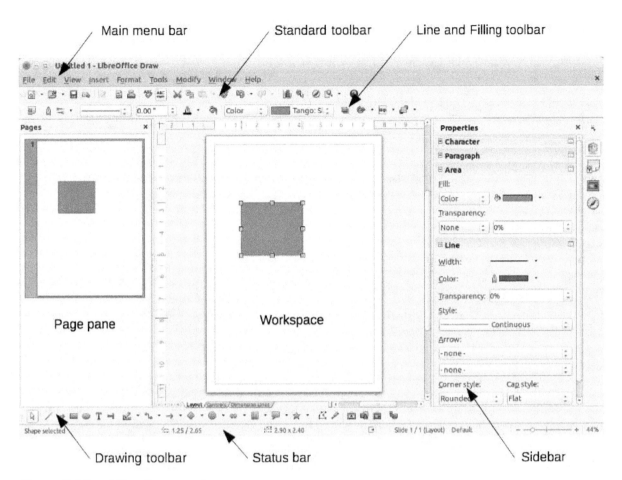

Figure 2: LibreOffice Draw workspace

Pages Pane

You can split drawings in Draw over several pages. Multi-page drawings are used mainly for presentations. The Pages Pane, on the left side of the Draw workspace in Figure 2, gives an overview of the pages that you create. If the Pages Pane is not visible on your setup, you can enable it by going to **View > Page Pane** on the main menu bar. To make changes to the page order, just drag and drop one or more pages into a new position.

Sidebar

On the right of the Workspace is the Sidebar, which gives you quick access to object properties and options. If the Sidebar is not visible on your setup, you can enable it by going to **View > Sidebar** on the main menu bar.

The Sidebar has four sections and to expand a section, either click on its icon or click on the small triangle at the top of the icons and select a section from the drop-down list. Only one section at a time can be open.

Properties

Clicking on the **Properties** icon ⬛ opens the **Properties** section of the Sidebar showing the options that are available for a selected object in your drawing. These options are similar to the options available when you use a Draw dialog.

Styles and Formatting

Clicking on the **Styles and Formatting** icon opens the **Styles and Formatting** section of the Sidebar showing the image styles that are available for a selected object in your drawing. Here you can edit and apply image styles. When you edit a style, the changes are automatically applied to all of the elements formatted with this style in your drawing.

Gallery

Clicking on the **Gallery** icon opens the **Gallery** section of the Sidebar opens the Draw gallery where you can insert an object into your drawing as a copy. This copy is independent of the original object in the Gallery.

Navigator

Clicking on the **Navigator** icon opens the **Navigator** section of the Sidebar opens the Draw navigator, in which you can quickly move to another object or another page in your drawing. It is recommended to give objects and pages in your drawing meaningful names so that you can easily identify them when using the Navigator.

Rulers

You should see rulers (bars with numbers) on the upper and left-hand sides of the Workspace. If they are not visible, you can enable them by selecting **View > Ruler** in the main menu bar. The rulers show the size of a selected object on the page using double lines (highlighted in Figure 3). When no object is selected, they show the location of the mouse pointer, which helps to position drawing objects more accurately.

You can also use the rulers to manage object handles and guide lines, making it easier to position objects.

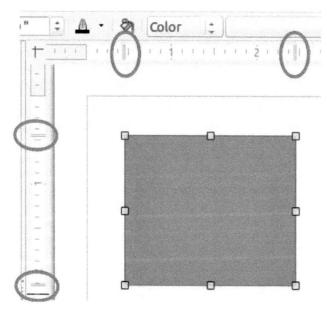

Figure 3: Rulers showing size of a selected object

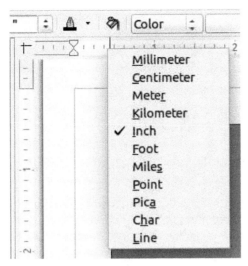

Figure 4: Ruler units

The page margins in the drawing area are also represented on the rulers. You can change the margins directly on the rulers by dragging them with the mouse. The margin area is indicated by the grayed out area on the rulers as shown in Figure 3.

To modify the measurement units of the rulers, which can be defined independently, right-click on the desired ruler, as illustrated for the horizontal ruler in Figure 4.

The default position of the zero for each of the rulers is located in the top left corner of the page where the left and top margins start. This zero position can be adjusted by clicking in the top left corner of the workspace (Figure 3) where the horizontal and vertical rulers meet and dragging to a new zero position.

Status bar

The Status bar is located at the bottom of the Draw window and includes several Draw-specific fields.

- **Information area** shows which action is being carried out, or which object type is selected.
- **Position** and **Object size** show different information depending on whether objects are selected or not.
  - When no object is selected, the position numbers show the current position (X and Y coordinates) of the mouse cursor.
  - When an object is selected and being resized with the mouse, the object size numbers show the size of the object (width and height).

Note	The sizes are given in the current measurement unit (not to be confused with the ruler units). This measurement unit is defined in **Tools > Options > LibreOffice Draw > General**.

  - If an object is selected, the position numbers shows the X and Y coordinates of the upper-left corner and the object size number pair displays the size of the object. These numbers do not relate to the object itself, but to the selection outline, which is the smallest possible rectangle that can contain the visible part or parts of the object; see *Chapter 3 Working with Objects and Object Points* for more information.
  - When an object is selected, a double-click in either of these areas opens the **Position and Size** dialog; see *Chapter 4 Changing Object Attributes* for more information.

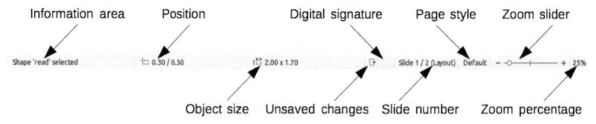

Figure 5: Draw status bar

- **Unsaved changes** are indicated whenever any change is made to the document but not yet saved to disk.

- **Digital signature** indicates if the document has been digitally signed. A double-click or right-click in this area opens the Digital Signatures dialog. A document must be saved at least once before it can be digitally signed. After a document is digitally signed, an indicator appears in this area.

- **Slide number** shows the sequence number for the current drawing page and the total number of pages created for the drawing. If you select an object, the information enclosed by parentheses indicates on which layer the object is placed within the drawing. In the example shown in Figure 5, the object is on the Layout layer of Slide 1 and there is a total number of one slide in the drawing.

- **Page style** shows which template is being used for the drawing.

- **Zoom slider** changes the zoom percentage of how the drawing appears on the computer display. Clicking on the plus (+) sign increases zoom and on the minus (-) sign decreases zoom. You can also drag the slider to increase or decrease the zoom percentage. The vertical bar in the middle of the *Zoom* slider represents a zoom percentage of 100%.

- **Zoom percentage** shows the level of zoom as a percentage. Double-clicking on the zoom percentage opens the **Zoom & View Layout** dialog. Right-clicking on the zoom percentage opens a menu where you can select a zoom level. See *Chapter 3 Working with Objects and Object Points* for more information on working with the zoom functions.

Toolbars

You can display or hide the various Draw toolbars, according to your needs. To display or hide a toolbar, click **View > Toolbars**. On the menu that appears, select which toolbar you want to display.

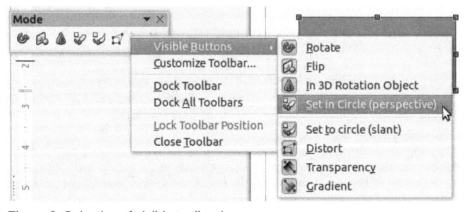

Figure 6: Selection of visible toolbar icons

You can also select the icons or buttons that you want to appear on toolbars. To change the visible icons or buttons on any toolbar, right-click in an empty area on the toolbar and select **Visible Buttons** from the context menu. Visible icons or buttons are indicated by a shaded outline around the icon as shown by the icons in Figure 6. Click on an icon to hide or show it in the toolbar.

Standard toolbar

The Standard toolbar (Figure 7) is the same for all LibreOffice components and is described in detail in the *Getting Started Guide*.

Figure 7: Standard toolbar

Drawing toolbar

The Drawing toolbar (Figure 8) is the most important toolbar in Draw. It contains all the necessary functions for drawing various geometric and freehand shapes, and for organizing them in the drawing. It is described in detail in *Chapter 2 Drawing Basic Shapes*.

Figure 8: Drawing toolbar

Line and Filling toolbar

The Line and Filling toolbar (Figure 9) lets you modify the main properties of a drawing object. The icons and pull-down lists vary according to the type of object selected. For example, to change the style of a line, click on the up and down arrows for *Line Style* and select the required style.

The functions on the Line and Filling toolbar let you change the color, style, and width of the line drawn, the fill color and style, and other properties of an object. The object must first be selected with a mouse click. If the selected object is a text frame, the Line and Filling toolbar changes to the Text Formatting toolbar (Figure 10).

Figure 9: Line and Filling toolbar

Text Formatting toolbar

The Text Formatting toolbar (Figure 10) is similar to the Formatting toolbar in Writer and only appears when a text object has been selected in your drawing. For an explanation of the functions on this toolbar, see *Chapter 4 Changing Object Attributes*. For information on adding and formatting text, see *Chapter 9 Adding and Formatting Text*.

Figure 10: Text Formatting toolbar

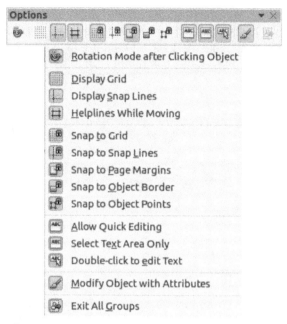

Figure 11: Options toolbar

Options toolbar

Use the Options toolbar (Figure 11) to activate or deactivate various drawing aids. The Options toolbar is not displayed by default. To display it, go to **View > Toolbars > Options** on the main menu bar. The tools available on this toolbar are shown in Figure 11 and described in greater detail in other chapters of this *Draw Guide*.

Floating and moving toolbars

Available toolsets

Many icons have a small triangle pointing downward to the right side of the icon. This triangle indicates that the icon has additional tools available. Click on the triangle to display the full set of tools (Figure 12).

You can "tear off" this toolset so it becomes a floating toolbar. Click the area at the bottom of the toolset, drag it across the screen to a location you want and then release the mouse button. To close a floating toolbar, click on the X on the right of the toolbar title.

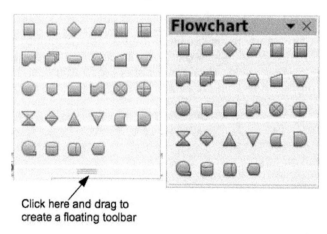

Click here and drag to
create a floating toolbar

Figure 12: Available toolset and floating toolbar

Note	When a toolset is made into a floating toolbar, the icon on the existing toolbar remains in the toolbar and always shows the last tool you used. This means that the icon you see on your screen may differ from the icon shown in this guide.

Tip	When you double-click on an icon on a toolbar, the command corresponding to that icon will become active and remain active. You can then repeat this action as often as you like. To exit from this mode, press the *Esc* key or click on another icon. Please note that this may not work for every icon on every toolbar.

Default toolbars

When you open Draw, the default set of toolbars are already docked or fixed in their positions at the top and bottom of the workspace. This default set of toolbars normally consist of the Standard, Line and Filling, and Drawing toolbars. These toolbars can be undocked and become floating toolbars.

- To undock a toolbar, move the mouse cursor to the far left of the toolbar and over the toolbar handle (Figure 13). The cursor will change shape, normally to a grabbing hand, but this is dependent on computer setup and operating system. Click and drag on the toolbar handle to move the toolbar until it becomes a floating toolbar. This floating-toolbar capability is common to all components of LibreOffice.

- To dock a floating toolbar at the top of the Draw workspace, press and hold the *Ctrl* key then double click on the title of the toolbar. The toolbar will move into available space at the top of the Draw workspace.

- An alternative method of docking a toolbar is to click in the toolbar title and drag the toolbar to the docked position that you require. This can be the top, bottom or one of the sides of the Draw workspace.

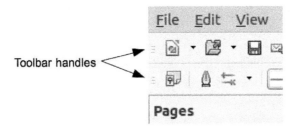

Figure 13: Toolbar handles

Customizing toolbars

You can customize toolbars in several ways to show or hide icons defined for a toolbar, see "Toolbars" and Figure 6 on page 22.

To add functions to a toolbar, move tools between toolbars, or create new toolbars:

1) Select **View > Toolbars > Customize** on the main menu bar, or right click in an empty area on a toolbar and select **Customize Toolbar** from the context menu to open the Customize dialog (Figure 14).

2) Select the **Toolbars** tab and the toolbar you want to change from the *Toolbar* drop-down list.

3) Select the desired function for that toolbar from the *Commands* list.

4) If necessary, reposition the new function on the *Commands* list using the up and down arrows.

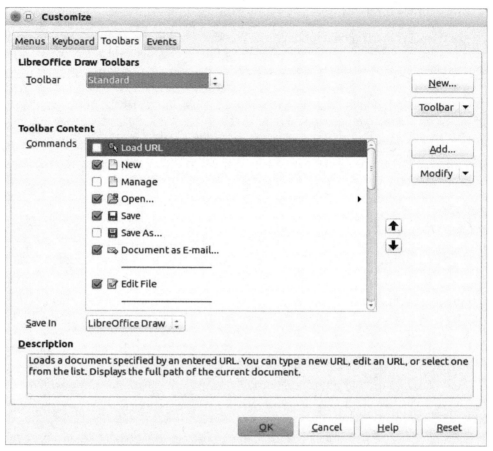

Figure 14: Customize dialog – Toolbars page

5) Click **Toolbar** and select how you want the toolbar to appear in Draw from the context menu – **Icons Only**, **Text Only**, **Icons & Text**, or **Restore Default Settings**.

6) Click **OK** to save your changes and close the dialog.

For more information when adding a new function, or modifying a toolbar, see the *Getting Started Guide*.

Choosing and defining colors

The Color dialog (Figure 15) displays the current color palette. It lets you rapidly select the color of the various objects (lines, areas, and 3D effects) in your drawing. The first box in the panel corresponds to none or no color. If the Color dialog is not displayed go to **View > Toolbars > Color Bar**. By default, the Colors dialog appears at the bottom of the Workspace and displays the current color palette. To make this dialog a floating dialog, hold down the *Ctrl* key and click at the top of the Colors dialog.

You can access several specialized color palettes in Draw, as well as change individual colors to your own taste. This is done using the Colors page in the Area dialog by selecting **Format > Area** on the main menu bar or clicking the **Area** icon on the Line and Filling toolbar, then selecting the **Colors** tab (Figure 16).

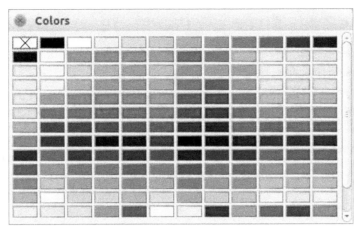

Figure 15: Colors dialog

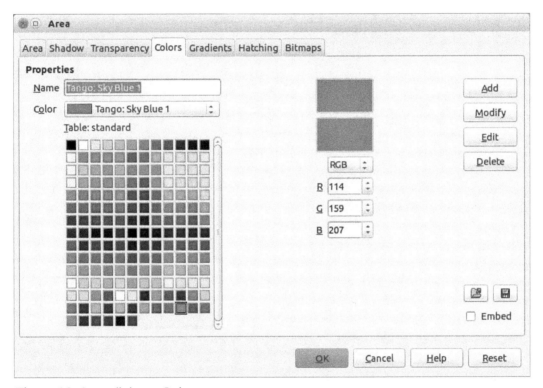

Figure 16. Area dialog – Colors page

To load another palette, click on the **Load Color List** icon . The file selector dialog asks you to choose one of the standard LibreOffice palettes (files with the file extension `*.soc`). For example, `web.soc` is a color palette that is adapted to creating drawings for placing in web pages. These colors will display correctly on workstations with screens capable of at least 256 colors.

The color selection box also lets you individually change any color by modifying the numerical values in the fields provided to the right of the color palette. You can use the color schemes known as CMYK (Cyan, Magenta, Yellow, Black) or RGB (Red, Green, Blue).

Click on the **Edit** button to open the Color dialog, where you can set individual colors, see the *Getting Started Guide* for more information. A more detailed description of color and options can also be found in *Chapter 11 Advanced Draw Techniques* in this guide.

Grid, snap, and help lines

Draw provides a grid and snap lines as drawing aids and these can be turned on or off by clicking on the **Display Grid** ⊞ or **Display Snap Lines** ┼ icons on the Options toolbar. The grid and snap lines are displayed only on the screen and are not shown on a printed drawing or when the drawing is used in another LibreOffice module. The color, spacing and resolution of the grid points can be individually chosen for each axis.

Help lines when moving objects can be displayed and these are turned on or off by clicking on the **Helplines While Moving** ⊞ icon on the Options toolbar. Showing the position of the object while moving it makes positioning the object much easier. If this function is activated, pairs of vertical and horizontal lines enclosing the object are shown while moving the object. These lines extend to the edges of the drawing area.

Draw also offers several snap functions to help you can position objects exactly in a drawing.

For more information on the grid, snap lines, snap functions, and help lines, see *Chapter 3 Working with Objects and Object Points*.

LibreOffice
The Document Foundation

Chapter 2
Drawing Basic Shapes

Introduction

You can create 2D and 3D objects in Draw. This chapter shows how to draw simple 2D objects. The following chapters describe how to work with and edit such objects. For more information on 3D objects, see *Chapter 7 Working with 3D Objects*.

All shapes, whether they are lines, rectangles, or more complicated shapes, are called *objects*. This is common notation in vector drawing software.

The drawing tools are found on the Drawing toolbar (Figure 17). This toolbar is normally located at the bottom of the workspace. If you do not see it, you can activate it by going to **View > Toolbars** on the main menu bar.

Figure 17: Drawing toolbar

As with all the components of LibreOffice, you can undock the Drawing toolbar and place it wherever you want to on the Draw workspace as a floating toolbar. You can also configure toolbars by adding, moving, hiding, or deleting toolbar icons. See *Chapter 1 Introducing Draw* for more information.

When you draw a shape, select one for editing or add text, the information field in the status bar (Figure 18) changes to reflect the action taken or in progress. See *Chapter 1 Introducing Draw* for more information on the status bar.

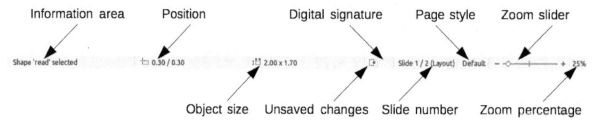

Figure 18: Draw status bar

Custom shapes

Draw also offers the ability to create custom shapes, which are the equivalent of *AutoShapes* in Microsoft Office. Custom shapes differ in their properties and are dealt with separately in the relevant chapters of this guide. The main differences relate to the behavior of 3D objects and text handling. Text frames in Draw have their own geometric format.

Drawing basic shapes

Basic shapes, including text, are treated as objects in Draw. The standard set of tools available for drawing basic shapes, from left to right on the Drawing toolbar, are shown in Figure 19.

The tools that are already placed on the Drawing toolbar are indicated by a darkened area around the icon, for example **Select**, **Line** and so on. The tools not on the Drawing toolbar do not have this darkened area around the icon, for example **To Curve**, **To Polygon**, and so on.

Please note that some of the icons on the Drawing toolbar will change shape according to the last tool used from the selection of available tools. The icons that have a small triangle to the right of the icon indicates that more tools are available. See "Drawing geometric shapes" on page 41 for information on the available shapes.

Select		Callouts	
Line		Stars	
Line Ends with Arrow		Points	
Rectangle		Glue Points	
Ellipse		To Curve	
Text		To Polygon	
Vertical Text		To 3D	
Curve		To 3D Rotation Object	
Connector		Fontwork Gallery	
Lines and Arrows		From File	
3D Objects		Gallery	
Basic Shapes		Insert	
Symbol Shapes		Controls	
Block Arrows			
Flowcharts		Extrusion On/Off	

Figure 19: Tools available for Drawing toolbar

Note	When you draw a basic shape or select one for editing, the information area at the left side in the status bar changes to reflect the present action: for example *Line created*, *Text frame xxyy selected*, and so on.

Straight lines

A straight line is the simplest element or object in Draw to create.

1) Click on the **Line** icon on the Drawing toolbar and place the cursor at the point where you want to start the line (Figure 20).
2) Click and drag the cursor while keeping the mouse button pressed.
3) Release the mouse button at the point where you want to end the line. When a line is selected, a large selection handle appears at the start of the line and a smaller selection handle appears at the end of the line.
4) Keep the *Shift* key pressed while you draw a line to restrict the drawing angle of the line to a multiple of 45 degrees (0, 45, 90, 135, and so on).

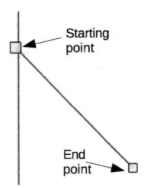

Figure 20: A straight line

Note	This is the default behavior of the *Shift* key. However, if the option *When creating or moving objects* in the *Snap position* section of **Tools > Options > LibreOffice Draw > Grid** has been selected, the action of the *Shift* key is the opposite. Lines will automatically be drawn at a multiple of 45 degrees *unless* the *Shift* key is pressed.

5) Keep the *Ctrl* key pressed while drawing a line to enable the end of the line to snap to the nearest grid point.

Note	This is the default behavior of the *Ctrl* key. However, if the **Snap to Grid** option on the **View->Grid** menu has been selected, the *Ctrl* deactivates the snap to grid activity.

6) Keep the *Alt* key pressed while drawing a line and the line extends outwards symmetrically in both directions from the start point. This lets you draw lines starting from the middle of the line.

7) When a line is drawn, it uses default attributes. To change any of these attributes, select the line by clicking on it, then use one of the following methods:

  • Use the tools on the Line and Filling toolbar to change line style, line width or line color.

  • Go to **Format > Line** on the main menu bar, or right-click and select **Line** from the context menu to open the Line dialog (Figure 21) to change line attributes.

  • Click on the **Properties** icon in the Sidebar to open the Properties section, then use the Line subsection (Figure 22) to change the line attributes.

8) If necessary, go to **Tools > Options > LibreOffice Draw > Grid** on the main menu bar to adjust the spacing (resolution) of the grid points. See *Chapter 3 Working with Objects and Object Points* for more information.

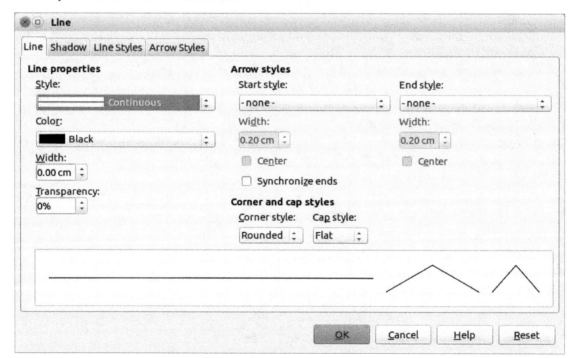

Figure 21: Line dialog – Line page

Figure 22: Sidebar Line subsection

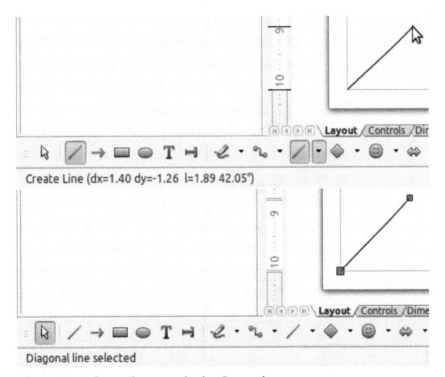

Figure 23: Information area in the Status bar

9) While you are working with a line (or any other element), use the information field on the Status bar to monitor your activity. A description of the current activity or selection is shown when you are working with elements and Figure 23 shows two examples.

Arrows

Arrows are drawn like lines because Draw classifies arrows as a subgroup of lines, that is lines with arrowheads. The information field on the status bar shows them only as lines. Click on the **Line Ends with Arrow** icon → to draw an arrow. The arrow head is drawn at the end point of the arrow when you release the mouse button.

Different types of lines and arrows

Click on the small triangle to the right of the **Lines and Arrows** → icon on the Drawing toolbar to open a pop-up toolbar with tools for drawing lines and arrows. Alternatively, go to **View > Toolbars > Arrows** on the main menu bar to open the Arrows toolbar as a floating toolbar. The **Lines and Arrows** icon on the Drawing toolbar always indicates the last tool used and may not be the same as the **Lines and Arrows** icon shown above. Figure 24 shows the tools that are available on the Arrows toolbar.

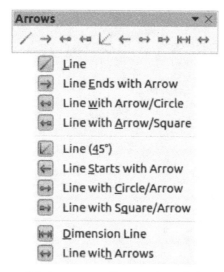

Figure 24: Arrows toolbar and available tools

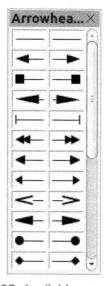

Figure 25: Available arrowheads

After drawing the line, you can change the arrow style by clicking on the **Arrowheads** icon ⇇ in the Line and Filling toolbar and select the arrow start and end options. Start options are on the left and end options are on the right in Figure 25.

Rectangles or squares

Drawing a rectangle is similar to drawing a straight line. Click on the **Rectangle** icon ▭ in the Drawing toolbar. As you draw the rectangle with the mouse cursor, the rectangle appears with the bottom right corner of the rectangle attached to the cursor.

Squares are rectangles with all sides of equal length. To draw a square, click on the **Rectangle** icon ▭ and hold down the *Shift* key while you draw a square.

Note	If the option *When creating or moving objects* has been selected in **Tools > Options > LibreOffice Draw > General**, the action of the *Shift* key is reversed. When the Rectangle tool is selected, a square is drawn. To draw a rectangle you have to press the *Shift* key when drawing. This *Shift* key reversal also applies when drawing ellipses and circles in "Ellipses and circles" on page 35.

To draw a rectangle or square from its center rather than the bottom right corner, position your cursor on the drawing, press the mouse button and then hold down the *Alt* key while dragging with the cursor. The rectangle or square uses the start point where you first clicked the mouse button as the center.

With the rectangle or square selected, you can quickly change border style, line width, or color, and the type of fill color or fill pattern using the tools on the Line and Filling toolbar. For more information on changing the attributes of a rectangle or square, see *Chapter 4 Changing Object Attributes*.

Ellipses and circles

To draw an ellipse (also called an oval), click on the **Ellipse** icon ⬭ on the Drawing toolbar. A circle is an ellipse with both axes the same length. To draw a circle, click on the **Ellipse** icon and hold down the *Shift* key while you draw a circle.

To draw an ellipse or circle from its center, position your cursor on the drawing, press the mouse button and then hold down the *Alt* key while dragging with the cursor. The ellipse or circle uses the start point (where you first clicked the mouse button) as the center.

With the ellipse or circle selected, you can quickly change border style, line width, or color, and the type of fill color or fill pattern using the tools on the Line and Filling toolbar. For more information on changing the attributes of an ellipse or circle, see *Chapter 4 Changing Object Attributes*.

Tip	To quickly insert a line, rectangle, ellipse, or text, press and hold the *Ctrl* key down and then click on one of the icons for line, rectangle, ellipse, or text. An object is drawn automatically in the center of the workspace area using default values. The object attributes can then be changed using the Line Fill toolbar or the information in *Chapter 4 Changing Object Attributes*. This works only if the icon has no associated toolbar; that is, no triangle or arrow on the right side of the icon.

Adding arc and segment tools to the Drawing toolbar

If you regularly draw arcs or segments (partial circles or ellipses), then you can add the Circles and Ovals toolbar (Figure 26) to the Drawing toolbar. The Circles and Ovals toolbar is an optional toolbar and you have to customize the Drawing toolbar to add this optional toolbar.

Figure 26: Circles and Ovals toolbar

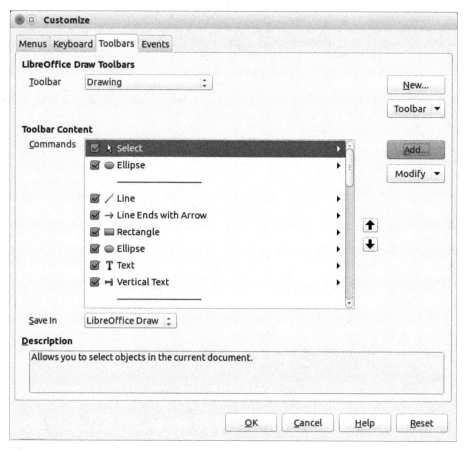

Figure 27: Customize dialog

1) Go to **View > Toolbars > Customize** on the main menu bar, or right-click in a blank area in the Drawing toolbar and select **Customize Toolbar** from the context menu to open the Customize dialog (Figure 27).

2) Select the **Toolbars** tab to open the Toolbars page of the Customize dialog.

3) Select *Drawing* from the **Toolbar** drop down list and click **Add** to open the Add Commands dialog (Figure 28).

4) Select *Drawing* in the **Category** list.

5) Scroll down and select the second *Ellipse* command in the **Commands** list. Check the **Description** section at the bottom of the dialog as this will indicate that you have selected the command for the Circles and Ovals toolbar.

6) Click **Add** and then click **Close**.

7) In the Customize dialog, make sure the new *Ellipse* command is selected and checked.

8) For clarity, click **Modify > Rename** and type in *Circles and Ovals* as the new name for this command, then click **OK**.

9) Use the up and down arrow buttons to move the new *Circles and Ovals* command to the desired position on the Drawing toolbar.

10) Click **OK** to save the customized Drawing toolbar and close the Customize dialog.

LibreOffice 4.3 Draw Guide

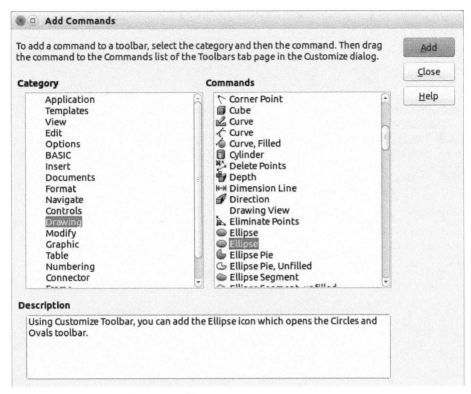

Figure 28: Add Commands dialog

Note	The icon used to open the Circles and Ovals toolbar is still called Ellipse and is not to be confused with the **Ellipse** icon that is one of the default tools placed on the left of the Drawing toolbar.

The new **Circles and Ovals** (Ellipse) icon appears on the Drawing toolbar with a small triangle to the right of it. Click on this triangle to open the Circles and Ovals toolbar (Figure 26). To make this toolbar into a floating toolbar, drag the toolbar onto the workspace area. The **Circles and Ovals** icon on the Drawing toolbar always indicates the last tool used and may not be the same as the **Circles and Ovals** icon shown above.

To help prevent any confusion, you can remove the standard **Ellipse** icon from the Drawing toolbar by opening the Customize dialog (Figure 27) and deselecting the first Ellipse command in the **Commands** list. Alternatively, select the first Ellipse command, click **Modify > Delete** to remove the Ellipse icon from the Drawing toolbar.

To return the Drawing toolbar to its default settings, open the Customize dialog, select the **Circles and Ovals** (Ellipse) icon, then click **Modify > Delete** to remove the icon from the Drawing toolbar.

Arcs or segments

1) To draw an arc or segment, select the appropriate icon in the Circles and Ovals toolbar (Figure 26).

2) Click and drag with the cursor to create a guide circle or ellipse.

3) Move the cursor to the position where you want the arc or segment to start. The status bar indicates the angle in degrees.

4) Click to start drawing the arc or segment, then move the cursor to create the arc or segment. The status bar shows the angle in degrees.

5) When you have drawn the arc or segment you require, click again to complete the arc or segment.

Curves or polygons

To draw a curve or polygon, click the **Curve** icon 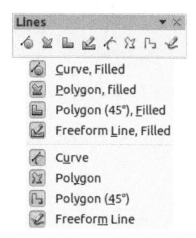 on the Drawing toolbar. Click on the triangle to the right of the icon to open the toolbar (Figure 29). The **Curve** icon on the Drawing toolbar always indicates the last tool used and may not be the same as the **Curve** icon shown above. Hovering the cursor over this icon gives a tooltip of Curve. If you open the floating toolbar, the toolbar title is Lines.

Figure 29: Curves (Lines) toolbar

Curves

1) Click and hold the left mouse button to create the starting point of your curve, then drag from the starting point to draw a line.
2) Release the left mouse button and continue to drag the cursor to bend the line into a curve.
3) Click to set the end point of the curve and fix the curve on the page. Only the first section of your curve is drawn as a curve.
4) To continue with your curve, click and drag the cursor to draw a straight line. Each mouse click sets a corner point and allows you to continue drawing another straight line from the last corner point.
5) Double-click to end the drawing of your curve.

If you selected a filled curve, the last point is automatically joined to the first point to close off the curve and fills it with the current standard fill color. A curve without filling will not be closed when you end the drawing.

Polygons

1) Click and draw the first line from the start point while holding the left mouse button held down.
2) Release the mouse button when you have reached the second point of your polygon and a line between the first and second points is drawn.
3) Move the cursor to where you want the next point point in your polygon and click the mouse button to draw the next line.
4) Double-click to end the drawing of your polygon.

If you selected a filled polygon, the last point is automatically joined to the first point to close off the polygon and fills it with the current standard fill color. A polygon without filling will not be closed when you end the drawing.

Polygons 45°

These polygons are drawn the same way as ordinary polygons above, but the angles between lines are restricted to 45 or 90 degrees when you create another point in your polygon.

Note	Holding down the *Shift* key when drawing lines with the Curve or Polygon tools will also restrict the angles between the lines to 45 or 90 degrees.

Freeform lines

Using the Freeform Line tools is similar to drawing with a pencil on paper.

1) Click and drag the cursor to the line shape you require.
2) Release the mouse button when you are satisfied with your freeform line and the drawing is completed.

If you selected a filled freeform line, the last point is automatically joined to the first point to close off the freeform line and fills it with the current standard fill color. A freeform line without filling will not be closed when you end the drawing.

Glue points and connectors

Glue points

All Draw objects have glue points, which normally are not displayed. Glue points become visible when the **Connectors** icon 🔗 on the Drawing toolbar is selected.

Most objects have four glue points (Figure 30). You can add more glue points and customize glue points using the **Gluepoints** toolbar (Figure 31). Go to **View > Toolbars > Gluepoints** on the main menu bar to open the toolbar.

Figure 30: Gluepoints

Figure 31: Gluepoints toolbar

Glue points are not the same as the selection handles of an object. The selection handles are for moving or changing the shape of an object, as described in *Chapter 3 Working with Objects and Object Points.*

Glue points are used to fix or glue a connector to an object so that when the object moves, the connector stays fixed to the object. For a more detailed description on the use of glue points, see *Chapter 8 Connections, Flowcharts and Organization Charts*.

Connectors

Connectors are lines or arrows whose ends automatically snap to a glue point of an object. Connectors are useful in drawing organization charts, flow diagrams, and mind-maps. When objects are moved or reordered, the connectors remain attached to a glue point. Figure 32 shows an example of two objects and a connector.

Draw offers a range of different connectors and connector functions. Click on the triangle to the right of the **Connector** icon 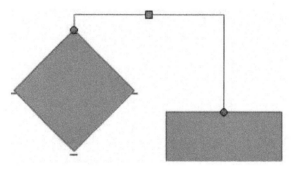 to open the Connectors toolbar (Figure 33). The **Connector** icon on the Drawing toolbar always indicates the last tool used and may not be the same as the **Connector** icon shown above.

For a more detailed description of the use of connectors, see *Chapter 8 Connections, Flowcharts and Organization Charts*.

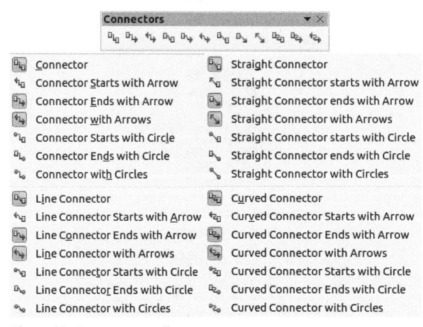

Figure 32: A connector between two objects

Connectors

Connector	Straight Connector
Connector Starts with Arrow	Straight Connector starts with Arrow
Connector Ends with Arrow	Straight Connector ends with Arrow
Connector with Arrows	Straight Connector with Arrows
Connector Starts with Circle	Straight Connector starts with Circle
Connector Ends with Circle	Straight Connector ends with Circle
Connector with Circles	Straight Connector with Circles
Line Connector	Curved Connector
Line Connector Starts with Arrow	Curved Connector Starts with Arrow
Line Connector Ends with Arrow	Curved Connector Ends with Arrow
Line Connector with Arrows	Curved Connector with Arrows
Line Connector Starts with Circle	Curved Connector Starts with Circle
Line Connector Ends with Circle	Curved Connector Ends with Circle
Line Connector with Circles	Curved Connector with Circles

Figure 33: Connectors toolbar

Drawing geometric shapes

The icons for drawing geometric shapes are located on the Drawing toolbar and each geometric shape is explained in the following sections. Clicking on the triangle to the right of the icon opens a floating toolbar giving access to the tools for that geometric shape.

The use of these tools for geometric shapes is similar to the tool used for drawing rectangles and squares. For more information, see "Rectangles or squares" on page 35.

The icons used on the Drawing toolbar for drawing geometric shapes always indicates the last tool used and may not be the same as the icons shown in the following sections.

Basic shapes

Click on the triangle to the right of the **Basic Shapes** icon  to open the Basic Shapes toolbar (Figure 34) for drawing basic shapes. This toolbar also includes a rectangle tool identical to the one already displayed on the Drawing toolbar.

Figure 34: Basic Shapes toolbar

Symbol shapes

Click on the triangle to the right of the **Symbol Shapes** icon  to open the Symbol Shapes toolbar for drawing symbols.

Figure 35: Symbol Shapes toolbar

Block arrows

Click on the triangle to the right of the **Block Arrows** icon  to open the Block Arrows toolbar for drawing block arrows.

Figure 36: Block Arrows toolbar

Figure 37: Flowcharts toolbar

Flowcharts

Click on the triangle to the right of the **Flowcharts** icon  to open the Flowchart toolbar for symbols used in drawing flowcharts. The creation of flowcharts, organization charts, and similar planning tools are further described in *Chapter 8 Connections, Flowcharts and Organization Charts*.

Callouts

Click on the triangle to the right of the **Callouts** icon to open the Callouts toolbar for drawing callouts.

Figure 38: Callouts toolbar

Stars and banners

Click on the triangle to the right of the **Stars** icon to open the Stars and Banners toolbar for drawing stars and banners.

Figure 39: Stars and Banners toolbar

Adding text to drawings and objects

In Draw you can add, insert, and format text to a drawing, objects, and shapes as follows:

- As a dynamic text frame, which is an independent Draw object and expands as you add more text within the frame.
- Text within a previously drawn object. This integrates text within the object and is placed within the boundary rectangle that surrounds an object. This boundary rectangle is not dynamic and care must be taken so that your text does not go outside of the object boundaries.

For more information on how to add, insert, and format text in a drawing or drawing objects, see *Chapter 9 Adding and Formatting Text*.

Chapter 3
Working with Objects and Object Points

Introduction

This chapter looks at the tools and functions that let you modify existing drawings. All of the functions apply to a selected object or a group of selected objects, which can be distinguished by selection handles on a rectangular frame that is large enough to contain the object. Where several objects are selected, the frame around the objects corresponds to the smallest rectangle that can contain all of the objects. This frame is called the selection rectangle.

Note	The color and shape of the selection handles will change depending on the tool and function that has been selected to change the object properties. The color of the selection handles also depends on the computer operating system and how the computer has been set up.

Selecting objects

Direct selection

The easiest way to select an object is to click directly on it. For objects that are not filled, click on the object outline to select it. One click selects; a second click deselects. To select or deselect more than one object, hold the *Shift* key down while clicking.

Selection by framing

You can also select several objects at once by dragging the mouse cursor around the objects. This draws a rectangle around the objects, and only objects that lie entirely within the rectangle will be selected.

To select multiple objects by framing, the Select icon on the Drawing toolbar must be active.

Note	When you drag the mouse cursor to select multiple objects, the selection rectangle being drawn is also known as a marquee.

Selecting hidden objects

If objects are located behind others and not visible, they can still be selected.

- For computers using a Windows or Mac operating system.

  Select the object in front of the hidden objects, then press the *Alt* key and click to select the hidden object. If there are several hidden objects, keep holding down the *Alt* key and clicking until you reach the object you want. To cycle through the objects in reverse order, hold down the *Alt+Shift* keys and click.

- For computers using a Linux operating system.

  Press the *Tab* key to cycle selection through the objects in your drawing, stopping at the hidden object you want to select. To cycle through the objects in reverse order, press *Shift+Tab*. This is a very quick way to reach an object, but it may not be practical if there a large number of objects in a drawing.

When you select a hidden object, its selection handles will appear through the objects covering it.

Arranging objects

In a complex drawing, several objects may be stacked on top of one another. To rearrange the stacking order by moving an object forward or backward using one of the following methods:

- Select an object, go to **Modify > Arrange** on the main menu bar, or right-click on the object and select **Arrange,** then select one of the following:
  - – **Bring to Front**
  - – **Bring Forward**
  - – **Send Backward**
  - – **Send to Back**
  - – **In Front of Object**
  - – **Behind Object**

- Select an object, then use one of the following keyboard shortcuts:
  - – *Ctrl+Shift++* (bring to front)
  - – *Ctrl++* (bring forward)
  - – *Ctrl+-(*send backward)
  - – *Ctrl+Shift+-* (send to back)

- Select an object, then click on the small triangle to the right of the **Arrange** icon on the Line and Filling toolbar to open the Position toolbar, giving access to the arrangement options as shown in Figure 40.

Figure 40: Position toolbar

Positioning and adjusting objects

Using zoom

To help in the positioning and adjustment of objects, Draw has a zoom function that reduces or enlarges the screen display of the current drawing. For example, zoom in to place objects onto your drawing with greater position; zoom out to see the complete drawing. You can control zooming three ways: from the Status bar, Zoom dialog, or Zoom toolbar.

Note	Zooming is handled differently on Linux and Windows operating systems. A document saved with a 100% zoom factor in Windows is displayed at a larger zoom factor in Linux.

Status bar

The zoom controls are located on the right side of the status bar (Figure 41); these controls give you quick and easy access to zooming.

Figure 41: Status bar zoom controls

- Click on the minus sign to reduce the zoom factor.

- Click on the plus sign to increase the zoom factor.

- Click and hold on the slide control and move it to increase or decrease the zoom factor.

- Right-click on the zoom percentage number and select a zoom factor from the context menu that opens.

- Double-click on the zoom percentage number and select a zoom factor from the Zoom & View Layout dialog (Figure 42) that opens.

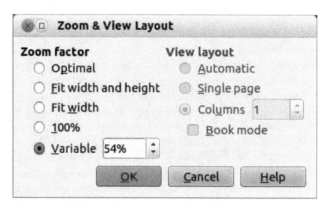

Figure 42: Zoom & View Layout dialog

Zoom layout dialog

Go to **View > Zoom > Zoom** on the main menu bar or double-click on the zoom percentage figure on the Status bar (Figure 41) to open the **Zoom & View Layout** dialog (Figure 42), where you can increase or reduce the zoom factor. The current zoom percentage is displayed on the Status bar.

Zoom factor

Sets the zoom factor at which to display the current document and all documents of the same type that you open thereafter.

- *Optimal* – resizes the display to fit the width of the text in the document.

- *Fit width and height* – displays the entire page on your screen.

- *Fit width* – displays the complete width of the document page. The top and bottom edges of the page may not be visible.

- *100%* – displays the document at its actual size.

- *Variable* – enter a percentage in the box for the zoom factor at which you want to display the document.

View layout

For text documents, you can set the view layout. Reduce the zoom factor to see the effects of different view layout settings.

- *Automatic* – automatic view layout displays pages side by side, as many as the zoom factor allows.

- *Single page* – single page view layout displays pages beneath each other, but never side by side.

- *Columns* – in columns view layout you see pages in a given number of columns side by side. Enter the number of columns.

- *Book mode* – in book mode view layout you see two pages side by side as in an open book. The first page is a right page with an odd page number.

Zoom toolbar

Go to **View > Toolbars > Zoom** to open the **Zoom** toolbar (Figure 43). The tools on this toolbar are as follows:

- **Zoom In** – displays the slide at two times its current size. Click once on the tool, then move the cursor onto the object and click again. You can also select the **Zoom In** tool and drag a rectangular frame around the area you want to enlarge.

- **Zoom Out** – displays the drawing at half its current size each time the tool is clicked.

- **Zoom 100%** – displays the drawing at its actual size.

- **Zoom Previous** – returns the display of the drawing to the previous zoom factor you applied. You can also use the keyboard shortcut *Ctrl +, (Comma)*.

- **Zoom Next** – undoes the action of the **Previous Zoom** command. You can also the keyboard shortcut *Ctrl +. (Period)*.

- **Zoom Page** – displays the whole drawing on your screen.

- **Zoom Page Width** – displays the complete width of the drawing. The top and bottom edges of the slide may not be visible.

- **Optimal** – resizes the display to include all of the objects on the slide.

- **Object Zoom** – resizes the display to fit the object(s) you selected.

- **Shift** – moves the drawing within the Draw workspace. Place the cursor on the drawing and drag to move the drawing. When you release the cursor, the last tool you used is automatically selected.

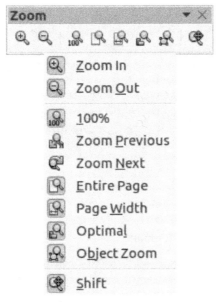

Figure 43: Zoom toolbar

Moving and adjusting object size

When moving an object or changing its size, check the left-hand area of the status bar at the bottom of the Draw window (Figure 44). From left to right, this area shows what object is selected, its position on the drawing in X/Y coordinates and dimensions of the object. The units of measurement are those selected in **Tools > Options > LibreOffice Draw > General**.

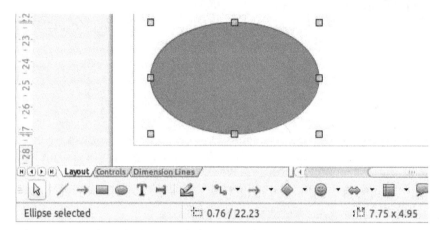

Figure 44: Left end of status bar when working with objects

Moving objects

To move an object (or a group of objects), select it and then click within the object borders and hold down the left mouse button while dragging the mouse. During movement, a ghost image of the object appears to help with repositioning. When the object reaches its new location, release the mouse button.

Adjusting object size

To change the size of a selected object (or a group of selected objects), move the cursor to one of the selection handles. The cursor will change shape to indicate the direction of movement for that selection handle. As you change the size of the object, a ghosted image of the object appears. When you have reached the desired size of the object, release the mouse button.

The results depend on which selection handle you use. To resize an object along one axis, use a selection handle on one of the sides. To resize along both axes, use a corner selection handle.

Note	If you press the *Shift* key while resizing an object, the change in size will be carried out symmetrically with respect to the two axes so that the aspect ratio of the object remains the same. This *Shift* key behavior works on all selection handles.
	This is the default behavior of the *Shift* key. However, if *When creating or moving objects* has been selected in **Tools > Options > LibreOffice Draw > Grid**, the action of the *Shift* key is reversed: that is the aspect ratio will be preserved *unless* the *Shift* key is pressed.

Modifying arcs

The size of an arc can be changed by adjusting the positions of the start and end points of an arc.

Select an arc and click on the **Points** icon ⌘ on the Drawing toolbar. Two handles appear at the start and end of the arc (Figure 45). The start point of the arc is indicated by the larger of the two handles.

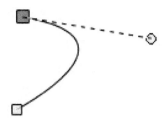

Figure 45: Modifying arcs

Click on one of these handles and drag it to a new position to change the shape of the arc. Also, when click on one of these handles, a control point appears and the end of a dashed line. Click on the end of this control point to also adjust the shape of the arc.

Rotating and slanting objects

Rotating objects

To rotate an object (or a group of objects), select the object, then go to rotation mode using one of the following methods:

- Click on the **Rotate** icon on the Line and Filling toolbar.

- Go to **View > Toolbars > Mode** on the main menu bar and select the **Rotate** icon on the Mode toolbar.

The selection handles will change shape and color (Figure 46). Also a center of rotation indicator will appear in the center of the object. As you move the cursor over the handles, the cursor changes shape. The corner handles are for rotating the object, and the top, bottom and side handles are to shear or slant the object.

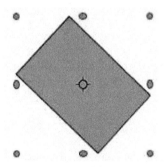

Figure 46: Rotating objects

Move the cursor to one of the corner handles, then click and hold the mouse button and start to move the cursor to rotate the object. A ghosted outline of the object being rotated appears and the current angle of rotation is shown in the status bar.

Note	Rotation works in a slightly different way for 3D objects because it occurs in a three dimensional space and not in a single plane. See *Chapter 7 Working with 3D Objects* for more information.

The rotation center is normally located at the center of an object. To change the position of the rotation center, click on the rotation center and drag until it is at the desired position. This rotation center can even be outside of the object.

Note	If you press the *Shift* key while rotating an object, rotation will be restricted to 15° of movement.
	This is the default behavior of the *Shift* key. However, if *When creating or moving objects* has been selected in **Tools > Options > LibreOffice Draw > Grid**, the action of the *Shift* key is reversed: that is rotation will be restricted to 15° of movement *unless* the *Shift* key is pressed.

Slanting objects

To slant an object, click on the **Rotate** icon, then use the handles located at the midpoints on the top, bottom and sides of a selected object. The cursor changes shape when it hovers over one of these midpoint handles indicating the direction of slanting. The axis used for slanting an object is the object edge directly opposite the midpoint handle being used to slant the object. This axis stays fixed in location while the other sides of the object move in relation to it as you drag the mouse cursor. Figure 47 shows a rectangle slanted using the selection handle at the top of the object.

Click and hold the mouse button, then start to move the cursor to slant the object. A ghosted outline of the object being slanted appears and the current angle of slanting is shown in the status bar.

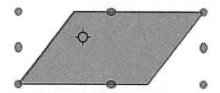

Figure 47: Slanting objects

Note	If you press the *Shift* key while slanting an object, slanting will be restricted to 15° of movement.
	This is the default behavior of the *Shift* key. However, if *When creating or moving objects* has been selected in **Tools > Options > LibreOffice Draw > Grid**, the action of the *Shift* key is reversed: that is slanting will be restricted to 15° of movement *unless* the *Shift* key is pressed.

Setting exact size and position

You can position and resize objects with the mouse, but this method is not exact. If you want to accurately position and size an object, you have to use the Position and Size dialog (Figure 48) or the Position and Size subsection (Figure 49) on the Sidebar.

- To open the Position and Size dialog, select the object, then go to **Format > Position and Size** on the main menu bar, or right-click on an object and select **Position and Size** from the context menu, or press the *F4* key.

- To open the *Position and Size* subsection on the Sidebar, select the object, then click on

  the **Properties** ⬚ icon on the Sidebar and click on the plus sign (+) next to the *Position and Size* title bar to open the subsection.

The options available in the Position and size dialog and the Position and Size subsection are similar. On the Sidebar, you cannot protect the position and size of an object or adapt an object to fit any text or set the base point position for position and size.

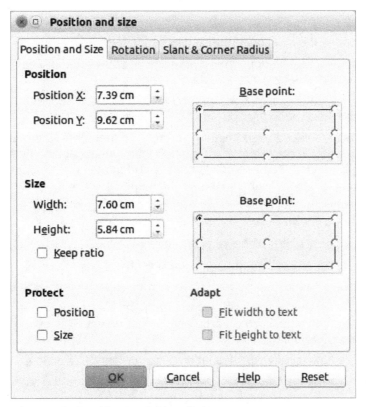

Figure 48: Position and Size dialog

Figure 49: Position and Size on the Sidebar

Position and Size

- **Position** – specify the location of the selected object on the page.
  - *Position X* – enter the horizontal distance that you want to move the object relative to the base point selected in the grid.
  - *Position Y* – enter the vertical distance that you want to move the object relative to the base point selected in the grid.
  - *Base point* – select a base point in the grid and then enter the amount that you want to shift the object relative to the base point that you selected in the Position Y and Position X boxes. The base points correspond to the selection handles on an object. This option is only available in the Position and Size dialog.
- **Size** – specify the amount by which you want to resize the selected object with respect to the selected base point.
  - *Width* – enter a width for the selected object.
  - *Height* – enter a height for the selected object.
  - *Keep ratio* – maintains proportions when you resize the selected object.
  - *Base point* – select a base point in the grid, and then enter the new size dimensions for the selected object in the Width and Height boxes. This option is only available in the Position and Size dialog.
- **Protect** – this option is only available in the Position and Size dialog.
  - *Position* – prevents changes to the position or the size of the selected object.
  - *Size* – prevents you from resizing the object.
- **Adapt** – specifies, if the size of a drawing object should be adjusted to fit the size of entered text. This option is only available in the Position and Size dialog.
  - *Fit width to text* – expands the width of the object to the width of the text, if the object is smaller than the text.
  - *Fit height to text* – expands the height of the object to the height of the text, if the object is smaller than the text.

The units of measurement used for X//Y coordinates and the width and height of the object are set by going to **Tools > Options > LibreOffice Draw > General**.

The default location of the base points for position and size is the upper left corner of the drawing area. You can temporarily change this base point to make positioning or dimensioning simpler by clicking on a position corresponding to the location of the base point you want to use. This change in base point is only valid for single use and the base point is reset to the standard position of top left corner when you close the Position and Size dialog.

Rotating objects

To accurately rotate an object, click on the *Rotation* tab of the Position and Size dialog (Figure 50). Use this dialog to define the rotation angle and the location of the pivot point. Alternatively, use the available options on the *Position and Size* subsection (Figure 49) on the Sidebar.

- **Pivot point** – the selected object is rotated around a pivot point that you specify. The default pivot point is at the center of the object. If you set a pivot point too far outside of the object boundaries, the object could be rotated off of the page. This option is only available in the Position and Size dialog.
  - *Position X* – enter the horizontal distance from the left edge of the page to the pivot point.
  - *Position Y* – enter the vertical distance from the top edge of the page to the pivot point.

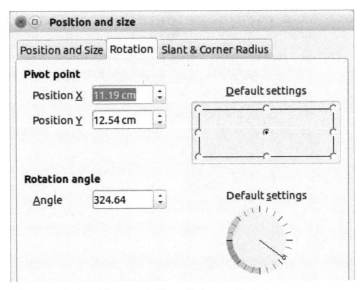

Figure 50: Position and Size dialog – Rotation page

- *Default settings* – select where you want to place the pivot point. Default position is the center of the object. Changing the rotation pivot point is only valid for single use. The pivot point is reset to default settings when you close the Position and Size dialog.

- **Rotation** – specify the number of degrees that you want to rotate the selected object, or click in the rotation grid.

  - *Angle* – enter the number of degrees that you want to rotate the selected object. This option is only available in the Position and Size dialog.

  - *Default settings* – click on the indicator to rotate the object. The number of degrees is shown in the *Angle* box as you rotate the indicator. This option is only available in the Position and Size dialog.

  - *Rotation* – click on the indicator to rotate the selected object, or set the angle in the text box, or select a a predetermined angle from the drop down list. This option is only available in the Position and Size subsection on the Sidebar.

  - *Flip* – flip the selected object either vertically or horizontally about its central axis. This option is only available in the Position and Size subsection on the Sidebar.

Slant and corner radius

To accurately set the corner radius or slant angle of an object, click on the *Slant & Corner Radius* tab of the Position and Size dialog (Figure 51). Options for slant and corner radius are only available in the Position and Size dialog.

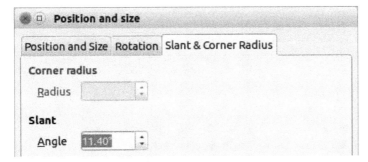

Figure 51: Position and Size dialog – Slant & Corner Radius page

- **Corner Radius** – you can only round the corners of a rectangular object. If this section is grayed out, then you cannot set a corner radius.
  - *Radius* – enter the radius of the circle that you want to use to round the corners. The larger the value for corner radius set, the rounder the corners of an object become.
- **Slant** – slants the selected object along the bottom edge of the object.
  - *Angle* – enter the angle of the slant axis. The slant angle relates to how much an object inclines or slants from its normal vertical position on a drawing.

Using grid and snap functions

In Draw, you can also position objects accurately and consistently using grid points, snap points and lines, object frames, individual points on objects, or page edges. This function is known as *Snap*.

It is easier to use snap functions at the highest practical zoom value for your drawing. You can use two different snap functions at the same time; for example, snapping to a guide line and the page edge. However, it is recommended to activate only those snap functions that you really need.

Configuring grid and snap functions

To configure the grid and snap functions in your drawing, go to **Tools > Options > LibreOffice Draw > Grid** to display the Grid dialog (Figure 52). The grid and snap functions can also be displayed and switched on or off using this dialog, right-clicking on your drawing and using the options in the context menu, or using the icons in the Options toolbar (Figure 53). If the Options toolbar is not open, go to **View > Toolbars > Options**.

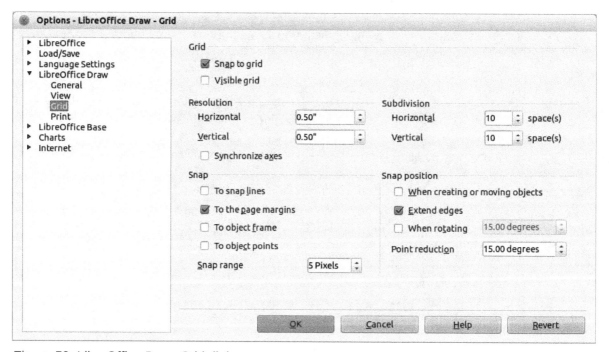

Figure 52: LibreOffice Draw Grid dialog

Figure 53: Options toolbar

- **Grid** – specifies the settings for the configurable grid on your document pages. This grid helps you determine the exact position of your objects. You can also set this grid in line with the magnetic snap grid. If you have activated the snap grid but wish to move or create individual objects without snap positions, keep the *Shift* key pressed to deactivate this function for as long as needed.
  - Snap to grid – specifies whether to move frames, drawing elements, and controls only between grid points. To change the status of the snap grip only for the current action, drag an object while holding down the *Ctrl* key.
  - Visible grid – specifies whether to display the grid.
- **Resolution**
  - Horizontal – defines the unit of measure for the spacing between grid points on the X-axis.
  - Vertical – defines the grid points spacing in the desired unit of measurement on the Y-axis.
- **Subdivision**
  - Horizontal – specify the number of intermediate spaces between grid points on the X-axis.
  - Vertical – specify the number of intermediate spaces between grid points on the Y-axis.
- **Synchronize axes** – specifies whether to change the current grid settings symmetrically. The resolution and subdivision for the X and Y axes remain the same.
- **Snap**
  - To snap lines – snaps the edge of a dragged object to the nearest snap line when you release the mouse button. You can also define this setting by using the **Snap to Snap Lines** icon on the Options toolbar.
  - To the page margins – specifies whether to align the contour of the graphic object to the nearest page margin. The cursor or a contour line of the graphics object must be in the snap range. In a drawing, this function can also be accessed with the **Snap to Page Margins** icon in the Options toolbar.
  - To object frame – specifies whether to align the contour of the graphic object to the border of the nearest graphic object. The cursor or a contour line of the graphics object must be in the snap range. In drawing, this function can also be accessed with the **Snap to Object Border** icon in the Options toolbar.
  - To object points – specifies whether to align the contour of the graphic object to the points of the nearest graphic object. This only applies if the cursor or a contour line of the graphics object is in the snap range. In a drawing, this function can also be accessed with the **Snap to Object Points** icon in the Options toolbar.
  - Snap range – defines the snap distance between the mouse pointer and the object contour. Snaps to a snap point if the mouse pointer is closer than the distance selected.
- **Snap position**
  - When creating or moving objects – specifies that graphic objects are restricted vertically, horizontally or diagonally (45°) when creating or moving them. You can temporarily deactivate this setting by pressing the *Shift* key.
  - Extend edges – specifies that a square is created based on the longer side of a rectangle when the *Shift* key is pressed before you release the mouse button. This

also applies to an ellipse (a circle will be created based on the longest diameter of the ellipse). When *Extend edges* is not selected, a square or a circle will be created based on the shorter side or diameter.

- *When rotating* – specifies that graphic objects can only be rotated within the rotation angle that you selected. If you want to rotate an object outside the defined angle, press the *Shift* key when rotating. Release the key when the desired rotation angle is reached.

- *Point reduction* – defines the angle for point reduction. When working with polygons, you might find it useful to reduce their editing points.

Snap to grid

Using Snap to Grid

Use the **Snap to Grid** function to move an object exactly onto a grid point in your drawing. This function can be switched on and off using one of three methods:

- Go to **View > Grid > Snap to Grid**.
- Right-click on your drawing and selecting **Snap to Grid** from the context menu.
- Click on the **Snap to Grid** icon on the Options toolbar.

Displaying grid

Displaying or turning off the grid in your drawing can be done using one of four methods:

- Go to **View > Grid > Display Grid.**
- Click on the **Display Grid** icon on the Options toolbar.
- Right-click on your drawing and select **Display Grid** from the context menu.
- Selecting *Visible grid* option in the Grid dialog (Figure 52 on page 54).

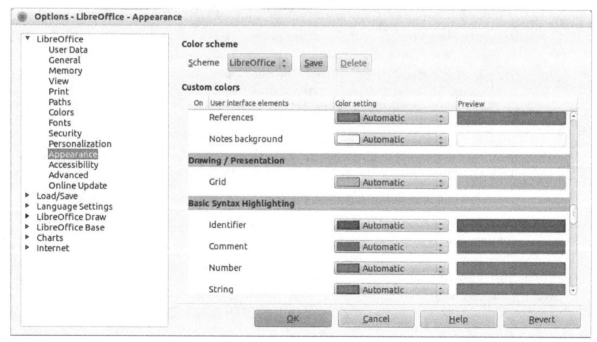

Figure 54: LibreOffice Appearance dialog

Changing color of grid points

By default the grid points are gray and, depending on you display and computer setup, are not always easy to see. To change the color of the grid points, go to **Tools > Options > LibreOffice > Appearance** to open the Appearance dialog (Figure 54). In the *Drawing/Presentation* section, select a more suitable color from the drop-down list.

Snap points and lines

Unlike the grid, snap lines and snap points are inserted by you when you want to position an object in a specific position on your drawing. Snap lines can either be horizontally or vertically and appear as dashed lines. Snap points appear as small crosses with dashed lines. Snap points and snap lines do not appear in printed output.

Inserting snap points and snap lines

To insert a snap point or snap line, go to **Insert > Insert Snap Point/Line** to open the New Snap Object dialog (Figure 55).

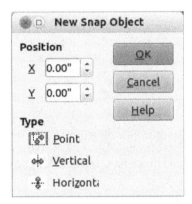

Figure 55: New Snap Object dialog

- **Position** – sets the position of a selected snap point or line relative to the top left corner of the page.
    - *X axis* – enter the amount of space you want between the snap point or line and the left edge of the page.
    - *Y axis* – enter the amount of space you want between the snap point or line and the top edge of the page.
- **Type** – specifies the type of snap object you want to insert.
    - *Point* – inserts a snap point.
    - *Vertical* – inserts a vertical snap line.
    - *Horizontal* – inserts a horizontal snap line.

Inserting snap lines using rulers

Snap lines, but not snap points, can be inserted using the vertical or horizontal rulers. If the rulers are not displayed, go to **Tools > Options > LibreOffice Draw > View** and select *Rulers visible*.

To insert a snap line, move the cursor to a ruler, then click and drag a snap line to the required position.

Displaying snap points and lines

Displaying or turning off snap points and lines in your drawing can be done using one of these methods:

- Go to **View > Grid > Display Snap Lines** on the main menu bar.

- Click on the **Display Snap Lines** icon 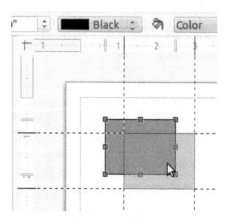 on the Options toolbar.

- Right-click on your drawing and select **Display Snap Lines** from the context menu.

Editing snap points and lines

To edit a snap point, right-click on the snap point and select **Edit Snap Point** from the context menu to open the New Snap Object dialog or drag it to a new position on your drawing.

To edit a snap line, right-click on the snap line and select **Edit Snap Line** from the context menu to open the New Snap Object dialog or drag the snap line to a new position on your drawing.

Deleting snap points and lines

To delete a snap point, drag it back to a ruler or right-click on the snap point and select **Delete Snap Point** from the context menu.

To delete a snap line, drag it back to the ruler or right-click on the snap line and select **Delete Snap Line** from the context menu.

Configuring snap range

To configure the snap range of when an object snaps to position, go to **Tools > Options > LibreOffice Draw > Grid** (Figure 52 on page 54) and enter the number of pixels to set the proximity of when the object will snap into position in the *Snap range* box. The default setting is 5 pixels.

Using guide lines

Guide lines (also known as help lines) are another function in Draw to help you position objects. Guide lines can be displayed while the object is being moved. They extend from the edges of the object to the rulers at the top and left side of your drawing and do not have a snap function (Figure 56).

To use guide lines, go to **Tools > Options > LibreOffice Draw > View** and select the *Snap Lines when moving* option or click the **Helplines While Moving** icon on the Options toolbar.

Figure 56: Using guide lines

Changing form of regular shapes

When drawing certain regular shapes, one or more dots are displayed in a different color to the selection handles when an object is selected. When the cursor hovers over one of these dots, it changes shape. Clicking and dragging on one of these dots modifies the shape of the object. For example, you can increase the corner radius of a rounded rectangle or square, change the angles of an arc, and so on.

These dots perform different functions according to the shape selected. These functions are listed in the following sections.

Basic shapes

- Rounded rectangles and squares – use the dot to change the radius of the curve that replaces the angled corners of a rectangle or square.
- Circle pie – use the dots to change the size of the filled sector.
- Isosceles triangle – use the dot to modify the triangle type.
- Trapezoid, parallelogram, hexagon, or octagon – use the dot to change the angle between the sides.
- Cross – use the dot to change the thickness of the four arms of the cross.
- Ring – use the dot to change the internal diameter of the ring.
- Block arc – use the dot to change both internal diameter and size of the filled area.
- Cylinder and cube – use the dot to change the perspective.
- Folded corner – use the dot to change the size of the folded corner.
- Frame – use the dot to change the thickness of the frame.

Symbol shapes

- Smiley face – use the dot to change the smile on the face.
- Sun, moon, heart – use the dot to change the shape of the symbol.
- Prohibited symbol – use the dot to change the thickness of the ring and the diagonal bar.
- Double bracket, left bracket, right bracket, double brace – use the dot to change the curvature of the bracket.
- Left brace, right brace – use the dots to change the curvature of the brace and the position of the point.
- Square bevel, octagon bevel, diamond bevel – use the dot to change the thickness of the bevel.

Block arrows

- Arrows – use the dot to change the shape and thickness of the arrows.
- Pentagon, chevron – use the dot to change the angle between the sides.
- Arrow callouts – use the dots to change the shape and thickness of the callouts.
- Circular arrow – use the dots to change the thickness and area of the arrow.

Callouts

- Callouts – use the dots to change the length, position and angle of the pointer.

Stars

- 4-point star, 8-point star, 24-point star – use the dot to change the thickness and shape of the star points.
- Vertical scroll, horizontal scroll – use the dot to change the width and shape of the scroll.
- Doorplate – use the dot to change the inward curvature of the corners.

Curves and polygons

Bézier curves

The editing of curves depends on the mathematics of Bézier curves[1]. Explaining Bézier curves goes beyond this scope of this chapter. See *Chapter 11 Advanced Draw Techniques* for more information on drawing and manipulating Bézier curves.

The editing of a Bézier curve consists in principle of moving points or tangents passing through these points. Each tangent has one control point at each end and a junction point where it meets the curve. The relative angle and distance between the control points determine the shape of the curve. Figure 57 shows what happens starting from a basic circle and changing only one point on the circle.

You can create many different shapes by moving either the junction point itself, or one or both of the round handle points at either end of the tangent. Draw offers more possibilities when you use the functions on the Edit Points toolbar.

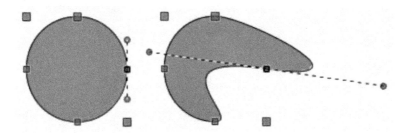

Figure 57: Creating different shapes by changing the tangent

Converting to curve or polygon

Before modifying the points on an object, you must convert the object to a curve or a polygon, depending on what kind of effect you want to produce.

After selecting an object, go to **Modify > Convert** on the main menu bar and select either **To Curve** or **To Polygon**. Alternatively, right-click on an object and select **Convert > To Curve** or **Convert > To Polygon** from the context menu.

After converting an object to a curve or polygon, click on the **Points** icon on the Drawing toolbar and the Edit Points toolbar opens (Figure 58). You can also open this toolbar using **View > Toolbars > Edit Points** on the main menu bar.

You will notice that after the conversion, the handles located in the corners of the selection rectangle have disappeared. This behavior is normal because the handles used with the tools on the Edit Points toolbar are located along the outline or trace of the object.

---

1 Bézier curves were invented by Pierre Bézier, an engineer working with the Renault car manufacturer, who developed the technique in the 1960s. The technology was intended to make modeling the surface of vehicles easier.

Edit Points toolbar

Open the Edit Points toolbar (Figure 58) by going to **View > Toolbars > Edit Points** on the main menu bar. It will then appear whenever you select an object that is a curve or polygon and the **Points** icon on the Drawing toolbar. Available tools on the Edit Points toolbar will depend on the object selected and which object point has been selected.

Figure 58: Edit Points toolbar

Tangents

Before you can use tangents on an object, you must convert the object to a curve. Go to **Modify > Convert > To Curve** on the main menu bar or right-click on the object and select **Convert > To Curve** from the context menu.

Note	Tangents are only used on curves. If an object has been converted to a polygon and a tangent is added, the object is automatically converted to a curve.

Symmetric transition

Symmetric Transition converts a corner point or a smooth point into a symmetrical point. Both control points of the corner point are aligned in parallel and have the same length. They can only be moved simultaneously and the degree of curvature is the same in both directions.

1) Convert the object to a curve and click on the selection handle where you want to place the tangent.

2) Click on the **Symmetric Transition** icon on the Edit Points toolbar.

3) Click and drag one of the tangent handles to change the shape of the object. Any movement of one tangent handle is carried over symmetrically to the other handle, as shown in Figure 59.

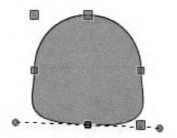

Figure 59: Symmetric transition

Smooth transition

Smooth Transition converts a corner point or symmetrical point into a smooth point. Both control points of the corner point are aligned in parallel, and can only be moved simultaneously. The control points may differentiate in length, allowing you to vary the degree of curvature.

1) Convert the object to a curve and click on the selection handle where you want to place the tangent.

2) Click on the **Smooth Transition** icon ✐ on the Edit Points toolbar so you can adjust separately the lengths on each side of a tangent to make a curve flatter or steeper.

3) Click and drag one of the tangent handles to change the shape of the object. This creates an asymmetric tangent; the curve is flatter on the longest side of the tangent (Figure 60).

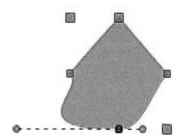

Figure 60: Smooth transition

Corner point

Use **Corner Point** tp convert the selected point or points into corner points. Corner points have two movable control points, which are independent from each other. A curved line, therefore, does not go straight through a corner point, but forms a corner.

It is possible to change independently the angle on each side of a tangent using the central point of the tangent as a corner point.

1) Convert the object to a curve and click on the selection handle where you want to place the corner point.

2) Click on the **Corner Point** icon ◥ on the Edit Points toolbar to create a corner point at the selected point (Figure 61).

3) Click and drag the end of one of the tangents to change its angle. Each tangent can be moved independently to create spikes and troughs in curves.

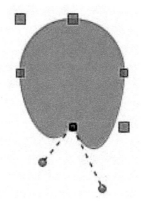

Figure 61: Corner point

Tangent rotation

You can alter the angle by which a tangent relates to curve by clicking on one of the end points of the tangent and rotating it with the cursor. As you change the angle of the tangent, the shape of the curve changes in response (Figure 62).

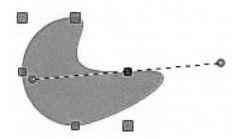

Figure 62: Tangent rotation

Points

Moving points

Move Points activates a mode in which you can move points. The cursor displays a small empty square when resting on a point. Drag that point to another location. The curve on both sides of the point follows the movement; the section of the curve between the next points changes shape.

Point at the curve between two points or within a closed curve and drag the mouse to shift the entire curve without distorting the form.

1) Make sure the object is converted to a curve.

2) Click on the **Move Points** icon ⬆ on the Edit Points toolbar to move any of the points when an object has been converted to a curve or polygon.

3) Hover over a point until the cursor changes shape, then drag the point to create a new shape. Figure 63 illustrates how an ovoid or egg shape was created from a circle by dragging the right hand side point to the right.

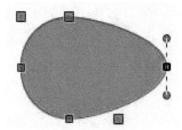

Figure 63: Moving points

Inserting points

Insert Points activates a mode in which you can insert points. You can also move points in this mode, just as in the move mode. If, however, you click on the curve between two points and move the cursor a little while holding down the mouse button, you insert a new point. The point is a smooth point and the lines to the control points are parallel and remain so when moved.

If you wish to create a corner point, you must first insert either a smooth or a symmetrical point which is then converted to a corner point by using Corner Point.

1) Make sure the object is converted to a curve.

2) Click on the **Insert Points** icon ![icon] on the Edit Points toolbar to add an extra point to an existing curve or polygon.

3) Click on the object border at the spot where you want to insert a point. The tangent type associated with the new point depends on where the point has been added to the object border. Figure 64 shows a new point added to the top right of an ovoid shape.

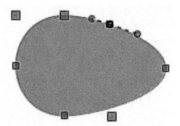

Figure 64: Inserting points

Deleting points

Select a point on the border of the object, then use the **Delete Points** icon ![icon] on the Edit Points toolbar to delete one or more selected points from the border of the object. To select several points, click on those points while holding down the *Shift* key. The resulting curve automatically changes shape around the remaining points. You can also delete selected points by pressing the *Del* key on the keyboard.

Figure 65 shows what happens when the right point was deleted from a circle. The left image is a curve with the right point deleted. The right image is a curve where points have been converted to a line (see "Converting curves or lines" on page 66) and the right point has been deleted. This forms a straight line is formed between the two points on either side of the deleted point.

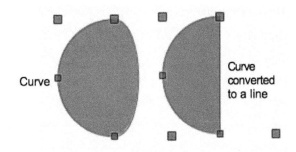

Figure 65: Deleting points

Eliminating points

The **Eliminate Points** icon only functions on lines with multiple points. These lines are created when a curve is converted to a line using the **Convert to Curve** icon on the Edit Points toolbar (see "Converting curves or lines" on page 66). The process of eliminating points from a line to create a straight line is shown in Figure 66.

1) Select a line with multiple points where the points have been converted to a line.
2) Click on the **Points** icon on the Drawing toolbar. The Edit Points toolbar should open. If it does not open, then go to **View > Toolbars > Edit Points** on the main menu bar to open it.
3) Use the mouse cursor to select the point on the line that you want to eliminate. The selected point will be emphasized.

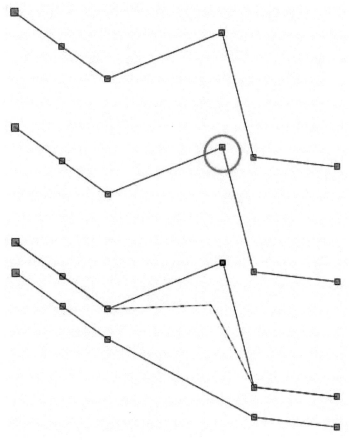

Figure 66: Eliminating points

4) Make sure the **Eliminate Points** icon is active. The area around the icon becomes shaded when active. If it is not active, click on the Eliminate Points icon.

5) Accurately position the mouse cursor over the selected point, then click and start dragging the selected point. As you drag, a dotted line forms between the two neighboring points.

6) When this dotted line appears to be a straight line between the two neighboring points, release the mouse button. The selected point is eliminated and a straight line now exists between the two neighboring points.

Converting curves or lines

Curves and lines can be easily converted to each other using the **Convert to Curve** icon on the Edit Points toolbar. When a curve is converted to a line, a straight line is created between selected points on a curve. When a line is converted to a curve, a curve is created between selected points on a line.

1) Select a curve or line and then select the points on the curve or line where you want to do the conversion.

2) Click on the **Convert to Curve** icon and a curve is converted into a line or a line is converted into a curve (Figure 67).

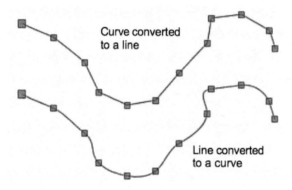

Figure 67: Converting curves and lines

Splitting curves

1) Select a point on the curve.

2) Click on the **Split Curve** icon to split or cut a curve at the location of the selected point. If the object is filled, it will be emptied because the curve that represented the object border is no longer closed (Figure 68).

3) To separate a curve at several points simultaneously, keep the *Shift* key pressed down and select all of the points at which the cut should occur, then click on the **Split Curve** icon.

4) Deselect the curve, then drag and drop segments to move them away from the original curve.

The point where you split the curve is now larger than the remaining points visible on the curve, except for the curve start point which is also larger than the other points.

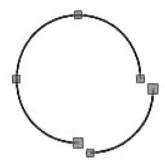

Figure 68: Splitting curves

Closing curves

1) Select an open and existing curve (Figure 69).

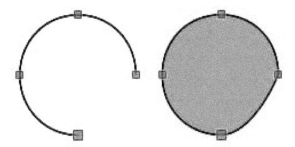

Figure 69: Closing curves

2) Select a point of the curve. Note that the start point of a curve is larger than the other points visible on the curve.

3) Click on the **Close Bézier** icon to close the curve. If the open curve was originally a closed and filled curve, then the original color will fill the curve when it is closed.

Rotating and distorting curves

1) Select the curve, then click on the **Rotate** icon on the Line and filling toolbar or the Mode toolbar. The points on the curve change color and shape (Figure 70).

2) Select one of the points on the curve and drag it to a new position to distort the curve. Movement will be restricted to the original border of the curve.

3) Select one of the control points at the end of the tangent line and rotate the distorted curve by dragging the cursor. The distorted curve will rotate about the center of rotation.

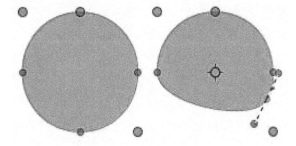

Figure 70: Rotating and distorting curves

Chapter 4
Changing Object Attributes

Formatting lines

In LibreOffice the term *line* indicates both a freestanding segment (line), the outer edge of a shape (border), or an arrow. In most cases the properties of the line you can modify are its style (solid, dashed, invisible, and so on), its width, and its color.

Line and Filling toolbar

To quickly format a line using the Line and Filling toolbar (Figure 71):

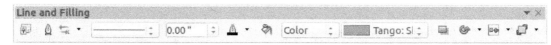

Figure 71: Line and Filling toolbar

1) Make sure the line is selected.
2) On the Line and Filling toolbar, select the line style you want to use from the **Line Style** drop-down list ⎯⎯⎯⎯⎯ .
3) On the Line and Filling toolbar, either type the line width in the **Line Width** text box 0.00 " , or use the up and down arrows to change the line width.
4) On the Line and Filling toolbar, click on the small triangle to the right of the **Line Color** icon 🛡 and select a color from the dialog that opens.

Figure 72: Sidebar Properties Line subsection

Sidebar

To quickly format a line using the Sidebar (Figure 72):

1) Make sure the line is selected in your drawing.

2) Click on the **Properties** icon ![icon] on the Sidebar, then click on the plus sign on the left of the Line title bar to open the **Line** subsection.

3) Use the various options in the **Line** subsection to format the width, color, transparency, and style of the selected line.

4) Select from the drop-down lists in the *Arrow* option to change the line into an arrow. The upper drop-down list adds an arrow head to the beginning of the line. The lower drop-down list adds an arrow head to the end of the line.

5) If the line is segmented, then select the type of *Corner style* and *Cap style* to use from the drop-down lists. For more information, see "Corner and cap styles section" on Page 73.

6) Deselect the line to save your changes to the line.

Line dialog

If you want to fully change the appearance of a line, then you need to use the Line dialog.

1) Select the line on your drawing.

2) Go to **Format > Line** on the main menu bar, or right-click on the line and select **Line** from the context menu, or select the **Line** icon ![icon] from the Line and Filling toolbar to open the Line dialog (Figure 73), where you can set various options for the selected line. This dialog consists of four pages: *Line*, *Shadow*, *Line Styles*, and *Arrow Styles*. The options on these pages are explained in the following sections.

3) When you have made all your changes to the selected line, click **OK** to close the dialog and save your changes. The preview box at the bottom of the dialog shows the effect of your changes on a line.

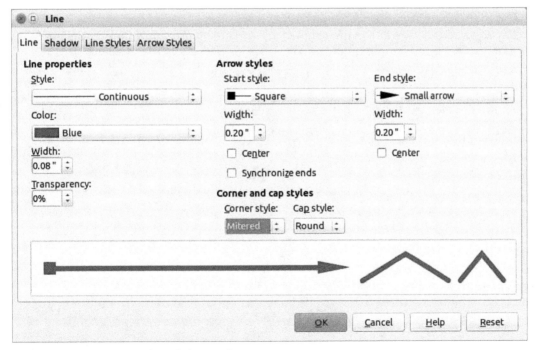

Figure 73: Line properties dialog – Line page

Line properties

The *Line* page is where you can set the basic parameters of the line and is divided into four sections as follows.

Line properties section

Use the *Line Properties* section on the left side to set the following parameters:

- **Line style** – several line styles are available from the drop-down list, but more line styles can be defined if necessary.
- **Color** – choose from the predefined colors in the drop-down list or create a new color.
- **Width** – specifies the thickness of the line.
- **Transparency** – sets the transparency of a line. Figure 74 shows the effects of different percentages in transparency levels to lines when placed over an object.

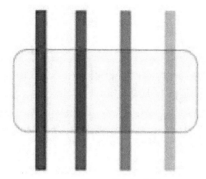

Figure 74: Line transparency effect (0%, 25%, 50%, 75% left to right)

Arrow styles section

The *Arrow styles* section of the *Line* dialog is only applicable to individual lines and is not used for lines that form the borders of a shape.

- **Style** – sets the style of the two ends of a line. The left drop-down menu is for where you start the line and the right drop-down menu is for where you end the line.
- **Width** – specifies the thickness of the arrow endings
- **Center** – moves the center of the arrow endings to the end point of the line. Figure 75 shows the effects of selecting this option.
- **Synchronize ends** – makes the two line ends identical.

Figure 75: Default arrowheads (left) and centered arrowheads (right)

Corner and cap styles section

Corner and cap styles determine how the connection between two segments looks. To appreciate the difference between these styles, choose a thick line style and observe how the preview changes.

- **Corner style** – select the shape to be used at the corners of the line. In case of a small angle between lines, a mitered shape is replaced with a beveled shape.

- **Cap style** – select the style of the line end caps. The caps are added to inner dashes as well.

Arrowheads

A quick way to set the arrowheads for a selected line is to click on the **Arrow Style** icon in the Line and Filling toolbar to open the *Arrowheads* menu (Figure 76). Here you can select one of the many predefined arrowhead styles for the start and ending of the selected line.

Note	Arrowheads are only applicable to lines. They have no effect on the border of an object.

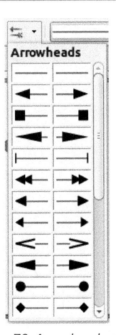

Figure 76: Arrowheads menu

Line shadows

Use the *Shadow* page (Figure 77) of the Line dialog to add and format the line shadow. The settings on this page are the same as those for shadows applied to other objects and are described in "Formatting shadows" on page 90.

A quicker way to apply a shadow to a line is using the **Shadow** icon on the Line and Filling toolbar. The main disadvantage of using the **Shadow** icon is that the shadow appearance will be constrained by the shadow settings of the default graphics style.

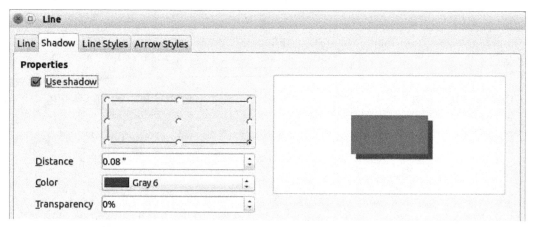

Figure 77: Line properties dialog – Shadow page

Line styles

Use the *Line Styles* page (Figure 78) of the Line dialog to create new line styles as well as to load previously saved line styles. It is normally better to create new styles when necessary than modify predefined styles.

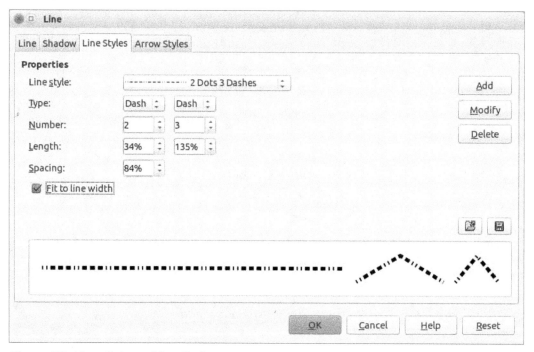

Figure 78: Line dialog – Line Styles page

Creating line styles

To create a new line style:

1) Choose **Format > Line** on the main menu bar, or right-click on the line and select **Line** from the context menu, or select the **Line** icon 🖊 on the Line and Filling toolbar to open the Line dialog.

2) Click on the **Line Styles** tab.

3) Select from the **Line style** drop-down menu a style similar to the style you want to create.

4) Click **Add** and type a name for the new line style in the dialog that opens, then click **OK**.

5) Now define the new style. Start by selecting the line type for the new style. To alternate two line types (for example, dashes and dots) within a single line, select different types in the two **Type** boxes.

6) Specify the **Number** and **Length** (not available for dot style) of each of the types of line selected.

7) Set the **Spacing** between the various elements

8) If necessary, select **Fit to line width** so that the new style fits the width of the selected line.

9) The new line style created is available only in the current document. If you want to use the line style in other documents, click the **Save Line Styles** icon 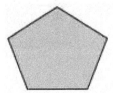 and type a unique filename in the *Save as* dialog that opens. Saved styles have the file extension of .sod.

10) To use previously saved line styles, click the **Load Line Styles** icon and select a style from the list of saved styles. Click **Open** to load the style into your document.

11) If necessary, click on the **Modify** button to change the name of the style.

12) Click **OK** to close the dialog and save any changes you have made.

Arrow styles

Use the *Arrow Styles* page (Figure 79) of the Line dialog to create new arrow styles, or modify existing arrow styles, or load previously saved arrow styles.

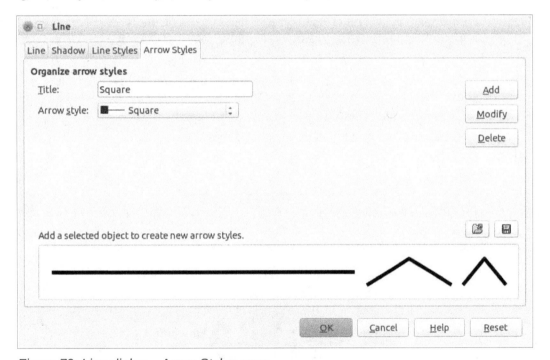

Figure 79: Line dialog – Arrow Styles page

Figure 80: Using shapes for arrow styles

Creating arrow styles

To create a new arrow style:

1) First draw a curve in the shape you want to use for the arrowhead, or create a shape and convert to a curve. The top of the shape must face upward, as shown in Figure 80, because this becomes the point of the arrow.

Note	The arrowhead must be a curve, which is something you can draw without lifting a pencil from the paper. For example, a star can be a curve, but a smiley face cannot be a curve because you have to reposition the pencil on the paper to draw eyes and a mouth on the face.

2) Select the shape and, if necessary, right-click and choose **Convert > To Curve** to convert the shape to a curve. If the shape is already a curve, **To Curve** will not be available.

3) With the selection handles showing, select **Format > Line** from the menu bar, or right-click and choose **Line** from the pop-up menu.

4) Go to the *Arrow styles* page, click the **Add** button, type a name for the new arrow style, and click **OK**. The new arrowhead style will be shown in the preview.

5) Now you can access the new style from the Arrow style list. When you select the name of the new style, it is shown at the bottom of the dialog.

6) The new arrowhead style created is available only in the current document. If you want to use this arrowhead style in other documents, click the **Save Line Styles** icon 🖫 and type a unique filename in the *Save as* dialog that opens. Saved styles have the file extension of .sod.

7) To use previously saved arrowhead styles, click the **Load Line Styles** icon 📂 and select the style from the saved list of styles. Click **Open** to load the style into your document.

8) If necessary. click on the **Modify** button to change the name of the style.

9) Click **OK** to close the dialog and save any changes you have made.

Formatting fill area

The term **area fill** refers to the inside of an object, which can be a uniform color, gradient, hatching pattern, or bitmap as shown in Figure 81. An area fill can be made partly or wholly transparent and can throw a shadow.

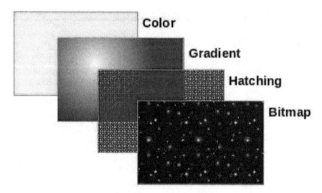

Figure 81: Different types of area fill

Line and Filling toolbar

Tools on the Line and Filling toolbar (Figure 71) provide a wide number of default fillings readily available to quickly format graphic objects. If this toolbar is not showing, go to **View > Toolbars > Line and Filling** on the main menu bar. To format the area of an object:

1) Select an object so that the selection handles are displayed.

2) Click on the left **Area Style/Filling** 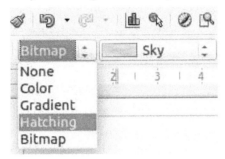 drop-down list and select the type of fill required (*None*, *Color*, *Gradient*, *Hatching*, or *Bitmap*) (Figure 82).

3) Click on the right **Area Style/Filling** drop-down list and select one of the available options for the selected type of area fill as shown in Figure 83, Figure 84, Figure 85 and Figure 86. For more information on area fills, see "Area dialog" on Page 78.

4) Deselect the object to save your changes to the object.

Figure 82: Area fill types

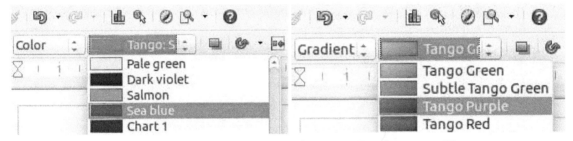

Figure 83: Color area fill   *Figure 84: Gradient area fill*

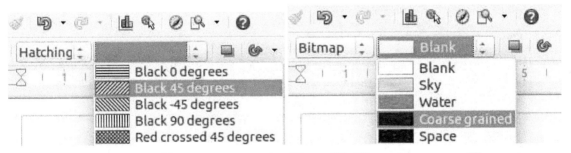

Figure 85: Hatching area fill   *Figure 86: Bitmap image area fill*

Figure 87: Sidebar Properties Area subsection

Sidebar

To quickly format the area of an object using the Sidebar (Figure 87):

1) Make sure the object is selected in your drawing.

2) Click on the **Properties** icon ⬚ on the Sidebar, then click on the plus sign on the left of the Area titlebar to open the **Area** subsection.

3) Use the various options in the drop-down lists of the **Area** subsection to format the fill and transparency of the object. For more information on area fills, see "Area dialog" below.

4) Deselect the object to save your changes.

Note	If you have selected a transparency, the options available will depend on the type of transparency selected. For more information on transparencies, see "Transparency formatting" on Page 90.

Area dialog

Use the Area dialog to apply existing area fills with greater control or create your own area fill.

1) Select the object you wish to edit.

2) Go to **Format > Area** on the main menu bar, or click on the Area icon ⬚ on the Line and Filling toolbar, or right-click on the object and select **Area** to open the Area dialog.

3) Click on the *Area* tab to open the Area page and to apply an area fill. LibreOffice includes several area fills already defined, but you can create area fills yourself. See "Creating new area fills" on page 80 for more information.

4) Select the type of area fill from the drop-down list: *None*, *Color*, *Gradient*, *Hatching*, or *Bitmap*. Types of area fill are explained below.

5) Select the style of area fill from the options that become available. The number of available options will depend on the type of area fill selected above.

6) Click **OK** to close the dialog and save your changes. The area fill will then appear in the selected object.

Figure 88: Area dialog – Area page available colors

Types of area fill

- **Color fills** – select **Color** from the *Fill* drop-down list and then select your required color from the list of available colors (Figure 88). A preview of the selected color appears at the bottom of the dialog.

- **Gradient fills** – select **Gradient** from the drop-down list and then select your required gradient from the list of available gradients (Figure 89). You can override the number of steps (increments) that should be applied to the gradient transition. To do so, deselect the **Automatic** option under *Increments* and then enter the number of steps required in the box to the right. A preview of the selected gradient appears at the bottom of the dialog.

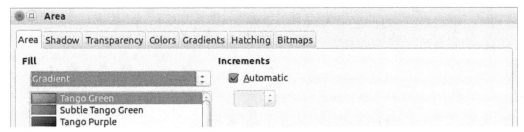

Figure 89: Area dialog – Area page available gradients

- **Hatching fills** – select **Hatching** from the drop-down list and then select your required hatching from the list of available hatchings (Figure 90). You can apply a different background color by selecting the **Background color** option and choosing a color from the drop-down list. A preview of the selected hatching appears at the bottom of the dialog.

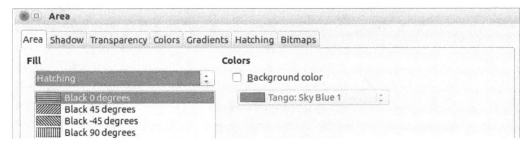

Figure 90: Area dialog – Area page available hatchings

- **Bitmap fills** – select **Bitmaps** from the drop-down list and then select your required bitmap from the list of available bitmaps (Figure 91). You can customize a large number of parameters. A preview of the selected bitmap appears at the bottom of the dialog.

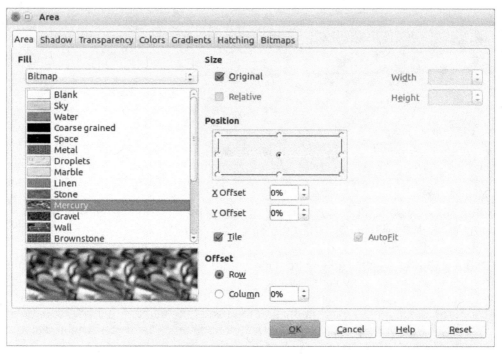

Figure 91: Area dialog – Area page available bitmaps

Creating new area fills

The following sections describe how to create new fills and how to apply them.

Although you can change the characteristics of an existing fill and then click the **Modify** button, it is recommended that you create new fills, or modify custom fills rather than the predefined ones, as these may be reset when updating LibreOffice.

Creating custom colors

On the *Colors* page (Figure 92), you can modify existing colors or create your own. You can also specify a new color either as a combination of the three primary colors Red, Green, and Blue, (RGB notation) or by percentages of Cyan, Magenta, Yellow, and Black (CMYK notation).

Creating new color

1) Select the object you wish to edit.

2) Go to **Format > Area** on the main menu bar, or click on the Area icon 🗔 on the Line and Filling toolbar, or right-click on the object and select **Area** to open the Area dialog.

3) Click on the *Colors* tab to open the Colors page.

4) Enter a name for the new color in the *Name* box.

5) Select whether to define the color in RGB or CMYK. For RGB, specify the red (R), green (G) and blue (B) component on a 0 to 255 scale. For CMYK, specify the cyan (C), magenta (M), yellow (Y) and black (K) components from 0% to 100%.

6) Click the **Add** button. The color is now added to the *Color* drop-down list.

7) Click **OK** to save your changes and close the dialog.

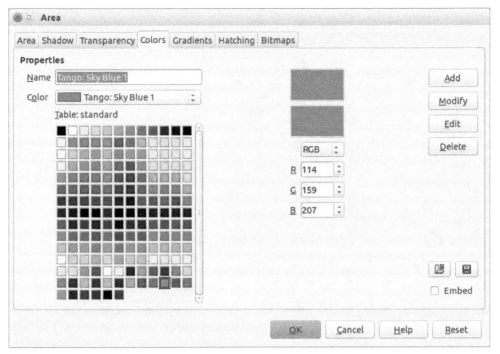

Figure 92: Area dialog – Colors page

Modifying colors

1) Select the object you wish to edit.
2) Go to **Format > Area** on the main menu bar, or click on the Area icon 🖼 on the Line and Filling toolbar, or right-click on the object and select **Area** to open the Area dialog.
3) Click on the *Colors* tab to open the Colors page.
4) Select the color to modify from the list.
5) Enter the new values that define the color in RGB or CMYK.
6) Modify the name as required.
7) Click **Modify** to save your changes.
8) Click **OK** to close the dialog.

Editing colors

1) Select the object you wish to edit.
2) Go to **Format > Area** on the main menu bar, or click on the Area icon 🖼 on the Line and Filling toolbar, or right-click on the object and select **Area** to open the Area dialog.
3) Click on the *Colors* tab to open the Colors page.
4) Select the color to edit from the list.
5) Click on the **Edit** button to open the Color Picker dialog (Figure 93).
6) Modify the color components as required using RGB, CMYK or HSB (Hue, Saturation, Brightness).
7) Click **OK** to exit the Color Picker dialog.
8) Modify the name as required.
9) Click **Modify** on the Color dialog to save your changes.
10) Click **OK** to close the dialog.

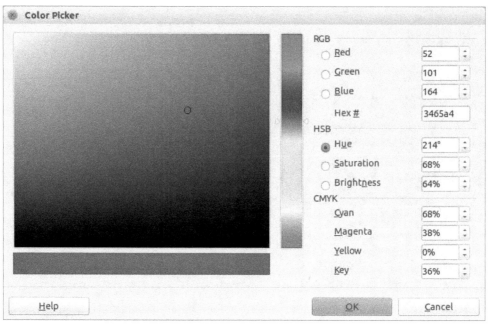

Figure 93: Color Picker dialog

Saving and using new colors

Any new color created is available only in the current document. If you want to use this color in other documents, click the **Save Color List** icon and type a unique filename in the **Save as** dialog that opens. The saved colors list has the file extension of .soc.

To use a previously saved color list, click the **Load Color List** icon and select from the file open dialog. Click **Open** to load the saved color list into Draw.

Tip	You can also add custom colors using **Tools > Options > LibreOffice > Colors**. This method makes the color available to all components of LibreOffice.

Creating custom gradients

To create a new gradient or to modify an existing one, select the Gradients tab from the Area dialog (Figure 94). Several types of gradients are predefined and in most cases changing the *From* and *To* colors will be sufficient to obtain the desired result.

It is highly recommended that you create a new gradient even if you just want to change the two colors, rather than modifying the predefined ones, which should only be used as starting points.

Creating new gradients

1) Select the object you wish to edit.

2) Go to **Format > Area** on the main menu bar, or click on the Area icon on the Line and Filling toolbar, or right-click on the object and select **Area** to open the Area dialog.

3) Click on the *Gradients* tab to open the Gradients page.

4) Select the *From* and *To* colors from the drop-down lists.

5) Select the type of gradient from the drop-down list: *Linear, Axial, Radial, Ellipsoid, Square* or *Rectangular*. A preview of the gradient type is shown in the dialog.

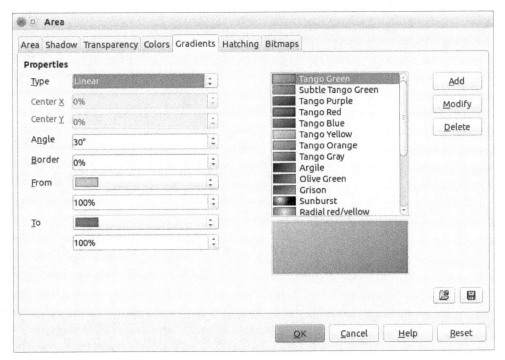

Figure 94: Area Dialog – Gradients page

6) Set all the properties as desired (very often the default values will work well). The properties used to create a gradient are summarized in Table 2. Depending on the type of gradient selected, some properties may be grayed out.

7) Click **Add** to add the newly created gradient to the list.

8) Type a name for the new gradient in the dialog that opens and click **OK**.

9) Click **OK** to close the dialog.

Table 2: Gradient properties

Property	Meaning
Center X	For Radial, Ellipsoid, Square and Rectangular gradients, modify these values to set the horizontal offset of the gradient center.
Center Y	For Radial, Ellipsoid, Square and Rectangular gradients, modify these values to set the vertical offset of the gradient center.
Angle	For all the gradient types, specifies the angle of the gradient axis.
Border	Increase this value to make the gradient start further away from the border of the shape.
From	The start color for the gradient. In the edit box below enter the intensity of the color: 0% corresponds to black, 100% to the full color.
To	The end color for the gradient. In the edit box below enter the intensity of the color: 0% corresponds to black, 100% to the full color.

Modifying gradients

1) Select the object you wish to edit.

2) Go to **Format > Area** on the main menu bar, or click on the Area icon 🎨 on the Line and Filling toolbar, or right-click on the object and select **Area** to open the Area dialog.

3) Click on the *Gradients* tab to open the Gradients page.

4) Select the gradient to modify from the list.

5) Enter the new values for the properties that become available for change. See Table 2 for more information on gradient properties.

6) Click **Modify** to save your changes.

7) Click **OK** to close the dialog.

Saving and using new gradients

The new gradient created is available only in the current document. If you want to use this gradient in other documents, click the **Save Gradients List** icon  and type a unique filename in the **Save as** dialog that opens. The saved gradients list has the file extension of .sog.

To use a previously saved gradients list, click the **Load Gradients List** icon and select from the file open dialog. Click **Open** to load the saved gradients list into Draw.

Advanced gradient controls

As discussed in "Creating custom gradients" on page 82, gradient properties can be configured using the properties given in the dialogs shown in Figure 94 and Table 2. However, LibreOffice provides advanced controls for gradients as follows.

1) Select the object you wish to edit.

2) Go to **Format > Area** on the main menu bar, or click on the Area icon on the Line and Filling toolbar, or right-click on the object and select **Area** to open the Area dialog.

3) Click on the *Gradients* tab to open the Gradients page (Figure 94).

Figure 95: Mode toolbar

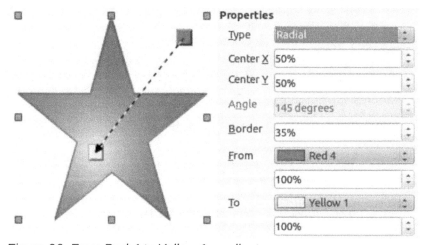

Figure 96: From Red 4 to Yellow 1 gradient

4) Select the type of gradient you want to use for the object from the *Type* drop-down list. Properties you can adjust will depend on the gradient type you have selected and these are explained below.

5) Go to **View > Toolbars > Mode** on the main menu bar, click on the **Effects** icon on the Line and Filling toolbar to open the Mode toolbar.

- Click on the **Gradient** icon in the **Mode** toolbar (Figure 95). This displays a dashed line connecting two colored squares. The colors show the *From* and *To* colors that are used for the selected gradient (Figure 96).

- For **linear gradients** – move the square corresponding to the *From* color to change where the gradient starts (border value). Move the square corresponding to the *To* color to change the orientation (angle value).

- For **axial gradients** – move the *To* color to change both the angle and border properties of the gradient. Only the square corresponding to the *To* color can be moved.

- For **radial gradients** – move the *From* color to modify the border property to set the width of the gradient circle. Move the *To* color to change the point where the gradient ends (Center X and Center Y values).

- For **ellipsoid gradients** – move the *From* color to modify the border property to set the size of the gradient ellipsoid. Move the *To* color to change the angle of the ellipsoid axis and the axis itself.

- For **square and rectangular gradients** – move the *From* color to modify the border to set the size of the gradient square or rectangle and the angle of the gradient shape. Move the *To* color to change the center of the gradient.

6) Click **OK** to save your changes and close the Area dialog.

Note	Moving the squares will have different effects depending on the type of gradient. For example, for a linear gradient, the start and end squares of the gradient will always be situated to either side of the center point of the object.

Creating custom hatching patterns

To create new hatching patterns or modify existing ones, select the *Hatching* tab of the Area dialog (Figure 97). As with gradients and colors, it is better to create a new hatching pattern rather than modify a predefined one. The properties that can be set for a hatching pattern are shown in Table 3.

Table 3: Hatching pattern properties

Property	Meaning
Spacing	Determines the spacing between two lines of the pattern. As the value is changed the preview window is updated.
Angle	Use the mini map below the numerical value to quickly set the angle formed by the line to multiples of 45 degrees. If the required angle is not a multiple of 45 degrees, just enter the desired value in the edit box.
Line type	Set single, double or triple line for the style of the pattern.
Line color	Use the list to select the color of the lines that will form the pattern.

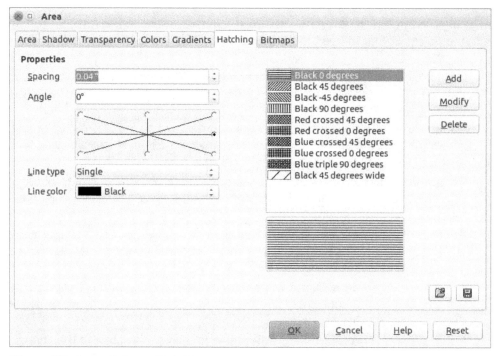

Figure 97: Area dialog – Hatching page

Creating new hatching patterns

1) Select the object you wish to edit.

2) Go to **Format > Area** on the main menu bar, or click on the Area icon 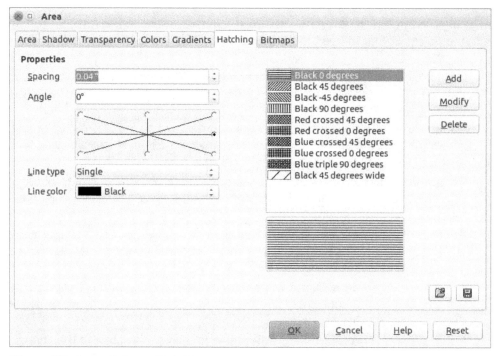 on the Line and Filling toolbar, or right-click on the object and select **Area** to open the Area dialog.

3) Click on the *Hatching* tab to open the Hatching page.

4) Select as a starting point a pattern similar to the one that will be created.

5) Modify the properties of the lines forming the pattern. A preview is displayed in the window below the available patterns. More information on hatching properties is shown Table 3.

6) Click **Add** and type a name for the new gradient in the dialog that opens, then click **OK**.

7) Click **OK** to close the dialog.

Modifying hatching patterns

1) Select the object you wish to edit.

2) Go to **Format > Area** on the main menu bar, or click on the Area icon on the Line and Filling toolbar, or right-click on the object and select **Area** to open the Area dialog.

3) Click on the *Hatching* tab to open the Hatching page.

4) Select the hatching pattern to modify from the list.

5) Enter the new values for the properties that become available for change. See Table 3 for more information on gradient properties.

6) Click **Modify** to save your changes.

7) Click **OK** to close the dialog.

Saving and using new hatching patterns

The new hatching pattern created is available only in the current document. If you want to use this hatching pattern in other documents, click the **Save Hatches List** icon 💾 and type a unique filename in the **Save as** dialog that opens. The saved hatches list has the file extension of .soh.

To use a previously saved hatches list, click the **Load Hatches List** icon 📂 and select from the file open dialog. Click **Open** to load the saved hatches list into Draw.

Working with bitmap fills

1) Select the object you wish to edit.
2) Go to **Format > Area** on the main menu bar, or click on the Area icon 🎨 on the Line and Filling toolbar, or right-click on the object and select **Area** to open the Area dialog.
3) Click on the *Area* tab to open the Area page.
4) Select *Bitmap* from the *Fill* drop-down list (Figure 91 on Page 80).
5) Select from the list of bitmaps the one to be used to fill the area. Note that any imported bitmaps will become available in the list.
6) Set the size, position and offset parameters (as applicable). See Table 4 for more information on bitmap properties. The best way to acquire understanding of these parameters is to use them. Figure 91 on Page 80 shows some examples of bitmap fills and the parameters used.
7) Click **OK** to close the dialog.

Original bitmap

Original size
Anchor to left corner
No offset

Original size
Anchor middle
30% column offset

Relative size
35% width 25% height
Anchor top left corner
No offset

Figure 98: Examples of bitmap fill

Table 4: Bitmap fill properties

Property	Meaning
Size – Original	Select this box to retain the original size of the bitmap.
Size – Relative	To rescale the object, deselect Original and select Relative. The Width and Height edit boxes are enabled.

Property	Meaning
Size – Width	When Relative is selected 100% means that the bitmap original width will be resized to occupy the whole fill area width, 50% means that the width of the bitmap will be half that of the fill area.
Size – Height	When Relative is selected 100% means that the bitmap original height will be resized to occupy the whole fill area height, 50% means that the height of the bitmap will be half that of the fill area.
Position – Anchor Map	Select from the map the place within the area to which the bitmap should be anchored.
Position – Tile	When this option is selected, the bitmap will be tiled to fill the area. The size of the bitmap used for the tiling is determined by the Size settings.
Position – X offset	When Tile is enabled, enter in this box the offset for the width of the bitmap in percentage values. 50% offset means that Draw will place the middle part of the bitmap at the anchor point and start tiling from there.
Position – Y offset	This will have a similar effect to the X offset, but will work on the height of the bitmap.
Position – Autofit	Stretches the bitmap to fill the whole area. Selecting this option disables all the size settings.
Offset – Row	If Tile is enabled, offsets the rows of tiled bitmaps by the percentage entered in the box so that two subsequent rows are not aligned.
Offset – Column	If Tile is enabled, offsets the columns of tiled bitmaps by the percentage entered in the box so that two subsequent columns of bitmaps are not aligned.

Creating and importing bitmaps

You can add (import) new bitmap fills or create your own pattern on an 8x8 grid using the *Bitmaps* tab of the Area dialog (Figure 99).

Creating bitmap fills

1) Select the object you wish to edit.

2) Go to **Format > Area** on the main menu bar, or click on the Area icon on the Line and Filling toolbar, or right-click on the object and select **Area** to open the Area dialog.

3) Click on the *Bitmap* tab to open the Bitmap page.

4) Select **Blank** as the bitmap type to activate the **Pattern Editor**.

5) Select the **Foreground** and **Background** colors.

6) Start creating the pattern by clicking with the left mouse button the squares (pixels) that you want in the foreground color. Use the right mouse button to apply the background color. Check the preview window to see if the desired effect is achieved.

7) Click **Add** to save the pattern and type a name for the new gradient in the dialog that opens, then click **OK**.

8) Click **OK** to close the dialog.

Note	You can only modify bitmaps that you have created in LibreOffice. The bitmaps supplied with LibreOffice or imported bitmaps cannot be changed or modified using LibreOffice.

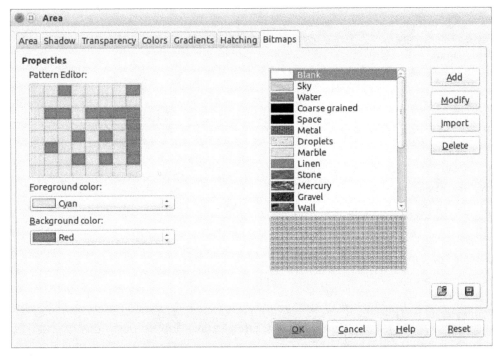

Figure 99: Creating a new bitmap

Modifying bitmaps

1) Select the object you wish to edit.

2) Go to **Format > Area** on the main menu bar, or click on the Area icon on the Line and Filling toolbar, or right-click on the object and select **Area** to open the Area dialog.

3) Click on the *Bitmap* tab to open the Bitmap page.

4) Select a bitmap that you have created from the list.

5) Make the changes to your bitmap using the **Pattern Editor** and the color drop-down lists.

6) Click **Modify** to save your changes.

7) If necessary, type a new name in the dialog that opens and click **OK**.

8) Click **OK** to close the dialog.

Importing bitmaps

To import a bitmap created in another program:

1) Click **Import** and a file browser dialog opens.

2) Browse to the directory containing the bitmap file and select it, then click **Open**.

3) Type a name for the imported bitmap and click **OK**.

Saving and using new bitmaps

The new bitmap created is available only in the current document. If you want to use this bitmap in other documents, click the **Save Bitmap List** icon and type a unique filename in the **Save as** dialog that opens. The saved bitmap list has the file extension of .sob.

To use a previously saved bitmap list, click the **Load Bitmap List** icon and select from the file open dialog. Click **Open** to load the saved bitmap list into Draw.

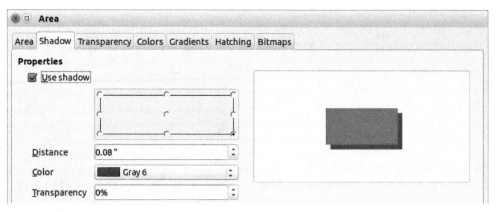

Figure 100: Area dialog – Shadow page

Formatting shadows

Shadowing can be applied to lines, shapes and text.

To quickly apply a shadow to a line or shape only, first select the object and then click on the **Shadow** icon ![shadow icon] in the Line and Filling toolbar. The shadow applied using this method cannot be customized and is set to default settings.

For a more control when adding shadows to an object, you have to use the Shadow page on the Area dialog (Figure 100) as follows:

1) Select the object you wish to edit.

2) Go to **Format > Area** on the main menu bar, or click on the Area icon ![area icon] on the Line and Filling toolbar, or right-click on the object and select **Area** to open the Area dialog.

3) Click on the *Shadow* tab to open the Shadow page.

4) Select **Use shadow** and the shadow options become active.

5) In **Position** select the direction in which the shadow is cast.

6) In **Distance** enter a distance in the text box to set spacing between the object and the shadow.

7) In **Color** select a color form the drop-down list to determine the color of the shadow.

8) In **Transparency** enter a percentage in the text box to determine the amount of transparency for the shadow.

9) Click **OK** to save your changes and close the dialog.

Transparency formatting

Transparency is applicable to objects as well as shadows. To apply transparency to lines, refer to "Formatting lines" on page 70; for shadows, refer to "Formatting shadows" above.

To apply transparency to objects using the Transparency page on the Area dialog (Figure 101):

1) Select the object you wish to edit.

2) Go to **Format > Area** on the main menu bar, or click on the Area icon ![area icon] on the Line and Filling toolbar, or right-click on the object and select **Area** to open the Area dialog.

3) Click on the *Transparency* tab to open the Transparency page.

4) To create a uniform transparency, select **Transparency** and enter a percentage in the text box.

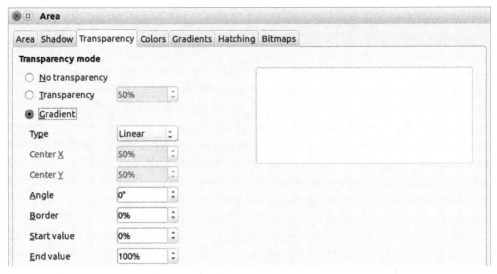

Figure 101: Area dialog – Transparency page

5) To create a gradient transparency (so that the area becomes gradually transparent) select **Gradient** and select the type of gradient transparency from the drop-down list: *Linear*, *Axial*, *Radial*, *Ellipsoid*, *Quadratic* or *Square*.

6) Set the parameters for the type of the gradient transparency you selected above. Refer to Table 5 for a description of the properties. The available parameters will depend on the type of gradient transparency selected above.

7) Click **OK** to save your changes and close the dialog.

Table 5: Gradient transparency properties

Property	Meaning
Center X	For Radial, Ellipsoid, Quadratic and Square gradients, modify these values to set the horizontal offset of the gradient center.
Center Y	For Radial, Ellipsoid, Quadratic and Square gradients, modify these values to set the vertical offset of the gradient center.
Angle	For Linear, Axial, Ellipsoid, Quadratic and Square gradient, specifies the angle of the gradient axis.
Border	Increase this value to make the gradient start further away from the border of the object.
Start value	Value for the starting transparency gradient. 0% is fully opaque, 100% means fully transparent.
End value	Value for the ending transparency gradient. 0% is fully opaque, 100% means fully transparent.

Using styles

Suppose that you want to apply the same area fill, line thickness, and border to a set of objects. This repetitive process can be greatly simplified by the use of styles. Styles allow you to define a formatting template (a style) and then to apply that style to multiple objects. For more information on styles, see the *Writer Guide Chapter 6 Introduction to Styles*.

Linked drawing object styles

Drawing object styles support inheritance; that is, a style can be linked to another (parent) style so that it inherits all the formatting settings of the parent. You can use this property to create families of styles.

For example, if you need multiple boxes that differ in color but are otherwise identically formatted, the best way to proceed is to define a generic style for the box including borders, area fill, font, and so on. Then create a number of hierarchically dependent styles which differ only in the fill color attribute. If you then need to change the font size or the thickness of the border, it is sufficient to change the parent style and all the other linked styles will change accordingly.

Creating drawing object styles

You can create a new drawing object style in the following ways:

- Using the Styles and Formatting dialog.
- Using the Styles and Formatting section on the Sidebar.
- From a selected object.

Note	In LibreOffice Draw, only Drawing Object Styles are available in the Styles and Formatting dialog and the Styles and Formatting section on the Sidebar.

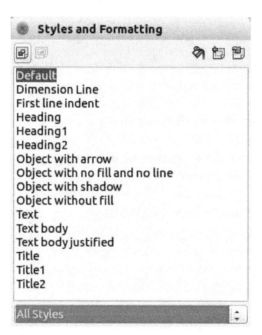

Figure 102: Styles and Formatting dialog

Styles and Formatting dialog

1) Click on the **Styles and Formatting** icon on the Line and Filling toolbar or go to **Format > Styles and Formatting** on the main menu bar or press the *F11* key to open the Styles and Formatting dialog (Figure 102).
2) Select a style you want to use in the Styles and Formatting dialog.
3) Right-click and select **New** to open the Image Styles dialog (Figure 103).

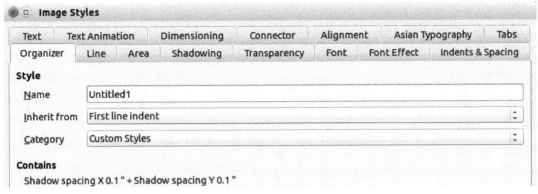

Figure 103: Image Styles dialog – Organizer page

4) Click on the *Organizer* tab to the Organizer page.

5) Give your new drawing object style a memorable file name.

6) Use the various pages and available options in the Image Styles dialog to format and categorize your new style.

7) Click **OK** when finished to save your new drawing object style and close the dialog.

The Image Styles dialog consists of several pages that may be grouped as follows:

- *Organizer* – contains a summary of the style and its hierarchical position.

- *Font*, *Font Effects*, *Indents & Spacing*, *Alignment*, *Tabs* and *Asian Typography* – set the properties of the text inserted in a text box or in a graphic object.

- *Dimensioning* – used to set the style of dimension lines.

- *Text*, *Text Animation*, *Connector*, *Line*, *Area*, *Shadowing*, and *Transparency* – determine the formatting of an object.

Note	When styles are linked, changing a color (for example) will change the color in all linked styles. Sometimes this is exactly what you want; at other times you do not want the changes to apply to all linked styles. It pays to plan ahead.

Sidebar Styles and Formatting section

Make sure your object is selected and click on the **Styles and Formatting** icon ⬚ on the Sidebar to open the Styles and Formatting section. This section is identical to the Styles and Formatting dialog. To create a new drawing object style, see the procedure given in "Styles and Formatting dialog" above.

Using a selected object

You can create a new drawing object style from an object that has already been formatted.

1) Select the object you want to use to create your new style.

2) Open the Styles and Formatting dialog or the Styles and Formatting section on the Sidebar.

3) Click the **New Style from Selection** icon ⬚ .

4) In the Create Style dialog that opens, type a name for the new style. This dialog also shows existing custom styles that are available.

5) Click **OK** to save the new style.

Modifying drawing object styles

To modify an existing style:

1) Right-click on the style in the Styles and Formatting dialog or the Styles and Formatting section on the Sidebar.
2) Select **Modify** from the context menu to open the Image styles dialog (Figure 103).
3) Make the required changes to the style.
4) Click **OK** to save your changes and close the dialog.

Updating from a selection

To update a drawing object style from a selected object:

1) Select an object that uses the format you want to adopt as a style.
2) In the Styles and Formatting dialog or the Styles and Formatting section on the Sidebar, select the style you want to update and then click the **Update Style** icon .

Applying drawing object styles

You can apply a drawing object style using the Styles and Formatting dialog or the Styles and Formatting section on the Sidebar. First make sure that the styles are shown (Figure 102), then do one of the following:

- Select the object to which you want to apply a style and double-click on the name of the style you want to apply.

- Click the **Fill Format mode** icon , position the cursor on the object to be styled and click the mouse button. This mode remains active until you turn it off, so you can apply the same style to several objects. To quit Fill Format mode, click the **Fill Format mode** icon again or press the *Esc* key.

- When Fill Format mode is active, a right-click anywhere in the document cancels the last Fill Format action. Be careful not to accidentally right-click and thus undo actions you want to keep.

Tip	At the bottom of the Styles and Formatting dialog or the Styles and Formatting section on the Sidebar there is a drop-down list. Here you can choose to show all styles or groups of styles such as applied styles or custom styles.

Deleting drawing object styles

You cannot delete any of the predefined styles in LibreOffice, even if you are not using them. You can only delete user-defined (custom) styles. However, before you delete a custom style, make sure the style is not in use. If an unwanted style is in use, make sure you replace it with another style. To see which style are in use, choose *Applied Styles* in the drop-down list at the bottom of the Styles and Formatting dialog.

To delete a custom style, right-click on the style in the Styles and Formatting dialog and choose **Delete** on the context menu. If the style is in use, a warning message will appear; you can click **Yes** to delete the style anyway. If the style is not in use, no confirmation message appears.

Figure 104: Mode toolbar and available tools

Applying special effects

As well as the basic actions of moving and resizing an object, a number of special effects can also be applied to objects in Draw. Several of these effects are readily available in the Mode toolbar (Figure 104). If the Mode toolbar is not showing, select it from **View > Toolbars > Mode**.

The tools available on the Mode toolbar are described in the following sections with the exception of the 3D rotation tool, which is described in *Chapter 7 Working with 3D Objects*.

Rotating objects

Rotation of an object can be carried out manually or using a dedicated dialog, just like changing object position and size.

Manual rotation

1) Click on an object and the selection handles will show.

2) Click the **Rotate** icon in the Line and Filling or Mode toolbars or click again on the selected object. The selection handles change shape and color (Figure 105).

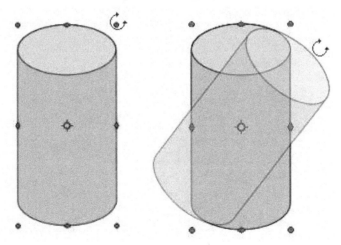

Figure 105: Object selected for rotation

3) If necessary, click and drag the pivot point for rotation to change the way an object is rotated. The pivot point is a circle and appears, by default, in the middle of the selected object. Normally the center of an object will be just fine, but on some occasions you may wish to rotate around a corner or even around a point outside the object.

4) Move the mouse over one of the corner handles and the cursor changes shape.

5) Click the mouse and move in the direction in which you want to rotate the object. Only the corner selection handles are active for rotation.

6) To restrict the rotation angles to multiples of 15 degrees, press and hold the *Shift* key while rotating the object. This is very handy for rotating objects through a right angle, for example from portrait to landscape.

7) When satisfied release the mouse button.

Sidebar rotation

To rotate an object using the Sidebar:

1) Click on an object and the selection handles will show.

2) Click on the **Properties** icon ⬛ on the Sidebar, then click on the plus sign (+) next to the *Position and Size* subsection to open this subsection (Figure 106).

3) Click on the selected object again to change the selection handles into rotation handles.

4) Click on and then rotate the rotation indicator in Rotation or enter the rotation angle in the text box or select a predetermined rotation angle from the drop-down list.

5) When satisfied with the rotation of the object, click outside the object and the object is rotated.

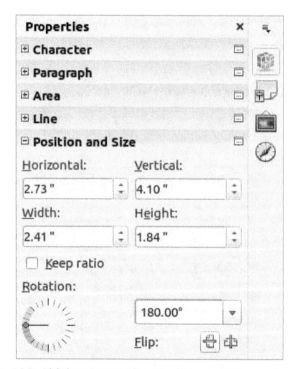

Figure 106: Sidebar Properties Position and Size subsection

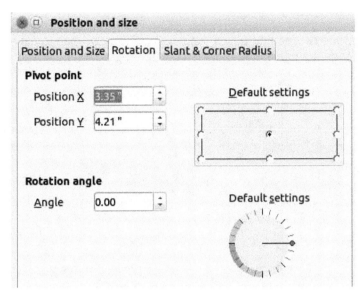

Figure 107: Position and Size dialog – Rotation page

Rotation dialog

Instead of rotating an object manually or using the Sidebar, you can use the Rotation dialog (Figure 107) for more precise control when rotating an object.

1) Select the object so that the selection handles are displayed.

2) Press *F4* key, or select **Format > Position and Size** on the main menu bar, or right-click on the object and select **Position and Size** from the context menu to open the Position and Size dialog.

3) Click the *Rotation* tab to open the Rotation page.

4) In the **Pivot point** section, enter a figure in **Position X** and/or **Position Y** boxes to reposition the pivot point relative to the top left corner of the drawing, or select a position for the pivot point in **Default settings**. The default position for the pivot point is the center of the object.

5) In the **Rotation angle** section, enter an angle in the **Angle** box by which to rotate the object, or click and drag the **Rotation Angle** indicator in **Default settings** until you reach the required angle. As you click and drag, the angle is shown in the **Angle** box.

6) Click **OK** to save your changes and close the dialog.

Flipping objects

Quick flipping

The quickest and easiest method to flip an object horizontally or vertically is as follows:

1) Select an object and the selection handles will be displayed.

2) Go to **Modify > Flip** and select **Horizontally** or **Vertically** on the main menu bar, or right-click and select **Flip > Horizontally** or **Flip > Vertically** from the context menu, or click on the vertical or horizontal **Flip** icons ⊕ ⊕ in the *Position and Size* subsection on the Sidebar and the selected object will be flipped to face the other direction.

Flip tool

The **Flip** tool on the Mode or Line and Filling toolbars can also be used to flip an object. Using this tool, you can also change the position and angle that the object flips over (Figure 108).

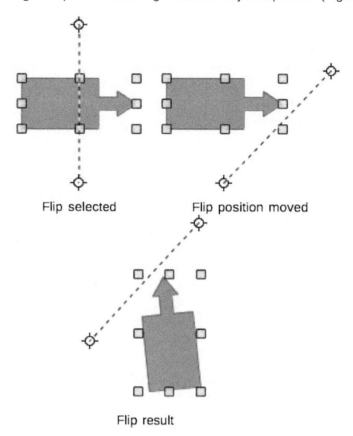

Flip selected   Flip position moved

Flip result

Figure 108: Using the Flip tool

1) Select an object and the selection handles will be displayed.

2) Click the **Flip** icon on the Mode toolbar and the *axis of symmetry* appears as a dashed line through the middle of the object. The object will be flipped about this axis of symmetry.

3) Click and drag one or both ends of the axis of symmetry to set the orientation of the axis.

4) Place the cursor over one of the object selection handles until it changes shape.

5) Click and drag the object across to the other side of the axis of symmetry until the object appears flipped over. The angle and position of the flip will depend on the angle and position of the axis of symmetry.

6) Release the mouse button and the object is flipped.

Note	If you press the *Shift* key while moving the axis of symmetry, it will rotate in 45 degree increments.

Mirror copies

At the moment there is no mirror command existing in Draw. However, mirroring an object can be emulated by using the **Flip** tool as follows:

1) Select the object you want to make a mirror copy of and copy the object to the clipboard.

2) Select the **Flip** tool on the Mode or Line and Filling toolbars.

3) Move the axis of symmetry to the desired location of the mirror axis, then flip the object.

4) Click on an empty area of the page to deselect the object.

5) Paste from the clipboard to put a copy of the object back into its original location and now you have a mirror copy.

6) If necessary, select both objects and realign them by going to **Modify>Alignment** on the main menu bar, or right-click and select **Alignment** from the context menu and then select the type of alignment.

Distorting images

Three tools on the Mode toolbar let you drag the corners and edges of an object to distort it.

- **Distort** ⬚ distorts an object in perspective.

- **Set to Circle (slant)** ⤸ creates a pseudo three-dimensional effect.

- **Set in Circle (perspective)** ⤸ creates a pseudo three-dimensional effect.

In all three cases you are initially asked if you want to transform the object to a curve. This is a necessary first step, so click **Yes**. Then you can move the object handles to produce the desired effect. The results of using these tools are shown in the following figures.

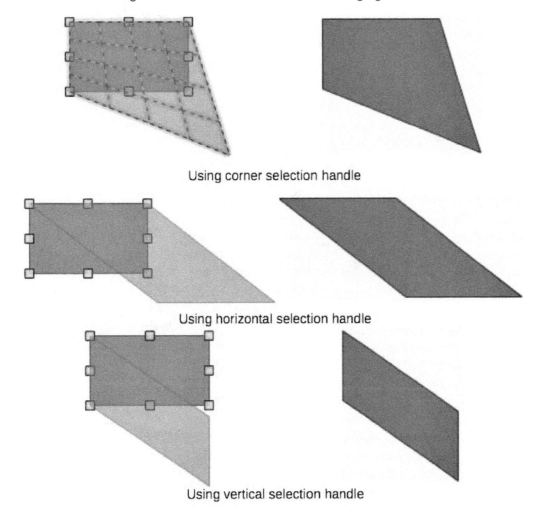

Using corner selection handle

Using horizontal selection handle

Using vertical selection handle

Figure 109: Distorting an object

Distorting

Select an object and click on the **Distort** icon ![distort icon] on the Mode toolbar. After converting to a curve as requested, move the handles to stretch the object. The corner handles distort the corners, the vertical midpoint handles distort the figure horizontally and the horizontal ones distort it vertically (Figure 109).

Setting in circle (perspective)

Select an object and click on the **Set in Circle (perspective)** icon ![set in circle icon] in the Mode toolbar. After converting to a curve, click and move one of the selection handles to give a pseudo three dimensional perspective) (Figure 110).

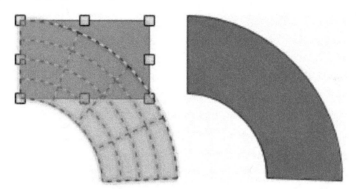

Figure 110: Setting an object to a circle with perspective

Setting to circle (slant)

Select an object and click on the **Set to Circle (slant)** icon ![set to circle slant icon] in the mode toolbar. After converting to a curve, click and move one of the selection handles to give a pseudo three dimensional slant perspective (Figure 111).

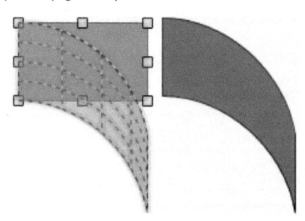

Figure 111: Setting an object to a circle with slant

Note	Transforming an object into a curve is a safe operation, but it cannot be reversed other than by clicking the **Undo** button.

Dynamic gradients

You can control transparency gradients in the same manner as color gradients and both types of gradient can be used together. With a transparency gradient, the direction and degree of object fill color changes from opaque to transparent. In a color gradient, the fill changes from one color to another, but the degree of transparency remains the same.

Two icons are present on the Mode toolbar to dynamically control transparency and color gradients. Even if you have not assigned transparency to an object with a color fill, you can control the transparency by clicking on the **Transparency** icon 🔧. This defines a transparency gradient and a dashed line connecting two squares appears on the object. Move the two squares to modify the gradient. You can define the direction of the gradient (vertical, horizontal, or at any angle) and the spot at which the transparency begins.

A regular color gradient is defined in the same manner. Select an object, then select a gradient fill from the Gradients page of the Area dialog (Figure 94 on page 83). The **Gradient** icon 🔧 is now active on the Mode toolbar. When you click on the gradient icon, a dashed line connecting two squares appears on the object, just as it does for a transparency gradient.

In both transparency gradient and gradient fill, click outside the object to set the gradient.

Note	Moving the squares will have different effects, depending on the type of gradient. For example, for a linear gradient, the start and end squares of the gradient will always be situated to either side of the center point of the object.

Example 1

A single color object and a transparency gradient, covering part of the underlying object. The gradient can be dynamically adjusted; the direction of transparency by moving the white square or the distance over which it is applied by moving the black square (Figure 112).

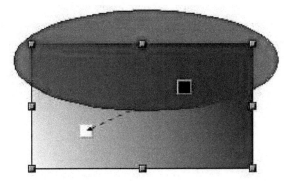

Figure 112: Example 1 of a dynamic gradient

Example 2

An object with a color gradient, completely covering another object. The gradient is adjusted dynamically by moving the squares – the color of the square relating to the increase or decrease in that color (Figure 113).

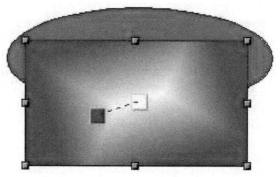

Figure 113: Example 2 of a dynamic gradient

Example 3

An object with both color and transparency gradients, partly covering the underlying object (Figure 114).

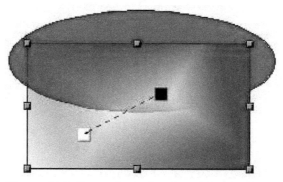

Figure 114: Example 3 of a dynamic gradient

Chapter 5
Combining Multiple Objects

Grouping, Combining, Merging, and Positioning

Grouping objects

Grouping of objects is similar to putting objects into a container. You can move the objects as a group and apply global changes to the objects within the group. A group can always be undone and the objects that make up the group can always be manipulated separately.

Temporary grouping

A temporary grouping is when several objects are selected. Any changes to object parameters that you carry out are applied to all of the objects within the temporary group. For example, you can rotate a temporary group of objects in its entirety.

To cancel a temporary grouping of objects, simply click outside of the selection handles displayed around the objects.

Grouping

To group objects together permanently:

1) Select the objects by clicking on each object in turn while holding down the *Shift* key, or use the **Select** icon 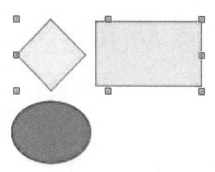 on the Drawing toolbar and draw a selection rectangle around the objects using the cursor. Selection handles will then appear around all the objects within the group (Figure 115).

2) Right-click on the group and select **Group** from the context menu, or go to **Modify > Group** on the main menu bar, or use the keyboard shortcut *Control+Shift+G*.

Figure 115: Grouping objects

When objects are grouped, any editing operations carried out on that group are applied to all objects within the group. If you click on one object in the group, the whole group is selected.

The objects within a group also retain their own individual properties and can be edited independently. See "Editing individual objects" on page 105 for more information.

Ungrouping

To undo or ungroup a group of objects:

1) Select the group of objects which is indicated by selection handles appearing around the group.

2) Right-click on the group and select **Ungroup** from the context menu, or go to **Modify > Ungroup** on the main menu bar, or use the keyboard shortcut *Control+Alt+Shift+G*.

Editing individual objects

You can individually edit an object within a group without ungrouping the group.

1) Right-click on the group and select **Enter group** from the context menu, or go to **Modify > Enter Group** on the main menu bar, or press the *F3* key, or double-click on the group. When you enter a group, objects outside the group cannot be selected for editing and appear pale (Figure 116).

2) Once inside the group, click on any object to individually edit it (Figure 117).

3) To leave a group, right-click on the group and select **Exit group** from the context menu, or go to **Modify > Exit Group** on the main menu bar, or use the keyboard combination *Ctrl+F3* key, or double-click outside the group.

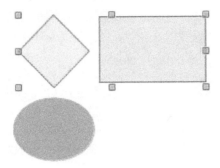

Figure 116: Entering groups

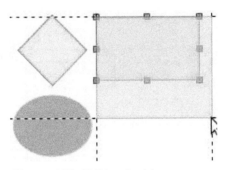

Figure 117: Editing inside a group

Nesting groups

You can create a group of groups, which is more commonly known as nesting groups. When you create nested groups, Draw retains the individual group hierarchy and remembers the order in which groups were selected. That is, the last individual group selected will be on top of all the other groups within a nested group.

Ungrouping and entering a nested group works in exactly the same way as for individual groups in "Grouping" and "Ungrouping" as above.

Combining objects

Combining objects is a permanent merging of objects that creates a new object. The original objects are no longer available as individual entities and cannot be edited as individual objects. Any editing of a combined object affects all the objects that were used when combination was carried out.

Combining

1) Select the objects you want to combine.

2) Right-click on the selection and select **Combine** from the context menu, or go to **Modify > Combine** on the main menu bar, or use the keyboard combination *Control+Alt+Shift+K*.

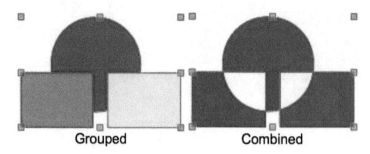

Grouped   Combined

Figure 118: Combining objects

At first glance, the results can seem rather surprising, but once you understand the rules governing combination in Draw, combining objects will become clearer.

- The attributes (for example, area fill) of the resulting object are those of the object furthest back. In Figure 118, it is the circle and Figure 119 it is the yellow rectangle.

- Where the objects overlap, the overlapping zone is either filled or empty depending on whether the overlap is even numbered or odd numbered. Figure 119 Shows that where the overlap number is even, you get an empty space and where the overlap number is odd, you get a filled area.

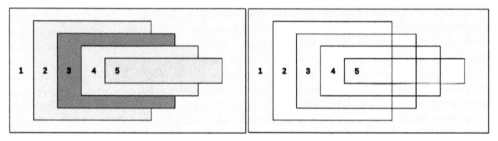

Figure 119: Area fill on overlapping objects

Tip	You can reorder objects so they are further back or further forward in the arrangement order. Right-click on the object and select **Arrangement** from the context menu. For more information, see "Arranging objects" on page 112.

Splitting combined objects

An object which has been combined from several objects can be split into individual objects by going to **Modify > Split** on the main menu bar, or right-clicking on the combined object and selecting **Split** from the context menu, or using the keyboard shortcut *Control+Alt+Shift+K*. However, the original objects will retain the formatting of the combined object and will **not** revert back to their original formatting.

In Figure 120, the left graphic is the original object, as shown on the left in Figure 119. The right graphic is the result of splitting and the individual objects have taken the formatting of the combined object, as shown on the right in Figure 119.

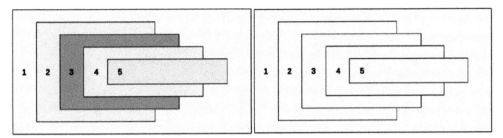

Figure 120: Splitting a combined object

Breaking combined objects

When an object is combined from several objects, the combined object can be broken into its constituent parts by going to **Modify > Break** on the main menu bar. This means that the original objects are broken into their constituent parts; for example, a rectangle will be broken into four separate lines and the area fill will be lost, as shown by the right graphic in Figure 121. The left graphic in Figure 121 is the original combined object.

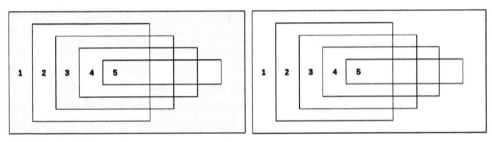

Figure 121: Breaking a combined object

Connecting lines

The constituent parts of an object can be connected together by selecting all the constituent parts of the object and going to **Modify > Connect** on the main menu bar. This connects the parts together and closes the object resulting in the area becoming filled with the area fill it had before the object was broken.

Merging, subtracting, or intersecting objects

After you have selected more than one object, the Merge, Subtract, and Intersect functions become available, allowing you to create a new object with a new shape. After selecting several objects, go to **Modify > Shapes** on the main menu bar or right-click on the selected objects and select **Shapes** from the context menu.

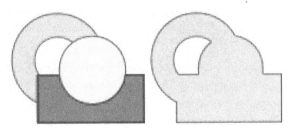

Figure 122: Merging objects

Merge

When you merge objects, a new object is created with a shape that follows the shape of the merged objects. The area fill of the merged object is determined by the area fill of the object that is at the rear of all the other objects, as shown in Figure 122.

Subtract

When you subtract objects, the objects at the front are subtracted from the object behind. This leaves a blank space that the subtracted objects occupied (Figure 123).

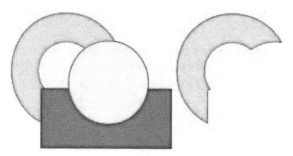

Figure 123: Subtracting objects

Intersect

When you intersect objects, the front objects and the exposed area of the object at the rear are removed. This creates a new object from the area of the object at the rear that was covered by the objects at the front (Figure 124).

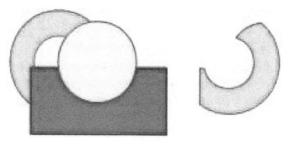

Figure 124: Intersecting objects

Practical example

The example in Figure 125 shows how you can use the merge, subtract, and intersect functions to create a knife with a wooden handle.

Figure 125: Creating a knife

Draw an ellipse and then a rectangle overlapping half of its width.	

Select both shapes, right-click, and select **Shapes > Subtract** from the context menu.	
Draw another rectangle and put it over the top half of the ellipse.	
Select both shapes, right-click, and select **Shapes > Subtract** from the context menu.	
Draw a small ellipse covering just the lower right corner.	
Select both shapes, right-click, and select **Shapes > Subtract** from the context menu. The knife blade shape is now complete.	
To make the handle, draw a rectangle and an ellipse.	
Merge the shapes together.	
Position the handle on the blade. Select the handle and blade, then group together to create a drawing of the knife.	

Duplication and cross fading

Duplication

Duplication makes copies of an object while applying a set of changes (such as color or rotation) to the duplicates.

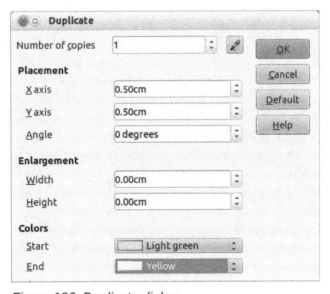

Figure 126: Duplicate dialog

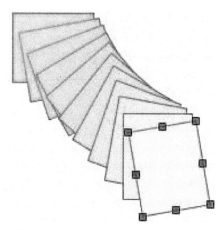

Figure 127: Duplication example

To duplicate an object or group of objects:

1) Select an object or group of objects.

2) Go to **Edit > Duplicate** on the main menu bar or use the keyboard shortcut *Shift+F3* to open the **Duplicate** dialog (Figure 126).

3) Select the number of copies, placement, enlargement, and the start and end colors for your duplicate copies.

4) Click **OK** and your duplicate copies are created. An example of a duplication is shown in Figure 127. Each duplicate object is a separate object.

5) To group the duplicate objects into one group, see "Grouping objects" on page 104.

6) To combine the duplicate objects into one object, see "Combining objects" on page 105.

The **Duplicate** dialog (Figure 126) has the following options:

- **Number of copies** – enter the number of copies you want to make.

- **Placement** – sets the position and rotation of a duplicate object with respect to the selected object.
    - *X axis*-- enter the horizontal distance between the centers of the selected object and the duplicate object. Positive values shift the duplicate object to the right and negative values shift the duplicate object to the left.
    - *Y axis* – enter the vertical distance between the centers of the selected object and the duplicate object. Positive values shift the duplicate object down and negative values shift the duplicate object up.
    - *Angle* – enter the angle (0 to 359 degrees) by which you want to rotate the duplicate object. Positive values rotate the duplicate object in a clockwise direction and negative values in a counterclockwise direction.

- **Enlargement** – sets the size of a duplicate object.
    - *Width* – enter the amount by which you want to enlarge or reduce the width of the duplicate object.
    - *Height* – enter the amount by which you want to enlarge or reduce the height of the duplicate object.

- **Colors** – sets the colors for the selected object and the duplicate object. If you make more than one copy, these colors define the start and end points of a color gradient.
    - *Start* – choose a color for the selected object.
    - *End* – choose a color for the duplicate object. If you are making more than one copy, this color is applied to the last copy.

Cross fading

Cross-fading transforms one object shape into another object shape. The result is a new group of individual objects that includes the start and end objects with the intermediate steps show the transformation from one object shape to another object shape.

To cross-fade two objects:

1) Select two objects and go to **Edit > Cross-fading** on the main menu bar to open the **Cross-fading** dialog (Figure 128).

2) Select the number of increments for the transformation.

3) If necessary, select **Cross-fade attributes** and **Same orientation**.

4) Click **OK** to perform the cross-fading. An example of cross-fading is shown in Figure 129. The object created is a group of objects.

5) To ungroup this group of objects so that you can use the individual objects, see "Ungrouping" on page 104.

Figure 128: Cross-fading dialog

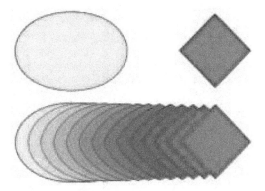

Figure 129: Cross-fading example

The **Cross-fading** dialog (Figure 128) has the following options:

- **Increments** – enter the number of shapes you want between the two selected objects.

- **Cross-fade attributes** – applies cross-fading to the line and fill properties of the selected objects. For example, if the selected objects are filled with different colors, a color transition between the two colors is applied.

- **Same orientation** – applies a smooth transition between the selected objects.

Arranging objects

When you combine, merge, subtract, or intersect objects, the end result varies depending on which object is at the front and which object is at the back. Each new object that you place on a drawing automatically becomes the front object and all the other objects move backwards in the positioning order. Arranging objects allows you to change the order in which objects are positioned.

First select one or more objects, then click on small triangle to the right of the **Arrange** icon on the Line and Filling toolbar to open a drop down list of positioning tools (Figure 130). The positioning tools available are as follows:

- **Bring to Front** – brings the selected object to the front of the group.
- **Bring Forward** – brings the selected object forward one step.
- **Send Backward** – sends the selected object one step backward.
- **Send to Back** – sends the selected object to the back of the group.
- **In Front of Object** – moves the selected object in front of another selected object.
- **Behind Object** – moves the selected object behind another selected object.
- **Reverse** – reverses the order of the selected objects. This tool is grayed out if only one object is selected.

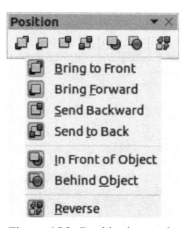

Figure 130: Positioning tools

Note	The drop down list of positioning tools can be turned into a floating toolbar by clicking at the bottom of the list and dragging it to a new position on your drawing workspace.

Aligning objects

To make your drawing look more professional, you can align objects with each other. Select one or more objects and click on small triangle to the right of the **Align** icon on the Line and Filling toolbar to open a drop down list of alignment tools (Figure 131). The alignment available tools are as follows:

- **Left** – aligns the left edges of the selected objects. If only one object is selected, the left edge of the object is aligned to the left page margin.

Figure 131: Alignment tools

- **Centered** – horizontally centers the selected objects. If only one object is selected, the center of the object is aligned to the horizontal center of the page.

- **Right** – aligns the right edges of the selected objects. If only one object is selected, the right edge of the object is aligned to the right page margin.

- **Top** – vertically aligns the top edges of the selected objects. If only one object is selected, the top edge of the object is aligned to the upper page margin.

- **Center** – vertically centers the selected objects. If only one object is selected, the center of the object is aligned to the vertical center of the page.

- **Bottom** – vertically aligns the bottom edges of the selected objects. If only one object is selected, the bottom edge of the object is aligned to the lower page margin.

Note	The drop down list of alignment tools can be turned into a floating toolbar by clicking at the bottom of the list and dragging it to a new position on your drawing workspace.

Distributing objects

Distributing objects allows you to space three or more objects evenly along the horizontal axis or the vertical axis. Objects are distributed using the outermost objects in the selection as base points for spacing.

Select at least three objects, then go to **Modify > Distribution** on the main menu bar or right-click and select **Distribution** from the context menu to open the Distribution dialog (Figure 132). The options available are explained as follows:

- **Horizontal** distribution specifies the horizontal distribution between the selected objects.
  - *None* – does not distribute the objects horizontally.
  - *Left* – distributes the selected objects so that the left edges of the objects are evenly spaced from one another.
  - *Center* – distributes the selected objects so that the horizontal centers of the objects are evenly spaced from one another.
  - *Spacing* – distributes the selected objects horizontally so that the objects are evenly spaced from one another.
  - *Right* – distributes the selected objects so that the right edges of the objects are evenly spaced from one another.

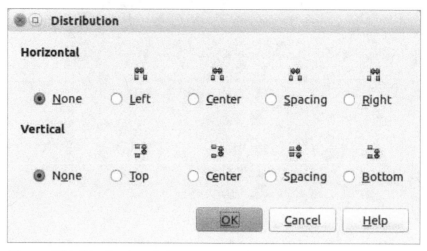

Figure 132: Distribution dialog

- **Vertical** distribution specifies the vertical distribution between the selected objects.
    - *None* – does not distribute the objects vertically.
    - *Top* – distributes the selected objects so that the top edges of the objects are evenly spaced from one another.
    - *Center* – distributes the selected objects so that the vertical centers of the objects are evenly spaced from one another.
    - *Spacing* – distributes the selected objects vertically so that the objects are evenly spaced from one another.
    - *Bottom* – distributes the selected objects so that the bottom edges of the objects are evenly spaced from one another.

Chapter 6
Editing Pictures

Raster Graphics

Introduction

Earlier chapters of the Draw Guide have dealt only with vector graphics. However, Draw also contains a number of functions for handling raster graphics (bitmaps) such as photographs and scanned pictures, including import, export, and conversion from one format to another.

Draw can read all the majority of graphic file formats. It has a subset of capabilities similar to raster graphics programs like Adobe Photoshop or Gimp.

Importing graphics

Inserting

To import graphic files into your drawing, go to **Insert > Image > From File** on the main menu bar or click the **From File** icon 🖼 on the Drawing toolbar opens the Insert Image dialog (Figure 133).

Draw contains import filters for the majority of graphic formats. If the file you want to import has a graphic format not covered by the import filters, then it is recommended to use one of the many free graphic conversion programs to convert the file into a format that Draw recognizes.

If you select the **Preview** option in the Insert Image dialog, a preview of the file is shown in the box on the right-hand side. This makes it much easier to select the file you want and also checks that Draw can import the file format used.

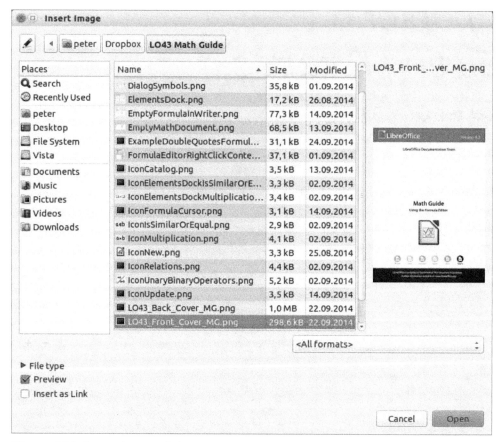

Figure 133: Insert Image dialog

Embedding

Embedding a graphic into a drawing makes the graphic a permanent part of the drawing. Any changes you make to an embedded graphic will only appear in the drawing; the original graphic file will not be affected.

Embedding happens when you import a graphic into a drawing using the Insert Image dialog, copying and pasting, scanning a graphic, or dragging and dropping.

The main advantage of embedding graphics into your drawing is that the graphic is always available no matter what computer is used to open the drawing.

The main disadvantage of embedding graphics is that it creates large file sizes, which may not be desirable if you have limited capacity for storing computer files. Also, if the original graphic is altered, then your drawing will not have an up to date version each time you open your document.

Note	When a graphic is embedded into a LibreOffice document or drawing, then the format of that graphic is automatically changed to PNG format. LibreOffice will only embed graphics into your document or drawing that can be converted into PNG format.

Linking

Linking a graphic to a drawing does not insert the graphic into the drawing, but a link is created to where the graphic file is located on your computer. Each time the drawing is opened, any linked graphics will be displayed in the drawing.

The main advantage of linking a graphic file to a drawing is if the original graphic file is altered or replaced by a new graphic with the same filename, then the next time you open the drawing, the latest version of the graphic will also open in the drawing.

The main disadvantage of linking graphics is that the link between the drawing and the graphic file must be maintained for linking to work correctly. If you move the drawing to another computer, then any linked files must also be moved to the same computer and the same folder on that computer.

To link a graphic file to your drawing, select the **Link** option in the Insert Picture dialog (Figure 133) before selecting the file and clicking on the **Open** button.

Note	When a graphic file is linked to a LibreOffice document or drawing, the format of the linked graphic is not changed.

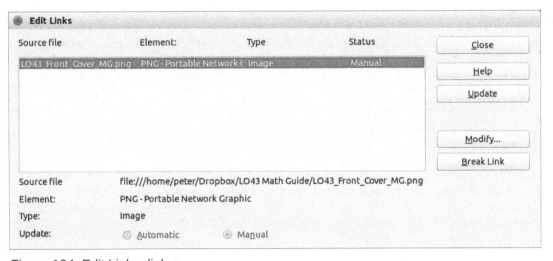

Figure 134: Edit Links dialog

Any changes made to a linked graphic within a LibreOffice drawing will apply only to that copy of the graphic placed into your the drawing and will not affect the original graphic file that has been linked to your drawing.

Links can be updated, modified, or broken as follows:

1) Go to **Edit > Links** on the main menu bar to open the **Edit Links** dialog (Figure 134).
2) Select the link to be edited.
3) Click on **Update**, **Modify** or **Break Link**, as appropriate.
   - **Update** – updates the selected link so that the most recently saved version of the linked file is displayed in the current document.
   - **Modify** – changes the source file for the selected link.
   - **Break Link** – breaks the link between the source file and the current document. The most recently updated contents of the source file are kept in the current document.
4) Click **Close** to close the dialog when you have finished editing the link.

Note	If you click **Break Link**, then the linked graphic becomes embedded in your drawing and the graphic format is converted to PNG.

Scanning

With most scanners you can directly insert a scanned image into a drawing or document. Scanned images are embedded using PNG format. Make sure that your scanner is configured for the computer and supported by the SANE system for a Linux operating system, or TWAIN for a Windows or Mac operating system.

To insert an image from the scanner:

1) Place a document, drawing, or photograph in the scanner and make sure that the scanner is switched on and ready.
2) If this is the first time the scanner has been used, go to **Insert > Image > Scan > Select Source** on the main menu bar to select the scanner. If the scanner has been used before, go to **Insert > Image > Scan > Request** on the main menu bar.

Note	If there is more than one scanning device connected to the computer, you will be able to select the device when you select the source. This selection will then become the default source when using scan requests until another device is used as the scanning source.

3) The rest of the procedure depends on the scanner driver, interface, and computer operating system. You will normally be required to specify scanning options such as resolution, scan window, and so on. Consult the documentation that came with the scanner for more information.
4) When the image has been scanned, Draw places it in the drawing. At this point it can be edited like any other graphic.

Copying and pasting

Copying a graphic and then pasting the graphic into another drawing is another way of embedding graphics into a drawing (this is also called using the clipboard). The copied graphic can be an image already embedded in another document or drawing, or it can be a graphic file such as a drawing, document or photograph.

After copying you can also choose the format when you paste a graphic into Draw using **Edit > Paste Special** on the main menu bar. Available formats will depend on the type of image copied onto the clipboard.

Dragging and dropping

Dragging and dropping is another method of embedding graphics into a drawing and can be used on graphics that have been embedded or linked. The way that dragging and dropping works is determined by the computer operating system. Behavior of dragging and dropping is normally controlled using the *Ctrl* or *Ctrl+Shift* keys in combination with the mouse.

Objects and images which are used frequently can be stored in the Draw Gallery. From the Gallery, a copy of the object or image can be simply dragged onto the drawing. Working with the Gallery is dealt with in *Chapter 10 Advanced Draw Techniques*.

File inserting

The command **Insert > File** on the main menu bar allows you to insert from an existing Draw drawing (*.ODG), an Impress presentation (*.ODP), a Writer document (*.ODT), or a document in Rich Text Format (RTF), HTML format, or plain text. Any text file will be contained within a text frame with paragraph and character formatting options available.

When inserting a file, normally the complete file will be inserted into your drawing. However, when selecting a Draw or Impress file, you can also select individual slides or individual objects for insertion into your drawing.

After selecting a Draw or Impress file and clicking on **Insert**, the Insert Slides/Objects dialog (Figure 135) opens. To access individual slides or objects, click on the expansion symbol (usually a + or a small triangle, depending operating system) to the left of the file name in the selection area.

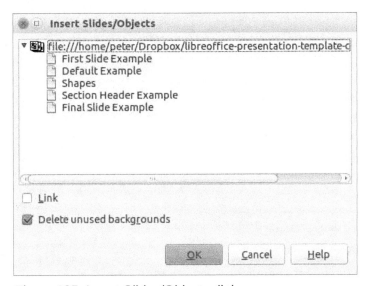

Figure 135: Insert Slides/Objects dialog

Select the slides or objects you want to insert and click **OK** to insert the selected items into your drawing.

If the inserted object was named in the source document, it keeps its original name unless the name already exists in the current document. If there is a name clash, you must give the object a new name before it is inserted. To rename an inserted object, right-click and choose **Name** from the context menu. Renaming has the advantage that the object is then listed in the Navigator.

Exporting the entire file

By default Draw saves drawings in the *.ODG format. Some software programs cannot open these files. To make your drawings available for other programs, you can export the file in various formats.

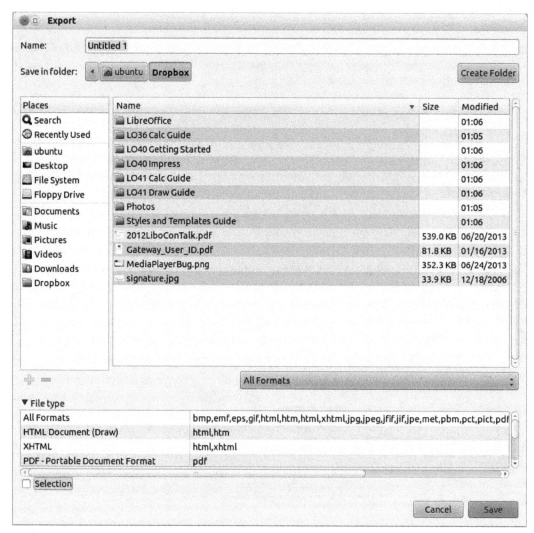

Figure 136: Exporting graphics

1) Select your file and go to **File > Export** on the main menu bar.
2) Select the required format from the **File type** list (Figure 136).
3) Click **Export**.
4) Depending on the format selected, another dialog will open allowing you to select the required options for the selected graphic format.
5) Click on **Export**, **Create**, or **OK** and your file will be exported as a new file in its new format.

Note	The format options in the **File type** list (EMF, HTML, XHTML, PDF, and SWF) only apply to complete files.

Exporting objects

To export individual objects from your drawing:

1) Select the objects and then go to **File > Export** on the main menu bar.
2) Select the required graphic format from the **File type** list.
3) Select the *Selection* option on the Export dialog (Figure 136).
4) Click **Export**.
5) Depending on the graphic format selected, another dialog will open allowing you to select the required options for that graphic format.
6) Click on **Export**, **Create**, or **OK** and your selected objects will be exported as a new file in its new format.

Formatting raster objects

Objects that are raster graphics can be formatted using the Format or context menus. The Picture toolbar is used to add or change filters and adjust the properties of lines, areas, and shadows.

The Transparency property in the Format menu does not relate to the transparency of the raster graphic itself but to the background area. To change the transparency of a raster graphic, you must use the Picture toolbar; see "Picture toolbar" below.

Some raster graphics may have a text element; for more information on formatting text, see *Chapter 9 Adding and Formatting Text*.

You can change position and size or rotate rotate raster graphics; for more information, see *Chapter 3 Working with Objects and Object Points*. Raster graphics can also be flipped (**Modify > Flip** on the main menu bar), but some metafile graphic formats may have problems flipping if they contain text.

Raster graphics included in a group behave like other objects when the properties of the group are modified.

It is recommended to name raster graphics using **Modify > Name** *on* the main menu bar or right-click and select **Name** on the context menu. Only named objects are visible in the Navigator and only named objects can be directly imported from another file.

Picture toolbar

The **Picture** toolbar will automatically appears when you select a picture (Figure 137). This can be in the main toolbar or as a floating toolbar. The tools available from left to right on the **Picture** toolbar are as follows:

- **Filter** – opens the Graphic Filter toolbar which is described in "Graphic filter toolbar" on page 124.
- **Graphics mode** – changes the display of the graphic from color to grayscale, black and white, or a watermark. This setting affects only the display and printing of the picture; the original picture file remains unchanged.
  - *Default* – the graphic is displayed unaltered in color.
  - *Grayscale* – the graphic is displayed in 256 shades of gray.
  - *Black/White* – the graphic is displayed in black and white.
  - *Watermark* – the brightness and contrast of the graphic are reduced to the extent that the graphic can be used as a watermark (background).

Figure 137: Picture toolbar

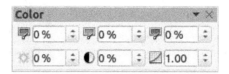

Figure 138: Color toolbar

- **Color** – opens the Color toolbar (Figure 138) to adjust the values of the RGB colors, brightness, contrast, and Gamma. These adjustments do not affect the original picture, but the values are stored in Draw as a separate formatting set.
  - *Red, Green, Blue* – select values between –100% (no color) to +100% (full intensity); 0% represents the original color value of the graphic.
  - *Brightness* – select a value between –100% (totally black) and +100% (totally white).
  - *Contrast* – select a value between –100% (minimum) and +100% (maximum).
  - *Gamma* – this affects the brightness of the middle color tones. Select a value between 0.10 (minimum) to 10 (maximum) Try adjusting this value if changing brightness or contrast does not give you the required result.

- **Transparency** – adjust the degree of transparency of the picture between 0% (opaque) and 100% (fully transparent).

- **Line** – opens the Line dialog. In this context, line refers to the outline of the border. See *Chapter 4 Changing Object Attributes* for more information.

- **Area** – opens the Area dialog, where you can edit color, gradient, hatching and fills of the background area that contains the picture — not the picture itself. To see the background, you must set the transparency of the picture to a suitably high value.

- **Shadow** – sets the default shadow effect around the picture.

- **Crop Image** – crops (trims) a picture. When you click on this tool, crop marks appear around the picture. Drag one or more of these marks to crop the picture to your desired size. For more accurate cropping, see "Cropping" on page 123.

- **Effects** – opens the Mode toolbar. See *Chapter 4 Changing Object Attributes* for more information.

- **Flip** – flips the selected object either horizontally or vertically. See *Chapter 4 Changing Object Attributes* for more information.

- **Position and Size** – opens the Position and Size dialog. See *Chapter 3 Working with Objects and Object Points* for more information.

- **Alignment** – opens the Alignment toolbar where you align an object in relation to other objects in the drawing. See *Chapter 5 Combining Multiple Objects* for more information.

- **Arrange** – opens the Arrange toolbar where you move a selected object either forward or backward in relation to other objects in the drawing. See *Chapter 5 Combining Multiple Objects* for more information.

Cropping

For more control and accuracy over cropping functions, select the picture and go to **Format > Crop Image**, or right-click and select **Crop Picture** from the context menu to open the **Crop** dialog (Figure 139).

Any changes made in the Crop dialog change only the display of the graphic. The original graphic file is not changed. If you want to export a cropped graphic, you must do it through **File > Export**. If you use **Save as Picture** from the context menu, the changes are not exported.

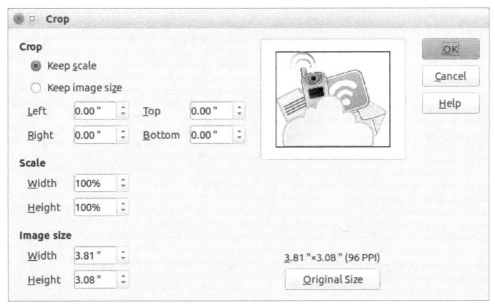

Figure 139: Crop dialog

Note	As an alternative to cropping, the **Position and Size** dialog has an option for keeping the width and height ratio fixed while changing one of the two dimensions. Changing values in one area (*Scale* or *Image Size*) will show up correspondingly in the other area.

Note	Take care with cropping operations. In the **Crop** dialog, the width and height are treated as independent values. Changing one without the other can result in significant distortion of the image and this may not be what you want.

Crop

Use this section of the **Crop** dialog to trim or scale the selected graphic, or to add white space around the graphic.

*   **Keep scale** – maintains the original scale of the graphic when cropping so that only the size of the graphic changes.
*   **Keep image size** – maintains the original size of the graphic when you crop so that only the scale of the graphic changes. To reduce the scale of the graphic, select this option and enter negative values in the cropping boxes. To increase the scale of the graphic, enter positive values in the cropping boxes.
*   **Left** and **Right** – if **Keep Scale** is selected, enter a positive amount to trim the left or right edge of the graphic, or a negative amount to add white space to the left or right of the

graphic. If **Keep image size** is selected, enter a positive amount to increase the horizontal scale of the graphic, or a negative amount to decrease the horizontal scale of the graphic.

- **Top** and **Bottom** – if **Keep Scale** is selected, enter a positive amount to trim the top or bottom of the graphic, or a negative amount to add white space above or below the graphic. If **Keep image size** is selected, enter a positive amount to increase the vertical scale of the graphic, or a negative amount to decrease the vertical scale of the graphic.

Scale

Use this section of the **Crop** dialog to change the scale of the selected graphic. In the **Width** and **Height** fields enter a value for the width or height of the selected graphic as a percentage.

Image size

Use this section of the **Crop** dialog to change the size of the selected graphic. In the **Width** and **Height** fields enter a value for the width or height of the selected graphic.

Above the **Original Size** button, the original size of the graphic is displayed. Clicking on this button and then clicking **OK** resets the inserted image to the original image size.

Graphic filter toolbar

After selecting a graphic and the Picture toolbar (Figure 137) has opened, click on the **Filter** icon to open the Graphic Filter toolbar (Figure 140). Draw offers eleven filter effects. Filters work on the current view of a graphic and they can be combined. Filters always apply to the entire graphic; it is not possible to use filters to edit only a part of the object.

Figure 140: Graphic Filter toolbar

| Note | If your graphic is linked, any graphic filters used are only applied to the current view. The original graphic is not changed. When you close the drawing, any filtering applied is lost. To keep a copy of the filtered graphic, export the graphic to create a copy with all the filters applied (**File > Export**). |
| | If your graphic is embedded, all graphic filters are applied directly on the embedded graphic and cannot be undone in a subsequent session. After you save and close the drawing, the graphic filter effects become permanent. If you do not want to retain a graphic filter, you must use **Edit > Undo** to cancel the filter effect before saving the file. |

Invert graphic filter

Clicking on the **Invert** icon inverts or reverses the color values of a color image (similar to a color negative), or the brightness values of a grayscale image. Apply the filter again to revert to the original graphic (Figure 141).

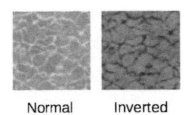

Normal   Inverted

Figure 141: Invert graphic filter

Smooth graphic filter

Clicking on the **Smooth** icon ◌ softens or blurs the image by applying a low pass filter reducing the contrast between neighboring pixels and produces a slight lack of sharpness (Figure 142). The **Smooth** icon also opens the Smooth dialog (Figure 143), where you can set the **Smooth Radius** parameter used for the Smooth filter when you click **OK**.

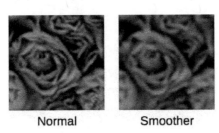

Normal   Smoother

Figure 142: Smooth graphic filter

Figure 143: Smooth dialog

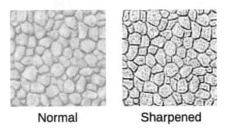

Normal   Sharpened

Figure 144: Sharpen graphic filter

Sharpen graphic filter

Clicking on the **Sharpen** icon 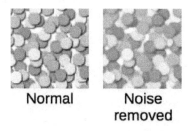 sharpens the image by applying a high pass filter, increasing the contrast between neighboring pixels emphasizing the difference in brightness. This will accentuate the outlines and the effect will be strengthened if you apply the filter several times (Figure 144).

Remove noise graphic filter

Clicking on the **Remove Noise** icon removes noise by applying a median filter by comparing every pixel with its neighbors. It then replaces extreme values of those pixels that deviate in color by a large amount from a mean value by a pixel with a mean color value. The amount of picture information does not increase, but because there are fewer contrast changes resulting in a graphic that looks smoother (Figure 145).

Normal   Noise
                removed

Figure 145: Remove Noise graphic filter

Normal   70% threshold   Inverted
                 value

Figure 146: Solarization graphic filter

Figure 147: Solarization dialog

Solarization graphic filter

Solarization is a phenomenon in photography in which the image recorded on a negative or on a photographic print is wholly or partially reversed in tone. Dark areas appear light or light areas appear dark. Solarization was originally a photochemical effect used during photographic film development and is now used in the digital world of computing to create a change or reversal of color (Figure 146 and Figure 147). Clicking on the **Solarization** icon ☐ opens the Solarization dialog, where you can define the threshold value for solarization. Entering a **Threshold value** above 70% reverses the color values (center picture in Figure 146). Selecting the **Invert** option causes all the colors to be inverted (right picture in Figure 146).

Aging graphic filter

Aging creates a look that resembles photographs developed in the early days of photography. All pixels are set to their gray values and then the green and blue color channels are reduced by the amount specified in the Aging dialog. Red color channel is not changed (Figure 148 and Figure 149). Clicking on the **Aging** icon ☐ opens the Aging dialog (Figure 149), where you can define the **Aging degree** and create an old look for your graphic as shown in the right picture in Figure 148.

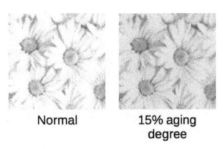

Normal   15% aging
                degree

Figure 148: Aging graphic filter

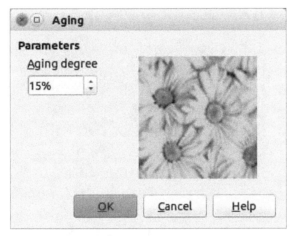

Figure 149: Aging dialog

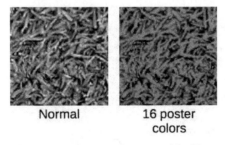

Normal   16 poster
                colors

Figure 150: Posterize graphic filter

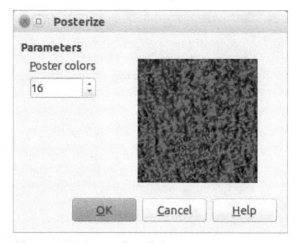

Figure 151: Posterize dialog

Posterize graphic filter

Posterizing reduces the number of colors in a graphic making it look flatter. When used on a photograph, posterizing can make the photograph look like a painting. Clicking on the **Posterize** icon ▨ opens the Posterize dialog, where you can define the number of **Poster colors** to produce the effect you want (Figure 150 and Figure 151).

Pop art graphic filter

Click on the **Pop Art** icon ▨ to change the colors of a graphic to a pop-art format (Figure 152).

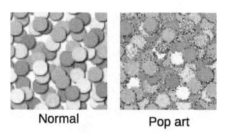

Normal   Pop art

Figure 152: Pop Art graphic filter

Charcoal sketch graphic filter

Click on the **Charcoal Sketch** icon ✎ to display the graphic as a charcoal sketch. The contours of the graphic are drawn in black and the original colors are suppressed (Figure 153).

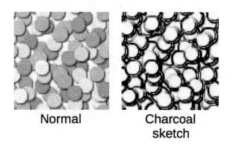

Normal   Charcoal
                sketch

Figure 153: Charcoal Sketch graphic filter

Relief graphic filter

The **Relief** graphic filter calculates the edges of a graphic in relief as if the graphic is illuminated by a light source. Clicking on the **Relief** icon opens the Emboss dialog, where you can select the position of the **Light source** producing shadows that differ in direction and magnitude (Figure 154 and Figure 155).

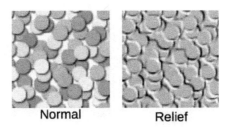

Normal   Relief

Figure 154: Relief graphic filter

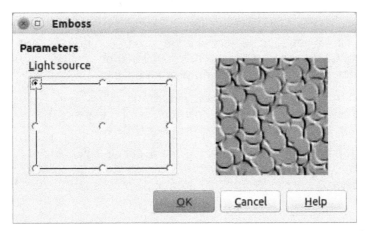

Figure 155: Emboss dialog

Mosaic graphic filter

The **Mosaic** graphic filter joins groups of pixels and converts them into a rectangular tile in a single color creating a graphic that appears to be a mosaic. The larger the individual rectangles created, the fewer details the mosaic graphic has.

Clicking on the **Mosaic** icon ![icon] opens the Mosaic dialog, where you can set the number of pixels used to create the **Width** and **Height** of each tile created. Selecting **Enhanced edges** will enhance the edges of each tile to create a sharper definition (Figure 156 and Figure 157).

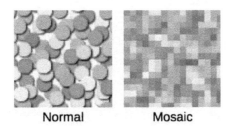

Normal   Mosaic

Figure 156: Mosaic graphic filter

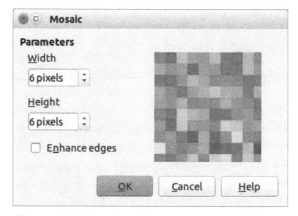

Figure 157: Mosaic dialog

Replacing colors

The **Color Replacer** allows you to replace or change a color in a graphic for another color or set the color as transparent. Up to four colors can be replaced at once. The tool works on the entire graphic and you cannot select an area of the graphic for editing.

The **Color Replacer** can only be used on embedded graphics. If you try to use the **Color Replacer** on a linked graphic, you will get the following error message *This graphic is linked to a document. Do you want to unlink the graphic in order to edit it?*

The selection list for replacement colors shows all the available colors in the current color palette of the drawing. You cannot define any new colors here but you can add colors to the available palette before using the Replace Color tool. For more information on this topic, see *Chapter 10 Advanced Draw Techniques*.

Replacing colors

To replace a color in a graphic, do as follows:

1) Go to **Tools > Color Replacer** on the main menu bar to open the Color Replacer (Figure 158).

2) Select a graphic to start using the Color Replacer.

3) Click on the **Pipette** icon to activate the color selection mode.

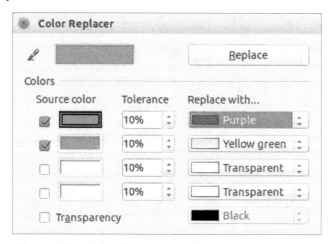

Figure 158: Color Replacer dialog

4) Move the cursor over the color you want to replace in the selected graphic and click on the color to be replaced.

5) A check box is now marked and the selected color appears in **Source color**.

6) Enter the amount of tolerance required for replacing the color in the **Tolerance** box. The default selection is 10% tolerance.

7) In **Replace with**, select a color from the drop-down list. *Transparent* is the default selection.

8) After selecting up to four colors for replacement, click **Replace** to replace the colors in the selected graphic.

9) There is no preview of the effect. If the result is not what you required, select **Edit > Undo** in the main menu bar and repeat the color replacement.

Replacing transparent areas

It is also possible to replace transparent areas in a graphic with a color.

1) Go to **Tools > Color Replacer** on the main menu bar to open the Color Replacer (Figure 158).

2) Make sure the graphic is NOT selected.

3) Select **Transparency** in the Color Replacer.

4) Select a color from the drop-down list next to **Transparency**.

5) Click **Replace** to replace the transparent areas with the selected color.

Tolerance parameter

The **Tolerance** parameter is used to set how much of the source color in the graphic is replaced by another color. To replace colors that are similar to the color you are replacing, enter a low value for the tolerance parameter. To replace a wider range of colors, enter a higher value for the tolerance parameter.

Conversion

Contour conversion

Converts a selected graphic to a contour by creating a polygon, or a group of polygons.

1) Make sure you have finished all your editing to a graphic, then select the graphic in your drawing.

2) Go to **Modify > Convert > To Contour** on the main menu bar, or right-click on the graphic and select **Convert > To Contour**. Your selected graphic is converted to a contour.

If the conversion creates a group of polygons (for example a text object), then **Modify > Enter Group**, or right-click on the converted graphic and select **Enter Group** from the context menu, or press the *F3* key to enter the group before selecting an individual polygon.

Note	Making sure you have finished all your editing to your graphic before converting to a contour is necessary as the graphic cannot be edited after conversion.

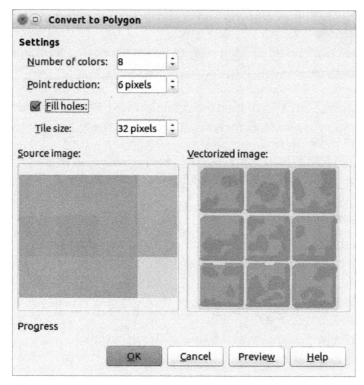

Figure 159: Convert to Polygon dialog

Polygon Conversion

Converts a selected graphic to a collection of polygons filled with color. The graphic also becomes a vector graphic and can be resized with no loss of image quality or distortion of any text. After conversion, you can break the graphic into groups of polygons and then split these groups into individual polygons. Breaking and splitting allows you to edit or delete individual colors within the graphic.

Converting

To convert a graphic to a polygon:

1) Select the graphic in your drawing.
2) Go to **Modify > Convert > To Polygon**, on the main menu bar, or right-click on the graphic and select **Convert > To Polygon** to open the Convert to Polygon dialog (Figure 159).
3) Select the **Number of colors** and **Point reduction** to be used in the conversion.
4) To prevent any blank areas appearing in your graphic, select **Fill holes** and the number of pixels to use for the **Tile size**.
5) Click **Preview** to check how your converted graphic will look.
6) Make any necessary changes to the settings and check the preview again.
7) If you are satisfied, click **OK** to convert your graphic to a polygon.

Conversion options and controls

- **Number of colors** – enter the number of colors to be displayed in the converted image. LibreOffice generates a polygon for each occurrence of a color in the image. The range for the number of colors is between 8 and 32.

- **Point reduction** – removes color polygons that are smaller than the pixel value you enter. The range for point reduction is between 0 and 32 pixels.

- **Fill holes** – fills the blank areas in the graphic that can be created when applying a point reduction.
- **Tile size** – enter the size of the rectangle for the background fill. The range of tile sizes is between 8 and 128 pixels.
- **Source picture** – preview of the original image.
- **Vectorized image** – preview of the converted image. Click **Preview** to generate the vectorized image.
- **Progress** – displays a progress bar during conversion.
- **Preview** – creates a preview of the converted image without applying any changes.
- **OK** – converts your graphic to polygons.

Breaking

After converting a graphic to polygons, you can break the graphic into groups of polygons. Each group of polygons consists of one color.

1) Convert your graphic to polygons, see "Converting" above.
2) Make sure your graphic is selected and go to **Modify > Break** on the main menu bar, or right-click on your graphic and select **Break** from the context menu to break your converted graphic into groups of polygons.
3) Click on a color in your graphic then drag the group of polygons filled with that color out of your graphic to create a new graphic OR press the *Delete* key and delete the color from your graphic.

Splitting

After converting a graphic to polygons and breaking the graphic into groups of polygons, you can then split these groups into individual polygons.

1) Convert your graphic to polygons, see "Converting" above.
2) Break your graphic into groups of polygons, see "Breaking" above.
3) Make sure your graphic is selected and go to **Modify > Split** on the main menu bar, right-click on the graphic and select **Split** from the context menu, or use the keyboard combination *Ctrl+Alt+Shift+K* to split groups of polygons into individual polygons.
4) Click on an individual polygon in your graphic and drag it out of your graphic or a polygon group OR press the *Delete* key and delete the polygon from your graphic.

Bitmap conversion

All drawing objects placed into a LibreOffice drawing are vector graphics and these vector graphics can be converted to a bitmap in PNG format. Any transparency effects in the original vector graphic are lost during conversion even though the PNG format used does support transparencies.

To convert a vector graphic to a bitmap, go to **Modify > Convert > To Bitmap** on the main menu bar or right-click on the graphic and select **Convert > To Bitmap** from the context menu.

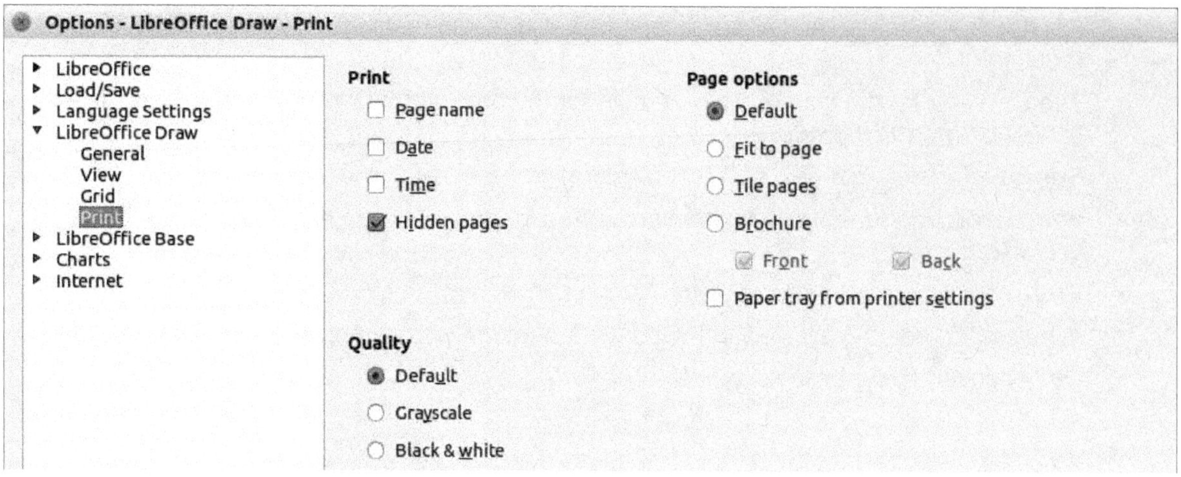

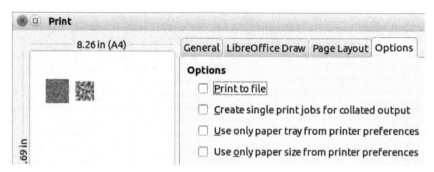

Figure 160: Options – LibreOffice Draw – Print

Figure 161: Print dialog – Options

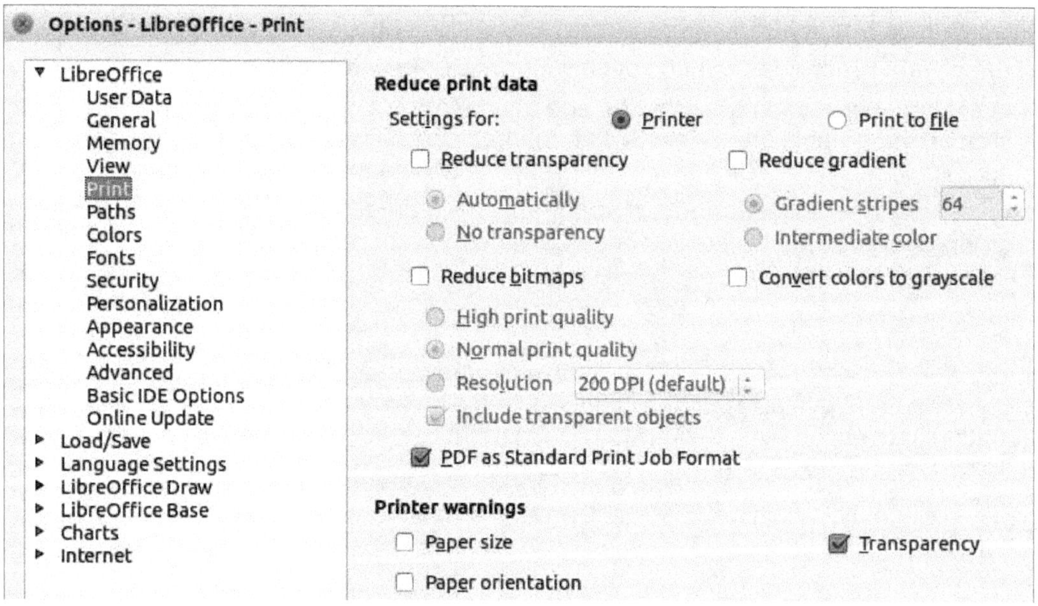

Figure 162: Options – LibreOffice – Print

Print options

If you have only a monochrome (single color) printer or are experiencing problems with printing, then the following settings may help with printing your drawing. You can set up printing so that all text and all graphics are printed either in grayscale or black and white.

The general settings are in **Tools > Options > LibreOffice Draw > Print** (Figure 160) and will only apply to all drawings that you print using LibreOffice Draw.

To set printing options for the current document only, go to **File > Print** or use the keyboard combination *Ctrl+P* and click on the **Options** tab in the Print dialog (Figure 161).

To set printing options for all the modules in LibreOffice, go to **Tools > Options > LibreOffice > Print** (Figure 162). These printing options allow you to reduce print data sent to a printer or file, and to give any printer warnings if the wrong paper size or orientation and transparency is set.

LibreOffice
The Document Foundation

Chapter 7
Working with 3D Objects

Introduction

Although Draw does not match the functionality of leading drawing or picture editing programs, it is capable of producing and editing 3D drawings and pictures. 3D objects can be created using one of the following methods:

- Extrusion – creates a 3D shape.
- Rotation – creates a 3D scene.
- Conversion – creates a 3D scene.
- Ready-made 3D objects which are 3D scenes.

3D object types

3D shapes

A 3D shape is created when a 2D object or text from the Fontwork Gallery is turned into 3D using extrusion with the **Extrusion On/Off** icon 🔲 on the Drawing or 3D-Settings toolbars. The Status bar displays *Shape selected* when this type of 3D object is selected.

A 3D shape can be viewed and edited in 2D mode by clicking on the **Extrusion On/Off** icon. To switch back to 3D mode, click the **Extrusion On/Off** icon again.

Any changes you want to make to the 3D effects used for a 3D shape are carried out using the 3D-Settings toolbar.

Note	The **Extrusion On/Off** icon only becomes available for use when you select a 2D object, or a 3D object that has been extruded from a 2D object.

3D scenes

3D scenes are built from objects which have dimensions using x, y, and z coordinates. The Status bar displays *3D scene selected* when a 3D object is selected that has been created from a 2D object using body rotation or conversion, or it is a ready-made 3D object that has been inserted into your drawing.

When you create a 3D scene from a selection of more than one 2D object, a group is automatically created. You can enter this 3D scene group so that you change the 3D effects and rotate the individual 3D objects within the group.

To enter the group, go to **Modify > Enter Group** on the main menu bar, or press the *F3* key, or right-click on the group and select **Enter Group** from the context menu.

To exit the group after you have finished your changes, go to **Modify > Exit Group** on the main menu bar, or use the *Ctrl+F3* key combination, or right-click on the group and select **Exit Group** from the context menu.

Note	You cannot ungroup into individual objects a 3D scene group that has been created from a selection of 2D objects.

Creating

Drawing toolbar

Before you begin creating 3D objects in your drawing, it is recommended that you add the LibreOffice 3D tools to the Drawing toolbar as follows:

1) Right-click in an empty area on the Drawing toolbar and select **Visible Buttons** from the context menu.

2) Select **To 3D** and **To 3D Rotation Object** from the available list of icons to place them on the Drawing toolbar as shown in Figure 163.

Figure 163: Drawing toolbar

Note	The **To 3D**, **To 3D Rotation Object**, and **Extrusion On/Off** icons only become active when a 2D object is selected in your drawing.

Extrusion

Extrusion is a procedure that creates a 3D shape from a 2D object. The 3D geometry is formed by extruding a polygon perpendicular to the plane of the given polygon using depth to create front, back, and side faces. The side faces are formed by connecting all corresponding single edges of the front and back faces.

Draw uses a default value for extrusion (depth) based on the size of a 2D object. This value can be changed after carrying out extrusion; see "3D-Settings toolbar" on page 145 for more information.

1) Draw an object using one of the shape tools on the Drawing toolbar.
2) Select the 2D object you want to convert to 3D.

Note	Extrusion only works on basic shapes, symbol shapes, block arrows, flowcharts, callouts, and stars that are included as a part of the default set of tools on the Drawing toolbar. Extrusion can also be used on any text created using the Fontwork Gallery.

Figure 164: Extruding a 3D object from a 2D object

3) Click the **Extrusion On/Off** icon ![icon] on the Drawing toolbar and the selected 2D object is converted into a 3D shape (Figure 164). The **Extrusion On/Off** icon used to create 3D shapes from 2D objects is included in the default set of tools for the Drawing toolbar.

4) Alternatively, click on the **Extrusion On/Off** icon ![icon] on the 3D-Settings toolbar and the selected 2D object is converted into a 3D shape. If the 3D-Settings toolbar is not visible, go to **View > Toolbars > 3D-Settings** on the main menu bar.

Rotation

To 3D rotation

To 3D rotation converts a 2D object into a 3D scene by rotating the object using the left edge of the bounding box around the object as the axis of rotation. Examples of rotation are shown in Figure 165, where a thick line has been used as an example object. The actual 3D shape created also depends on the angle and shape of the object being rotated.

1) Draw a line and make sure it is selected.

2) To convert the line into a 3D scene, click on the **To 3D Rotation Object** icon ![icon] on the Drawing toolbar, or go to **Modify > Convert > To 3D Rotation Object** on the main menu bar, or right-click on and select **Convert > To 3D Rotation Object** from the context menu.

Normal line   Curved line   Freeform line

Figure 165: Examples of using To 3D body rotation

In 3D rotation

In 3D rotation converts a 2D object into a 3D scene by rotating the object using a movable axis of rotation. A 2D object is rotated and slightly tilted with the central projection turned on so that the converted object is better recognized as a 3D scene (Figure 166).

Figure 166: Examples of rotating 2D objects to create a 3D objects

The default location of this rotation axis is the left edge of the bounding box around the object. However, this location and angle of rotation can be adjusted, allowing you to create 3D scenes that have different shapes. Examples of adjusting the rotation location and angle are shown in Figure 167 where a thick line has been used as an example object. The actual 3D scene created also depends on the angle and shape of the object being rotated.

1) Draw a line and make sure it is selected.

2) Click on the small triangle next to the **Effects** icon on the Line and Filling toolbar and select the **In 3D Rotation Object** icon ⚲ in the popup toolbar.

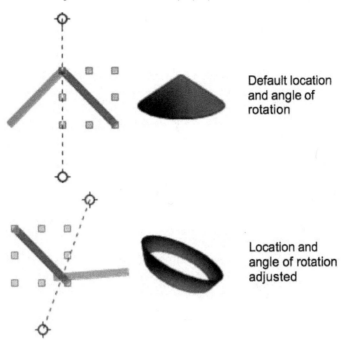

Figure 167: In 3D body rotation

3) Alternatively, go to **View > Toolbars > Mode** on the main menu bar to open the Mode toolbar and select the **In 3D Rotation Object** icon ⚲.

4) If necessary, adjust the position and angle of the rotation axis. This is shown as a dashed line with rotation points at each end.

5) Click anywhere outside the object and it is converted into a 3D scene.

Note	The shape of the Effects icon on the Line and Filling toolbar changes depending on the last Effects tool that was used on the Line and Filling or Mode toolbars.
	If the Effects icon is not visible on the Line and Filling toolbar, then right-click in an empty area on the toolbar and click on **Visible Buttons**, then select **Effects**.

Conversion

When a 2D object is converted to a 3D scene, it is slightly tilted and central projection turned on so that the converted object is better recognized as a 3D scene.

1) Select a 2D object in your drawing.

2) Go to **Modify > Convert > To 3D** or **To 3D Rotation object** on the main menu bar and the object is converted into a 3D scene.

3) Alternatively, right-click on the object and select **Convert > To 3D** or **To 3D Rotation object** from the context menu and the object is converted into a 3D scene.

Examples of conversion using **To 3D** are shown in Figure 166 on page 140 and for **To 3D Rotation object** conversion; see "To 3D rotation" on page 140 for more information.

Text

Draw treats text like an object which can be converted to 3D as easily as any other object in your drawing.

1) Click on the **Text** icon **T** on the Drawing toolbar.
2) Move the cursor onto your drawing and click once to create a text box, then type your text.
3) Click again on the text box to select it. Selection handles will show on the text box.
4) Click the **To 3D** icon on the Drawing toolbar, or go to **Modify > Convert > To 3D** or **To 3D Rotation object**, or right-click on the object and select **Convert > To 3D** or **To 3D Rotation object** from the context menu and the selected text is converted into a 3D scene.
5) See "Editing 3D objects" on page 143 on how to change the 3D effects for 3D text.

Fontwork

The Fontwork Gallery in Draw contains a set of templates allowing you to create artistic text for

your drawings. Click on the **Fontwork** icon on the Drawing toolbar to open the **Fontwork Gallery** (Figure 168). See the *Impress Guide Chapter 5 Managing Graphic Objects* for more information on the Fontwork Gallery and its tools.

After creating your text using the Fontwork Gallery, it can be converted to a 3D shape using the information in "Extrusion" on page 139, and into a 3D scene using "Rotation" on page 140, "Conversion" on page 141, or "Text" above.

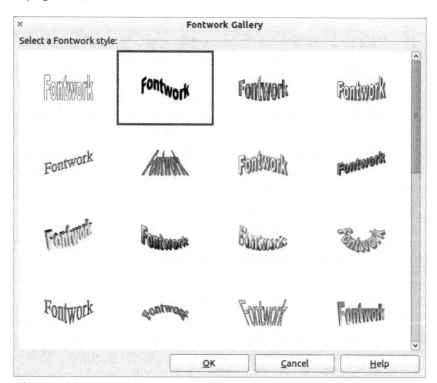

Figure 168: Fontwork Gallery

Ready-made 3D objects

LibreOffice has a collection of ready-made 3D objects available for immediate use. To access these ready-made 3D objects, go to **View > Toolbars > 3D Objects** on the main menu bar to open the **3D-Objects** toolbar or click on the **3D Objects** icon 🔲 on the Drawing toolbar to open a pop-up menu (Figure 169).

Creating 3D scenes using this toolbar is exactly the same as drawing basic shapes. See *Chapter 2 Drawing Basic Shapes* for more information.

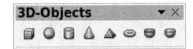

Figure 169: 3D Objects toolbar

Note	The shape of the **3D Objects** icon on the Drawing toolbar changes depending on the last tool that was used.
	If the **3D Objects** icon is not visible on the Drawing toolbar, then right-click in an empty area on the toolbar and click on **Visible Buttons** and select **3D Objects**.

Editing 3D objects

Note	Where 3D scenes have been created from more than one 2D object, a 3D scene group is automatically created. You cannot ungroup this 3D scene group and any editing carried out will affect all 3D objects within the group. To edit an individual 3D object within this 3D scene group, you must enter the group. See "3D scenes" on page 138 for more information.

Rotation

Rotating 3D scenes and shapes is similar to rotation for 2D objects (see *Chapter 3 Working with Objects and Object Points* for more information).

Using the mouse

Note	For 3D shapes that have been created using extrusion, see "3D-Settings toolbar" on page 145 for information on how to rotate 3D shapes about the horizontal or vertical axes.

1) Select a 3D object (3D scene or 3D shape), then click on the small triangle next to the **Effects** icon on the Line and Filling toolbar and select the **Rotate** icon 🌀 in the pop-up toolbar, or go to **View > Toolbars > Mode** on the main menu bar to open the Mode toolbar and select the **Rotate** icon 🌀 or go to **Modify > Rotate** on the main menu bar.

2) Click on a corner selection handle and hold the mouse button down until the cursor changes to a double-headed circular arrow.

3) Drag the cursor to rotate the 3D object around the rotation point ⊹ in exactly the same way as rotating a 2D object.

4) Release the mouse button when you are satisfied with the rotation effect.

5) Click on a center selection handle and hold the mouse button down until the cursor changes to parallel arrows. These center selection handles are not available for 3D shapes created using the extrusion method.

6) Drag the cursor to rotate the 3D object around the horizontal axis or the vertical axis. The left and right center selection handles are used for the horizontal axis. The top and bottom center selection handles are used for the vertical axis.

7) Release the mouse button when you are satisfied with the rotation effect.

Note	By default, the rotation point $\oplus$ is in the center of a selected 3D object. This rotation point can be moved to change the center of rotation and create a different effect when you carry out rotation. Move your cursor over the rotation point until it changes (normally a pointed fist), then click and drag the rotation point to a new position. Alternatively, click and drag on the 3D object to a new position when it is in rotation mode to move the object away from the default position for the center of rotation.

Using the Rotation dialog

1) Select the 3D object (3D scene or 3D shape).

2) Go to **Format > Position and Size** on the main menu bar, or right-click on the selected object and select **Position and Size** from the context menu, or press the *F4* key to open the Position and Size dialog (Figure 170).

3) Click on the **Rotation** tab to open the Rotation page.

4) In the **Rotation angle** section, enter the number of degrees for rotation in the *Angle* box.

5) Alternatively, click and drag the *Rotation Angle* indicator in *Default settings* until you reach the rotation angle you require. As you drag the indicator, the rotation angle is displayed in the *Angle* box.

6) In the **Pivot point** section, enter the X and Y coordinates in the *Position X* and *Position Y* boxes to adjust the location of rotation point.

7) Alternatively, select one of the position points in *Default settings* to adjust the location of the rotation point. The default location is in the center.

8) Click **OK** to save your changes and close the dialog.

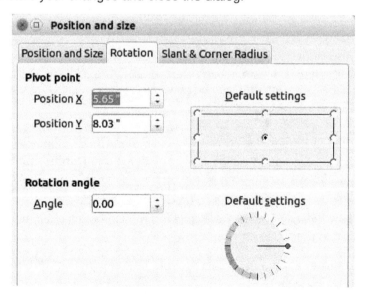

Figure 170: Rotation dialog

3D-Settings toolbar

The 3D-Settings toolbar (Figure 171) is only used to edit a 3D shape that has been created from a 2D object using extrusion (see "Extrusion" on page 139 for more information). To open the 3D-Settings toolbar, go to **View > Toolbars > 3D-Settings** on the main menu bar. The 3D-Settings toolbar only becomes active when a 3D shape has been selected.

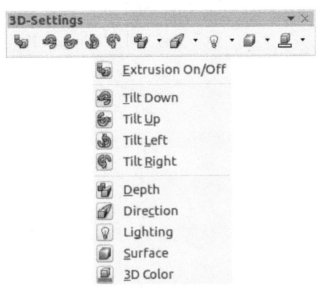

Figure 171: 3D-Settings toolbar

The tools available for editing 3D shapes are as follows. The result of any changes made using these editing tools is applied to the selected 3D shape immediately and the 3D effect is displayed.

- **Extrusion On/Off** – used to create a 3D shape from a 2D object. If necessary, can also be used to switch off the 3D effects created by extrusion allowing you to edit the underlying 2D object.

- **Tilt Down** – tilts the selected object downward (horizontal axis rotation) by 5 degrees each time the icon is used.

- **Tilt Up** – tilts the selected object upward (horizontal axis rotation) by 5 degrees each time the icon is used.

- **Tilt Left** – tilts the selected object left (vertical axis rotation) by 5 degrees each time the icon is used.

- **Tilt Right** – tilts the selected object right (vertical axis rotation) by 5 degrees each time the icon is used.

- **Depth** – opens a pop-up menu where you can set the extrusion depth from an object by a fixed or custom amount.

- **Direction** – opens a pop-up menu where you can set the view direction to create an extrusion in either a perspective or parallel projection.

- **Lighting** – opens a pop-up menu where you can set the direction and intensity of the lighting when creating an extrusion.

- **Surface** – opens a pop-up menu where you can set the surface of the extrusion as matt, plastic, metal, or wireframe display.

- **3D Color** – opens a pop-up menu where you can set the color used for the extrusion. This color does not have to be the same as the color used for the original 2D object.

3D effects

The **3D Effects** dialog (Figure 172) offers a wide range of possible settings for 3D objects created using the following methods. This dialog can also be used to convert a 2D object to 3D using the tools in the bottom left corner of the dialog.

To open the 3D Effects dialog, select the 3D object and right-click on the object then select **3D Effects** from the context menu to open the 3D Effects dialog.

Any 3D effects that you apply to a 3D scene are not carried out until you click on the **Assign** icon ✅. This allows you to make all the 3D effect changes before applying them to your 3D scene.

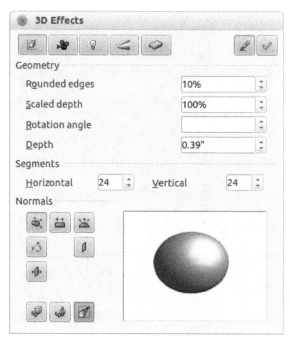

Figure 172: 3D Effects dialog - Geometry

Note	You can add a **3D Effects** icon ⊞ to the Drawing toolbar, or any other toolbar, by going to **View > Toolbars > Customize** or right-clicking in an empty area on the toolbar and selecting **Customize Toolbar**. When the **Customize** dialog opens, go to **Toolbars**, select the toolbar you want to use and click on the **Add** button to display the **Add Commands** dialog. The **3D Effects** icon is located in the **Options** category.

3D conversion

In the bottom left corner of all the pages in the Effects dialog are tools allowing you to convert a 2D object to a 3D object and to change the projection used in a 3D object.

- **Convert to 3D** – converts the selected object into a 3D scene. This tool works in the same way as "Conversion" on page 141.

- **Convert to Lathe Object** – converts a 2D object into a 3D scene using body rotation. This tool works in the same way as "To 3D rotation" on page 140.

- **Perspective On/Off** – switches perspective projection on or off for a 3D object. Perspective projection is where projecting lines from the center of projection pass through an imaginary plane until they meet at a point some distance from an object.

3D Effects – Geometry

On the **Geometry** page of the Effects dialog (Figure 172) you can make changes to the geometry of a 3D object.

- **Geometry** – defines the properties for a 3D scene or shape created from a 2D object.
    - *Rounded edges* – enter the amount by which you want to round the corners of a 3D shape as shown by the example in Figure 173. The default setting for rounded edges is 10%

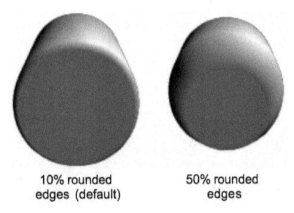

10% rounded   50% rounded
edges (default)   edges

Figure 173: Rounded edges example

- *Scaled depth* – enter the amount by which to increase or decrease the frontal area of the selected 3D object. Figure 174 shows an example where the scaled depth has been increased to 150% and then decreased to 50%. The default setting for scaled depth is 100%.

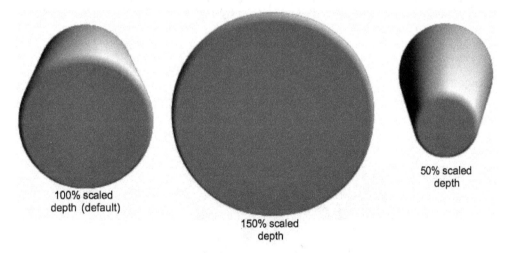

100% scaled
depth (default)

150% scaled
depth

50% scaled
depth

Figure 174: Scaled depth example

- *Rotation angle* – enter the angle in degrees to rotate a 2D object that has been converted to 3D using the **To 3D Rotation Object** tool. Figure 175 shows an example of a 2D circle converted to 3D and the rotation angle changed to 150 degrees.

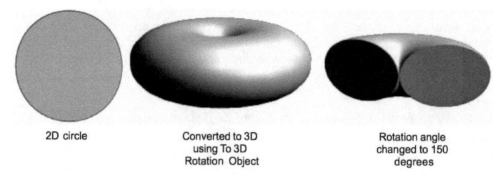

| 2D circle | Converted to 3D using To 3D Rotation Object | Rotation angle changed to 150 degrees |

Figure 175: Rotation angle example

– *Depth* – enter the extrusion depth for the selected 3D object. This option is not available for 2D rotation objects converted to 3D using the **To 3D Rotation Object** tool. Figure 176 shows an example of a 2D circle converted to a 3D cylinder with the extrusion depth increased to 3 cm.

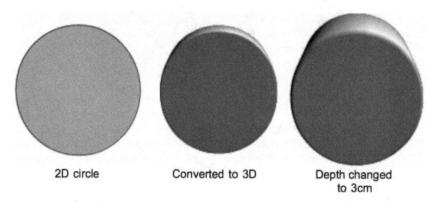

| 2D circle | Converted to 3D | Depth changed to 3cm |

Figure 176: Depth example

- **Segments** – changes the number of segments that Draw uses to draw a 3D rotation object. The higher the number of segments, the smoother the object surface will be. However, a high segment number may increase the time it takes to generate the 3D object on your display. Figure 177 shows the difference on a 3D sphere when the segments have been increased from 10 to 30 segments horizontally and vertically.

  – *Horizontal* – enter the number of horizontal segments to use in the selected 3D rotation object.

  – *Vertical* – enter the number of vertical segments to use in the selected 3D rotation object.

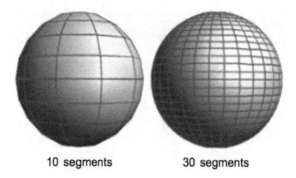

| 10 segments | 30 segments |

Figure 177: Segment example

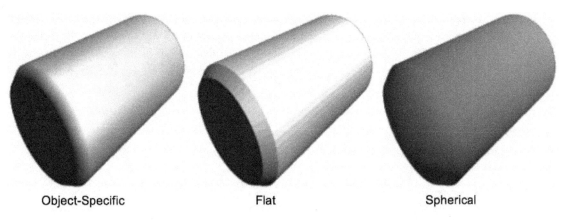

Object-Specific   Flat   Spherical

Figure 178: Object-Specific, Flat, and Spherical examples

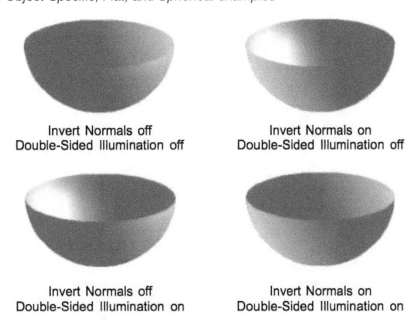

Invert Normals off
Double-Sided Illumination off

Invert Normals on
Double-Sided Illumination off

Invert Normals off
Double-Sided Illumination on

Invert Normals on
Double-Sided Illumination on

Figure 179: Invert Normals and Double-Sided Illumination examples

- **Normals** – modifies the rendering style of the 3D surface (Figure 178 and Figure 179).

  - *Object-Specific* – renders the 3D surface according to the shape of the object. For example, a circular shape is rendered with a spherical surface.

  - *Flat* – renders the 3D surface as polygons.

  - *Spherical* – renders a smooth 3D surface regardless of the shape of the object.

  - *Invert Normals* – inverts or reverses which side of the selected object is considered to be the outside face and which side is considered the inside face.

  - *Double-Sided Illumination* – lights an object from the outside and the inside of the object. To use as an ambient light source, click this button, and then click *Invert Normals*. This is a setting for the whole of the 3D scene and not fopr a single object within the scene.

  - *Double-Sided* – a 3D object has a front and back face. With *Double-Sided* switched off, only the front face of the object is rendered. The effect, when looking from outside, is that the object solid, but, when looking from inside, the front face is transparent. If there is no view to the inside face, normally for an extruded 3D object with solid texture, the *Double-Sided* should be switched off to improve performance during rendering. Any 3D object created using rotation often allow an inside view and it is recommended that Double-Sided is switched on. Which side of an object face is considered to be back or front is determined by the *Invert Normals* setting, that is the front side of a plane is the one the normal points away from.

3D Effects – Shading

On the Shading page of the Effects dialog (Figure 180) you can set the shading and shadow options for the selected 3D object.

- **Shading** – specifies the type of shading applied to a 3D object (Figure 181).
  - *Flat Mode* – assigns a single color of shading to a single segment on the surface of the object.
  - *Gouraud Mode* – blends shading colors across the segments.
  - *Phong Mode* – averages the shading color of each pixel in a segment based on the pixels that surround it, and requires the most processing power.

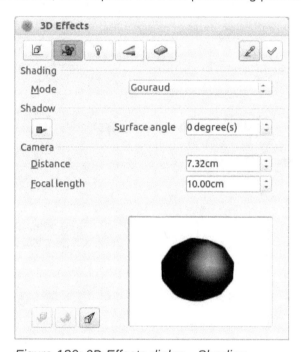

Figure 180: 3D Effects dialog - Shading

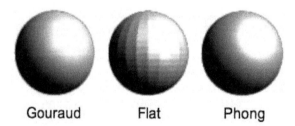

Figure 181: Shading mode examples

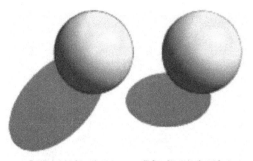

0 deg shadow   50 deg shadow

Figure 182: Example of using Shadow

- **Shadow** – adds or removes a shadow from a selected 3D object (Figure 182).
    - *3D Shadowing On/Off* ▣☞ – switches the shadowing on or off.
    - *Surface angle* – enter an angle from 0 to 90 degrees for casting a shadow.
- **Camera** – sets the camera options for a selected 3D scene as if you are actually using a camera to take a photograph (Figure 183).
    - *Distance* – enter the distance to leave between the camera and the center of the selected 3D scene. The default setting for distance is 2.6cm.
    - *Focal length* – enter the focal length of the camera lens, where a small value corresponds to a fish-eye lens and a large value to a telephoto lens. The default setting for focal length is 10cm.

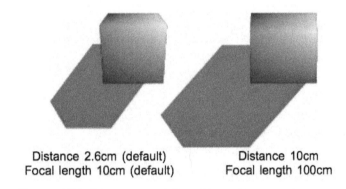

Distance 2.6cm (default)   Distance 10cm
Focal length 10cm (default)   Focal length 100cm

Figure 183: Distance and Focal Length examples

3D Effects – Illumination

On the Illumination page of the Effects dialog (Figure 184) you define how a 3D scene is lit and the settings apply to all 3D objects in a scene. You can specify the direction of the light source for the 3D scene, as well as the color of the light source and of the ambient light.

By default one light source is already selected when you open the Illumination page. However, you can select another light source or use more than one light source for illumination. A maximum of eight sources can be used and each light source can use a different color. Figure 184 shows three light sources selected with each color having a different color. At least one light source must be active; otherwise, the rendering and shading functions on 3D Effects will not function correctly.

1) Select a **Light source** icon 💡 to turn the required light source on. The icon changes to an illuminated bulb.

2) Press the space bar or click again on the selected light source so you can adjust the color and ambient light for the light source.

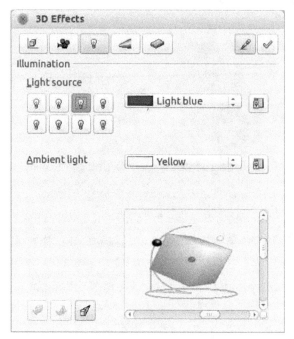

Figure 184: 3D Effects dialog - Illumination

3) Select a color for the light from the drop-down list for **Light source**. A different color can be used for each light source selected.

4) If necessary, select a color from the drop-down list for **Ambient light** to set the color of the surrounding light.

5) To deselect a light source, select the light source and click on it again.

The light source location and color are shown in the lower right corner of the Illumination page. The vertical slider bar adjusts the lighting angle and the horizontal slider bar rotates the light about the object. Alternatively you can click on the light point and drag the light source to where you want it.

To change the preview from a sphere to a cube, click on the small square to the right of the horizontal slider bar and below the vertical slider bar.

Each light source selected is shown as a small colored sphere in the color specified for it. The larger colored sphere indicates the active light source.

3D Effects – Textures

On the Textures page of the Effects dialog (Figure 185) you can set the properties of the surface texture for a selected 3D object. The Textures page is only available after you have set the **Area Fill** of a 3D object to *Gradient*, *Hatching* or *Bitmap*. For more information, see *Chapter 4 Changing Object Attributes*.

- **Type** – sets the color properties of the texture.

  - *Black & White* ◰ – converts the texture to black and white.

  - *Color* ▥ – converts the texture to color.

- **Mode** – shows or hides shading.

  - *Only Texture* ● – applies the texture without shading.

  - *Texture and Shading* ● – applies the texture with shading. To define the shading options for the texture, use the Shading page of this dialog.

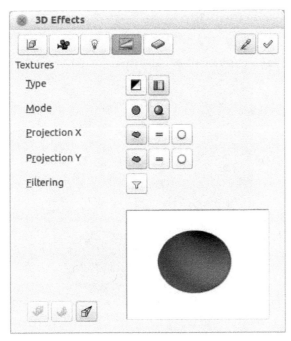

Figure 185: 3D Effects - Textures

- **Projection X** – sets the options for displaying the texture along the X axis. Only one of the three following options can be selected.
    - *Object-Specific* – automatically adjusts the texture for best fit based on the shape and size of the object. This is the default setting.
    - *Parallel* – applies the texture parallel to the horizontal axis and is mirrored on the rear side of the object.
    - *Circular* – wraps the horizontal axis of the texture pattern around an object.
- **Projection Y** – sets the options for displaying the texture along the Y axis. Only one of the three following options can be selected.
    - *Object-Specific* – automatically adjusts the texture for best fit based on the shape and size of the object. This is the default setting.
- *Parallel* – applies the texture parallel to the vertical axis and is mirrored on the rear side of the object.
    - *Circular* – wraps the vertical axis of the texture pattern around an object.
- **Filter** – filters out noise that can occur when you apply a texture to a 3D object.
    - *Filtering On/Off* – blurs the texture slightly to remove unwanted speckles.

Before Textures can be used, you must change the area fill of the 3D object as follows:

1) Select the 3D object.
2) Right-click on the 3D object and select **Area** from the context menu or go to **Format > Area** on the main menu bar to open the **Area** dialog.
3) From the **Fill** drop-down list, select *Gradient*, *Hatching* or *Bitmap*.
4) Select the fill from the list that appears and then click **OK**. The texture is then applied to the selected 3D object.

Figure 186: 3D Effects - Material

3D Effects - Material

On the Materials page of the Effects dialog (Figure 186) you can change the appearance of a 3D object to represent different materials. Materials and textures can be combined with each other and it is a matter of trial and error to achieve the desired result.

- **Material** – assigns a predefined color scheme or lets you create your own color scheme.
  - *Favorites* – select a predefined color scheme, or select a custom color scheme that has been user defined.
  - *Object color* – select the color that you want to apply to a 3D object.
  - *Illumination color* – select the color to illuminate the object and brightening parts of the object which lie in shadow making the object seem more illuminated.

- **Specular** – sets the light reflection properties for the selected object simulating the reflecting capacity of the surface. The position of the illuminated point is determined by the setting of the first light source.
  - *Color* – select the color that you want the object to reflect.
  - *Intensity* – enter the intensity of the specular effect.

- The **Color** icon 🔲 opens the **Color** dialog allowing you to define your own colors using the two-dimensional graphic and numerical gradient chart.

Tip	Do not use a very high brightness values for individual colors. These are all additive and it is easy to end up with a colored area that is white.

When you use individual color parameters additional effects can be produced, which are similar to the color parameters in "3D Effects – Illumination" on page 151.

Note	Metallic and glass surfaces do not simulate well because the appearance of these materials is produced using reflection.

3D-Settings toolbar editing

When 3D shapes have been created from 2D objects using the extrusion method, they are handled differently from 3D scenes. You have to use the tools on the 3D-Settings toolbar to make any changes to a 3D shape. These tools are highlighted in Figure 187.

- **Depth** 🔲 – sets the extrusion depth and direction from the pop-up options.

- **Direction** 🔲 – sets a view direction and a perspective or parallel projection from the pop-up options.

- **Lighting** 💡 – sets the lighting direction and lighting intensity from the pop-up options.

- **Surface** 🔲 – sets the surface material or use a wireframe display from the pop-up options.

- **3D Color** 🔲 – sets the extrusion color from the pop-up options.

Figure 187: 3D-Settings toolbar - editing

The result of any changes made using these editing tools is applied to the selected 3D shape immediately and the effect is displayed.

Note	The 3D Effects dialog described in "3D effects" on page 146 cannot be used on 3D shapes created using the Extrusion On/Off tool because the correct formatting results will not be achieved. If you have used the 3D Effects dialog in error, you can remove any incorrect formatting by going to **Format > Default Formatting** on the main menu bar.

Combining 3D objects

Multiple 3D objects can be grouped or combined together in the same way as 2D objects. See *Chapter 5 Combining Multiple Objects* for more information.

Note	When copying and pasting a 3D scene into another 3D scene, it is not pasted in as a scene, but the objects within the copied scene are pasted in.

Chapter 8
Connections, Flowcharts, and
Organization Charts

Connectors and glue points

Connectors and glue points were briefly introduced in *Chapter 2 Drawing Basic Shapes*. This section describes them in more detail and how to use them.

Connectors are lines or arrows whose ends automatically dock to a connection or glue point on an object. Connectors are useful when drawing, for example, flowcharts and organization charts. The connecting lines between objects remain intact even when objects are moved or rearranged. Also, if you copy an object with a connector, the connector is also copied.

Connectors

Draw has a comprehensive selection of connectors on a Connectors toolbar (Figure 188) to help you connect objects in, for example, a flowchart or organization chart. To open this toolbar, click the small triangle to the right of the Connector icon  on the Drawing toolbar. Note that this icon changes shape depending on the last connector tool used.

The Connector toolbar shown in Figure 188 displays a default set of connectors. If the connector you want to use is not displayed, then use one of the following methods to select the connector you want to use.

- Click on the small triangle on the right of the title bar and select your connector from the drop down list.
- Right click in a blank area on the toolbar and select **Visible Buttons** from the context menu. Click the connector you want to use and it is added to the Connectors toolbar.

Figure 188: Connector toolbar

Note	This toolbar can become a floating toolbar by clicking on the bottom of the pop-up toolbar and dragging it into your workspace.

Types of connectors

Connectors fall into four type groups:

- *Standard connectors* (Figure 189) – the line segments run vertically and horizontally. Draws a connector with one or more 90-degree angle bends. Click on an object glue point on an object, drag to a glue point on another object, then release.

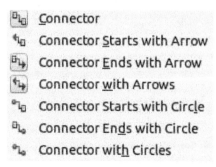

Figure 189: Standard connectors

- *Line connectors* (Figure 190) – consist of a line segment with two smaller segments at the ends. Draws a connector that bends near a glue point. Click on an object glue point, drag to a glue point on another object, then release. To adjust the length of the line segment between a bend point and a glue point, click the connector and drag the bend point.

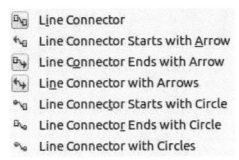

Figure 190: Line connectors

- *Straight connectors* (Figure 191) – consist of a single line. Draws a straight line connector. Click on an object glue point, drag to a glue point on another object, then release.

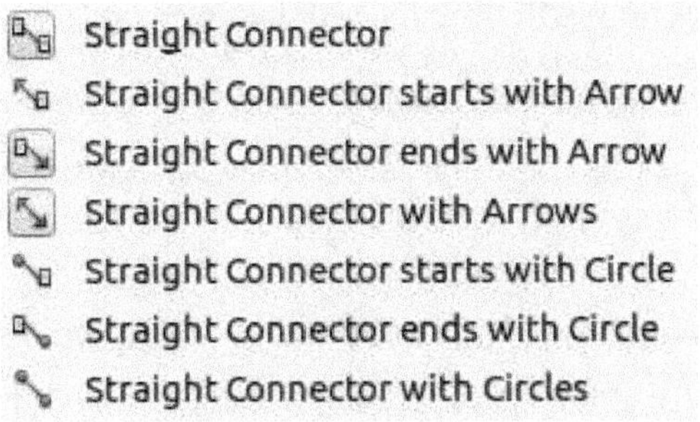

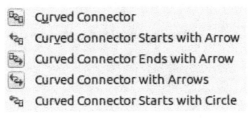

Figure 191: Straight connectors

- *Curved connectors* (Figure 192) – are based on Bézier curves and curve around objects. Draws a curved line connector. Click on an object glue point, drag to a glue point on another object, then release.

Figure 192: Curved connectors

Adding connectors

When you select a connector and move the mouse pointer over a filled object or the edge of an unfilled object, glue points appear. A glue point is a fixed point where you can attach a connector line. You can also add custom glue points to an object, see "Glue points" on page 161 for more information.

To draw a connector, select the connector type and click on a glue point on an object. Drag the cursor to a glue point on another object and then release. Figure 193 shows a line connector drawn between two objects. Remember not to drag the connector so that it overlaps or touches any objects and creates a confusing drawing. If this does happen, see "Modifying connectors" below on how to change the connector route to avoid any objects the connector crosses over.

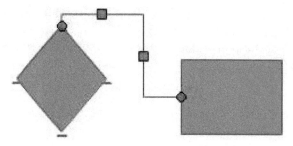

Figure 193: Connector between two objects

You can also drag a connector to an empty part of your document. When you release the mouse button, the unattached end of the connector is locked into place until you drag the end to a different location.

Modifying connectors

To detach or reposition a connector, click and drag either end of the connector line to a different location.

To change the connector route between objects avoiding any objects on the route, click on a control point on the connector line and drag it to a new position. In Figure 193, the control points are shown as small red squares at the point where the connector changes direction.

To modify a connector, right-click on the connector and select **Connector** from the context menu to open the Connector dialog (Figure 194). Use this dialog to change connector type and its properties.

- **Line skew** – defines the skew of the line and the dialog preview displays the result.
- **Line spacing** – sets the spacing for the connectors.
  - *Begin horizontal* – enter the amount of horizontal space you want at the beginning of the connector.
  - *Begin vertical* – enter the amount of vertical space you want at the beginning of the connector.
  - *End horizontal* – enter the amount of horizontal space you want at the end of the connector.
  - *End vertical* – enter the amount of vertical space you want at the end of the connector.

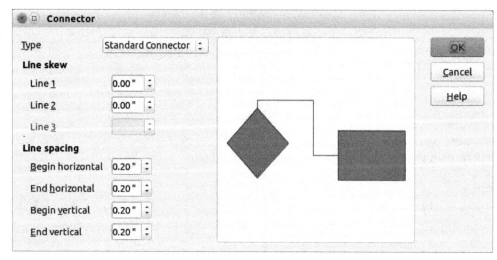

Figure 194: Connector dialog

Note	You cannot swap the ends of the connector using this dialog, that is start point becomes the end point and the end point becomes the start point. To swap the ends of a connector, you have to draw a new connector.

Glue points

Glue points are not the same as the selection handles of an object. The selection handles are for moving or changing the shape of an object; see *Chapter 3 Working with Objects and Object Points* for more information. Glue points are used to fix or glue a connector to an object so that when the object moves, the connector stays fixed to that object.

All Draw objects have glue points, which normally are not displayed and only become visible when the **Connectors** icon on the Drawing toolbar is selected. Note that the Connectors icon changes shape depending on the last connector tool used.

To add, customize or delete glue points to an object, go to **View > Toolbars > Gluepoints** on the main menu bar to open the Gluepoints toolbar (Figure 195). This toolbar only becomes active after you click on the **Glue Points** icon on the Drawing toolbar or select **Edit > Glue Points** on the main menu bar, or right click on a selected connector and select **Edit Points** from the context menu.

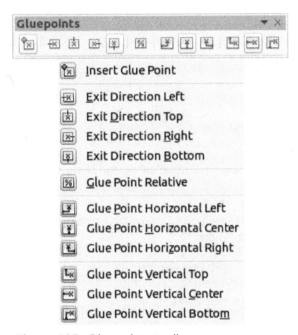

Figure 195: Gluepoints toolbar

Types of glue points

When the Gluepoints toolbar opens, only the six tools on the left of the toolbar are active. The remaining six tools on the right of the toolbar only become active when the **Glue Point Relative** icon is deselected.

With reference to Figure 195, the following briefly describes the function of each tool on the Gluepoint toolbar.

- **Insert Glue Point** – inserts a glue point where you click in an object.
- **Exit Direction Left** – connector attaches to the left edge of the selected glue point.

- **Exit Direction Top** – connector attaches to the top edge of the selected glue point.
- **Exit Direction Right** – connector attaches to the right edge of the selected glue point.
- **Exit Direction Bottom** – connector attaches to the bottom edge of the selected glue point.
- **Glue Point Relative** – maintains the relative position of a selected glue point when you resize an object. This tool is selected by default when the Gluepoint toolbar opens. The following six tools only become active when this tool is deselected.
- **Glue Point Horizontal Left** – when the object is resized, the current glue point remains fixed to the left edge of the object.
- **Glue Point Horizontal Center** – when the object is resized, the current glue point remains fixed to the center of the object.
- **Glue Point Horizontal Right** – when the object is resized, the current glue point remains fixed to the right edge of the object.
- **Glue Point Vertical Top** – when the object is resized, the current glue point remains fixed to the top edge of the object.
- **Glue Point Vertical Center** – when the object is resized, the current glue point remains fixed to the vertical center of the object.
- **Glue Point Vertical Bottom** – when the object is resized, the current glue point remains fixed to the bottom edge of the object.

Note	Each glue point you have added can have only one horizontal position and one vertical position. Only one of the horizontal position tools and one of the vertical position tools can be selected and used at any one time.

Adding glue points

By default, most objects normally have four glue points. To add extra glue points to an object or to an object that does not have glue points, proceed as follows:

1) Make sure no objects are selected and click on the **Glue Points** icon ✏ or select **Edit > Glue Points** on the main menu bar, or right click on a selected connector and select **Edit Points** from the context menu.

2) If the Gluepoints toolbar (Figure 195 on page 161) does not open, go to **View > Toolbars > Gluepoints** on the main menu bar.

3) Select the object and then the **Insert Glue Point** icon 🗔, or right click on a glue point you have previously inserted and select **Insert Point** from the context menu.

4) Move your cursor to a position where you want the glue point on an object and click to insert the glue point.

5) To move a glue point to another position, click on the glue point and drag it to its new position.

Tip	When adding, moving or customizing glue points, it is recommended to use the zoom function to make it easier to work with glue points. See *Chapter 3 Working with Objects and Object Points* for more information.

Customizing glue points

Only glue points that have added to an object can be customized. The default glue points included with an object cannot be customized.

1) Make sure no objects are selected and click on the **Glue Points** icon 🖊 or select **Edit > Glue Points** on the main menu bar, or right click on a selected connector and select **Edit Points** from the context menu.

2) If the Gluepoints toolbar (Figure 195 on page 161) does not open, go to **View > Toolbars > Gluepoints** on the main menu bar.

3) Make sure the object is not selected and double-click on a glue point that you have added to select the glue point.

4) Select the exit directions you want to use for connectors and double-click again on the glue point to customize the glue point.

5) To use horizontal and vertical positioning, click on the **Glue Point Relative** icon or right-click on the glue point and select **Adapt Position to Object** from the context menu to deselect this tool.

6) Select the horizontal and vertical positioning tools you want to use and double-click on the glue point to customize the glue point. Only one horizontal positioning tool and one vertical positioning tool can be used at any one time.

Deleting glue points

Only glue points that have added to an object can be deleted. The default glue points included with an object cannot be deleted.

1) Make sure no objects are selected and click on the **Glue Points** icon 🖊 or select **Edit > Glue Points** on the main menu bar.

2) Make sure the object is not selected and double-click on a glue point that you have added to select the glue point.

3) Right-click on the glue point and select **Cut** from the context menu, or press the *Delete* key on the keyboard, or go to **Edit > Cut** on the main menu bar.

Connector text

Text can be easily added to connectors, then formatted or edited to make, for example, your flowchart or organization chart easier to follow. See *Chapter 2 Drawing Basic Shapes* and *Chapter 9 Adding and Formatting Text* for more information on working with text.

Adding text

1) Select the connector.and the control points become active.

2) Click on the **Text** icon T or **Text Vertical** icon 🔲 on the Drawing toolbar and a flashing text cursor appears close to the connector. The Text Formatting toolbar replaces the Line and Filling toolbar.

3) Use the Text Formatting toolbar or **Format** and **Tools** on the main menu bar to change the default format of the text.

4) Type the text and, when you have finished typing the text and using the text tools, move the cursor away from the objects and connector and click to end the text mode. The Line and Filling toolbar then replaces the Text Formatting toolbar.

1) Click on the connector text to enter text editing mode. The Text Formatting toolbar replaces the Line and Filling toolbar under the menu bar.

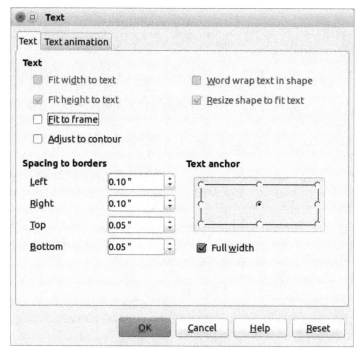

Figure 196: Text dialog

2) Perform any changes to the text using the text tools provided on the Text Formatting toolbar or **Format** and **Tools** on the main menu bar. You can also right-click on the text and select text tools from the context menu.

3) Right-click on the connector text and select **Text** from the context menu or go to **Format > Text** to open the Text dialog (Figure 196) where you can change the **Text anchor** and **Spacing to borders**.

Note	A connector has an invisible rectangle around it. **Text anchor** will position the text within this invisible rectangle and **Spacing to borders** will create margins between the text and the borders. These options are in addition to the standard text tools.

4) Click on the **Text Animation** tab where you can animate the text. However, this is not recommended unless you are going to display the drawing as part of a presentation. See the *Impress Guide* for more information on text animation.

5) When you have finished formatting and editing your text, move the cursor away from the objects and connector and click to end the text mode. The Line and Filling toolbar then replaces the Text Formatting toolbar.

Flowcharts

For drawing flowcharts (also known as flow diagrams), Draw has a **Flowchart** toolbar that includes a large selection of flowchart tools to help you to easily draw a flowchart.(Figure 197). Click on the small triangle to the right of the **Flowchart** icon ▣ on the Drawing toolbar to open the Flowchart pop up toolbar. Note that this icon changes shape depending on the last flowchart tool used.

Note	This toolbar can become a floating toolbar by clicking on the bottom of the pop-up toolbar and dragging it into your workspace.

Figure 197: Flowchart toolbar

1) When adding objects to your flowchart, see *Chapter 2 Drawing Basic Shapes* for information on how to draw and resize object shapes.

2) Add text to each flowchart shape to make it easily identified in the flowchart. See *Chapter 2 Drawing Basic Shapes* and *Chapter 11 Advanced Draw Techniques* for more information.

3) Use connections lines in your flowchart. This allows repositioning of an object in your chart while maintaining connections with the other objects in the chart. See "Connectors" on page 158 for more information.

4) Use the zoom, grid and snap functions to help in positioning objects in your flowchart. See *Chapter 3 Working with Objects and Object Points* for more information.

5) Use the alignment and distribution functions to give your flowchart a more professional look. See *Chapter 5 Combining Multiple Objects* for more information.

6) Duplicate objects when you require more than one of the same shape and size. See *Chapter 5 Combining Multiple Objects* for more information.

Organization charts

Draw does not have a toolbar for organization charts, but these charts are easily created using basic shapes, flowchart shapes, connection points and connector lines. Hierarchy in an organization is easily indicated using shading and/or color. When using shading and color in an organization chart, make sure that your selection provides a good contrast between the text and the shading or color to make the chart easy to read on a computer display or in a printed document.

An example of an organization chart is shown in Figure 198. This was drawn using the process shape from the Flowchart toolbar and connection lines.

1) When adding objects to your chart, see *Chapter 2 Drawing Basic Shapes* for information on how to draw and resize object shapes.

2) Add text to each object in the organization chart to make it easily identified in the chart. See *Chapter 2 Drawing Basic Shapes* and *Chapter 11 Advanced Draw Techniques* for mare information.

3) Use connections lines in your organization chart. This allows repositioning of an object in your chart while maintaining connections with the other objects in the chart. See "Connectors" on page 158 for more information.

4) Use the zoom, grid and snap functions to help in positioning objects in your chart. See *Chapter 3 Working with Objects and Object Points* for more information.

5) Use the alignment and distribution functions to give your organization chart a more professional look. See *Chapter 5 Combining Multiple Objects* for more information.

6) Duplicate objects when you require more than one of the same shape and size. See *Chapter 5 Combining Multiple Objects* for more information.

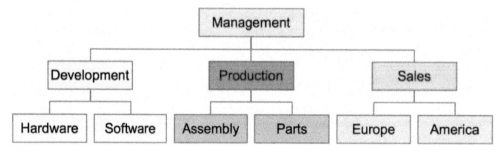

Figure 198: Example organization chart

Chapter 9
Adding and Formatting Text

Introduction

When text is used in drawings, it is contained in text boxes. This chapter describes how to create, format, use, and delete text. It also discusses the various types of text that can be inserted into a drawing. Finally, it provides information on how to insert special forms of text such as numbered or bulleted lists, tables, fields, and hyperlinks.

Using the text tool

To activate the text tool, click the **Text** icon **T** for horizontal text or the **Vertical Text** icon ⊢ for vertical text on the Drawing toolbar.

If the **Vertical Text** icon is not visible, first select the option *Show UI elements for East Asian writings* in **Tools > Options > Language Settings > Languages**. Second, right-click in a blank area on the Drawing toolbar and go to **Visible Buttons > Vertical Text** and the icon will be placed on the toolbar.

When the text tool is active, the Text Formatting toolbar (Figure 199) replaces the Line and Filling toolbar at the top of the drawing workspace. Click at the location where you want to position the text and a small text frame appears containing only the cursor.

When the **Text** icon is selected, you can select font type, font size, and other text properties before you start typing text. As you type the text, the left corner of the status bar indicates that you are in text edit mode and the position of your cursor (Figure 200).

Once you have finished typing your text and clicked outside the text frame or selected another tool from the Drawing toolbar, the Text Formatting toolbar is replaced by the default Line and Filling toolbar.

Figure 199: Text Formatting toolbar

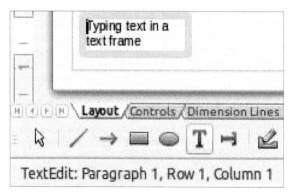

Figure 200: Text information on the status bar

Using text boxes

Using text boxes, you can place text anywhere on your drawing; for example, a caption for a shape; an explanatory note; a title block for the drawing similar to those used in engineering drawings.

Creating a text box

1) Click the **Text** icon T or the **Vertical Text** icon ⊢ on the Drawing toolbar.
2) Click and drag to draw a text box on the drawing. This sets the width. The height of the text box automatically increases as you type or add text.
3) Release the mouse button when you have reached the desired width for your text box. The cursor appears in the text box and the text box, depending on your computer system, has a border indicating edit mode.
4) Type or paste your text in the text box. The status bar at the bottom of the drawing workspace indicates that you are in text edit mode and the cursor position within the text box.
5) Click outside the text box to deselect it.

Moving, resizing and rotating text boxes

You can move, resize and rotate a text box just like any other object in your drawing. For more information, see *Chapter 3 Working with Objects and Object Points*. However, before you can move, resize, or rotate a text box, you must make sure the text box is in edit mode.

1) Click on the text to switch the text box into edit mode.
2) Move the cursor over the border. The cursor changes shape to the move symbol for your computer setup (for example, a clenched hand).
3) When the move symbol appears, click once again on the border and selection handles appear.
4) To quickly move a text box into a new position, place the cursor on the border (but not on a selection handle), click and drag to move the text box to a new position, then release the mouse button when the text box is in the desired position. A semi-transparent copy of the text box shows where your text box will be placed (Figure 201).

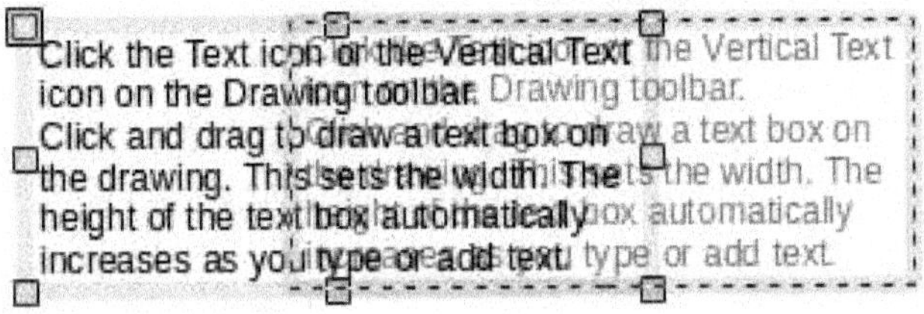

Figure 201: Moving a text box

5) To quickly resize a text box, move the cursor over one of the selection handles and the cursor changes shape to the resizing symbol for your computer setup (for example, a double-headed arrow). Click and drag the border to a new position to resize the text box, then release the mouse button when the text box reaches the desired size (Figure 202).

Note	Use the selection handles at the top and bottom of the text box to resize the text box height. Use the selection handles at the left and right side of the text box to resize the text box width. Use the corner selection handles to resize the height and width of the text box while maintaining the aspect ratio of the text box.

Tip	To maintain the aspect ratio of a text box while resizing, press and hold the *Shift* key, then click and drag. Make sure to release the mouse button **before** releasing the *Shift* key.

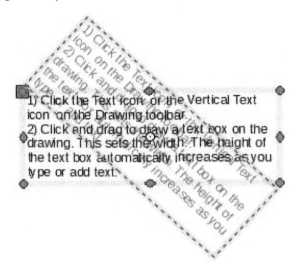

Figure 202: Resizing a text box

6) To quickly rotate a text box, click again on a selection handle to change the shape and color of the selection handles. Click and drag on a corner handle to rotate the test box, then release the mouse button when the text box is at the desired rotation angle. A ghosted outline of the text box being rotated appears and the current angle of rotation is shown in the status bar (Figure 203).

Figure 203: Rotating a text box

Note	When in rotation mode, the top, bottom, and side handles are not available for use on a text box.

7) To accurately control the position, size, and rotation angle of a text box, use the Position and Size dialog (Figure 204) or the Sidebar Position and Size subsection (Figure 205). See *Chapter 3 Working with Objects and Object Points* on how to use the Position and Size dialog or the Sidebar Position and Size subsection and for information on the options available.

Deleting text boxes

1) Click on the text to switch the text box into edit mode.
2) Move the cursor over the hashed border. The cursor changes shape to the move symbol for your computer setup (for example, a clenched hand).
3) When the move symbol appears, click once again on the hashed border and selection handles appear.
4) Press the *Delete* key.

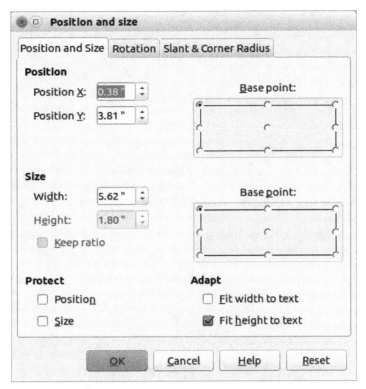

Figure 204: Position and Size dialog

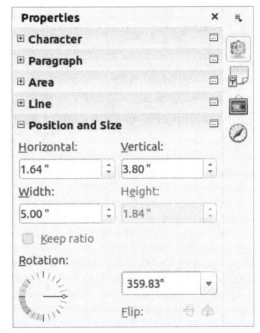

Figure 205: Sidebar Position and Size subsection

Using text with Draw objects

Text can be added to most Draw objects. The exceptions are control elements like buttons, list boxes, or 3D objects. An object is not dynamic and does not behave like a text frame. To keep text within the borders of the object, you have to use paragraphs, line breaks, smaller text size, increasing the object size, or a combination of all four methods.

To add text to an object:

1) Select the object.

2) Select the **Text** icon on the Drawing toolbar and a text cursor starts flashing in the center of the selected object.

3) Start typing your text (Figure 206). The status bar will indicate that you are editing text, as shown in Figure 200.

4) Alternatively, double-click on an object to enter text editing mode. If double-clicking does not work, then open the Options toolbar and select the **Double-click to edit Text** icon.

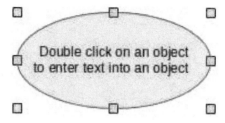

Figure 206: Adding text to an object

Inserting text

Pasting text

Text may be inserted into a text box or object by copying it from another document and pasting it into the text box or object on your drawing. However, pasted text may not match the formatting of the text that has already been included on your drawing. This may be what you want on some occasions, but in most cases it is better to make sure that text format is consistent throughout your drawing.

Pasting unformatted text

It is good practice to paste text without formatting and apply the formatting later so it matches the text already in your drawing or make the text fit within the borders of an object.

1) Copy the text you want to use, then move your cursor into position on the drawing.

2) Go to **Edit > Paste Special** on the main menu bar or use the keyboard shortcut

    Control+Shift+V or click on the small triangle next on the right of the **Paste** icon 📋 on the Standard toolbar.

3) Select **Unformatted text** from the dialog or context menu that appears. The text will be pasted at the cursor position and formatted to the default paragraph style of the text box or object.

Formatting pasted text

1) Select the text you have just pasted (see "Selecting text" on page 175 for more information).

2) Use the formatting tools that are available on the Text Formatting toolbar, or go to **Format** on the main menu bar and select a formatting tool from the drop-down menu, or right-click on the text and select a formatting tool from the context menu.

3) Alternatively, go to **Format > Styles and Formatting** or press the *F11* key to open the Styles and Formatting dialog. See "Using styles" on page 175 for more information.

Inserting special characters

To insert special characters, such as copyright, math, geometric, monetary symbols, or characters from another language:

1) Click on the **Text** icon **T** and then click in the text where you want to insert the character.

2) Go to **Insert > Special Character** on the main menu bar or right-click and select **Special Characters** from the context menu to open the **Special Characters** dialog (Figure 207).

3) Alternatively, click on the **Special Character** icon ⊞ on the Text Formatting toolbar to open the **Special Characters** dialog. If this icon is not visible, right-click in an empty area on the toolbar and select **Visible Buttons > Special Character** from the context menu and the icon will be placed on the toolbar.

4) Select the font and character subset from the *Font* and *Subset* options in the Special Characters dialog.

5) Select the character you want to insert. You may have to scroll to find the character you want.

6) Click **OK.**

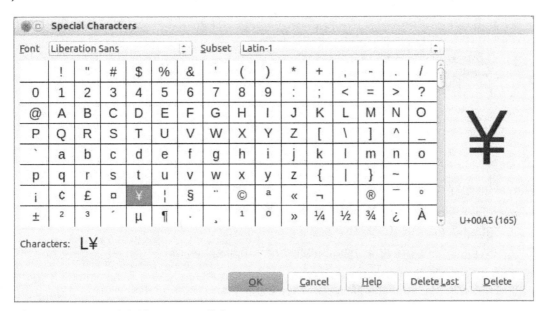

Figure 207: Special Characters dialog

Note	Characters you select will be inserted in the order they were selected, even if you accidentally click on the wrong character. Clicking on another character will only add it to the ones being inserted. Click **Delete** to delete all the characters selected, then click on the correct characters.

Inserting non-breaking spaces and hyphens

Where it is not desirable for words that are separated by a space or a hyphen to span over two lines, or where an optional hyphen is desired, you can insert a special formatting mark. Draw supports the following formatting marks:

- **Non-breaking space** – inserts a space that will keep bordering characters together on line breaks.
- **Non-breaking hyphen** – inserts a hyphen that will keep bordering characters together on line breaks.
- **Optional hyphen** – inserts an invisible hyphen within a word that will appear and create a line break once it becomes the last character in a line.
- **No-width optional break** – inserts an invisible space within a word that will insert a line break once it becomes the last character in a line. Only available when complex text layout (CTL) is enabled.
- **No-width no break** – inserts an invisible space within a word that will keep the word together at the end of a line. Only available when complex text layout (CTL) is enabled.
- **Left-to-right mark** – inserts a text direction mark that affects the text direction of any text following the mark. Only available when complex text layout (CTL) is enabled.
- **Right-to-left mark** – inserts a text direction mark that affects the text direction of any text following the mark. Only available when complex text layout (CTL) is enabled.

To insert a non-breaking space, or hyphens, or access the formatting marks:

1) Click on the **Text** icon and place the cursor in the text where you want to use formatting marks.

2) Go to **Insert > Formatting Mark** on the main menu bar, and select the formatting mark you want to use from the context menu that opens.

   A non-breaking space can also be inserted using the keyboard shortcut *Ctrl+Shift+Space*. A no-width optional break can be inserted using the keyboard shortcut *Ctrl+Slash*.

Formatting text

The appropriate use of text formatting can give text in a drawing a consistent look, making your drawing look more professional without any distracting elements.

Formatting text may require some intervention in three areas:

- Character attributes (for example, font color or emphasis)
- Paragraph attributes (for example, alignment or spacing)
- List attributes (for example, type of bullet or indent spacing)

In some cases it is quicker and more efficient to apply manual formatting; but in situations where you need to perform the same modifications to many different parts of the drawing, the use of styles is recommended.

Tip	Sometimes it is very useful to re-apply the default style to a selection of text removing any manual formatting applied to it, especially if a mistake has been made and you are not sure how to undo it. To revert back to the default style, select the manually formatted text and then select **Format > Default formatting** from the main menu bar.

Selecting text

All text

To select *all* the text in a text box:

1) Click on the **Text** icon on the Drawing toolbar and then click once on the text to turn on edit mode for the text box.

2) Click once on the border of the text box to display the selection handles.

3) Refer to "Character formatting" on page 177 and "Paragraph formatting" on page 179 for information on how to format the text.

Partial selection

To select only *part* of the text in a text box or an object:

1) Click on the **Text** icon on the Drawing toolbar and then click once on the text at the position where you want to start selecting text.

2) Select the text to be formatted using one of the following methods.

   – Click and drag the cursor over the text.

   – Press *Shift* then use the left or right arrow keys to select characters.

   – Press *Shift+Ctrl* then use the left or right arrow keys to select whole words.

   – Press *Shift+Home* to select text to the beginning of the line.

   – Press *Shift+End* to select text to the end of the line.

3) Refer to "Character formatting" on page 177 and "Paragraph formatting" on page 179 for information on how to format the text.

Using styles

Only drawing object styles are available in Draw to format text. Each drawing object style listed in the Styles and Formatting dialog (Figure 208) or the **Styles and Formatting** subsection (Figure 209) on the Sidebar has default settings for formatting and layout. You can create new styles and modify the styles supplied with Draw.

Figure 208: Styles and Formatting dialog

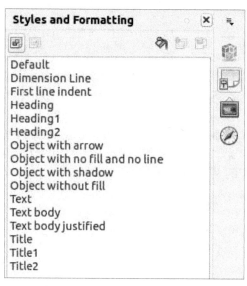

Figure 209: Sidebar Styles and Formatting subsection

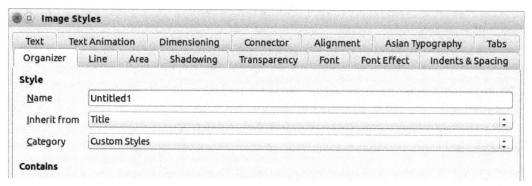

Figure 210: Image Styles dialog

Creating styles

1) Go to **Format > Styles and Formatting** on the main menu bar or press the *F11* key to open the Styles and Formatting dialog (Figure 208). Alternatively, click on the **Styles and Formatting** icon ▣ on the Sidebar to open the **Styles and Formatting** subsection (Figure 209).

2) Right-click on a style name and select **New** from the context menu to open the Image Styles dialog (Figure 210).

3) On the **Organizer** page, type a unique name for your style and select which style your new style will inherit attributes from. Any new style is automatically placed into the Custom Styles category.

4) Use the various pages in the Image Styles dialog to set all the attributes for your text and/or paragraph.

5) Click **OK** when finished and your new style is added to the list in Styles and Formatting.

Alternatively, select your text and carry out all the formatting changes to the text, then click on the

New Style from Selection icon ▣ to open the Create Style dialog. Type a unique style name and click **OK** to close the Create Style dialog. Your new style is added to the list in Styles and Formatting.

Modifying styles

1) Go to **Format > Styles and Formatting** on the main menu bar or press the *F11* key to open the Styles and Formatting dialog (Figure 208). Alternatively, click on the **Styles and Formatting** icon  on the Sidebar to open the **Styles and Formatting** subsection (Figure 209).

2) Right-click on the style to be modified and select **Modify** from the context menu to open the Image Styles dialog (Figure 210).

3) Use the various pages in the Image Styles dialog to change any of the attributes for your text and/or paragraph.

4) Click **OK** when finished making changes and the style is saved with the new format attributes.

Alternatively, select your text and perform all the changes to format, then select a style in Styles and Formatting list. Click on the **Update Style** icon and the style is saved with the new format attributes.

Character formatting

Characters can be formatted independently from the format used for a paragraph of text. This character formatting will also override any formatting that has been applied using a drawing object style.

Note	If the text box has been selected, then any character formatting to text will be applied to all of the text contained within the text box. For more information about selecting text, see "Selecting text" on page 175.

Figure 211: Character dialog

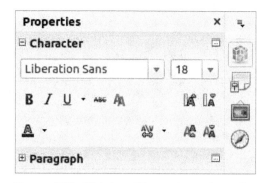

Figure 212: Sidebar Character subsection

1) Click on the **Text** icon, then select the characters you want to format. See "Selecting text" on page 175 for information on how to select text.

2) Go to **Format > Character** on the main menu bar, or click the **Character** icon on the Text Formatting toolbar, or right-click on the selected character and select **Character** from the context menu to open the **Character** dialog (Figure 211).

3) Make your changes to the character formatting using the options available in the tabbed pages in the Character dialog, then click **OK** to save your changes.

   To cancel any changes you have made to the character format, click **Reset** and the characters revert back to the original paragraph formatting.

Alternatively, use the tools available on the Text Formatting toolbar (Figure 199 on page 168) or in the **Character** subsection (Figure 212) on the Sidebar to format the characters.

Alternatively, right-click on the selected text and use the options available in the context menu (**Font**; **Size** and **Style**).

Note	Selecting **Format > Text** on the main menu bar, or right-clicking on selected text and then selecting **Text** from the context menu, opens the Text dialog. The Text dialog is used to format a text box or an object that contains text and any text animation applied to text within a text box or object.

Character formatting options

The formatting options in the tabbed pages of the Character dialog are used as follows:

- **Font** – select the desired font type, its base attributes (*Italic*, **Bold**, Language, and so on) as well as the size. A sample of the font is displayed in the lower part of the dialog. This font page is also available when creating or modifying a graphics style. If support for Asian language and Complex Text Layout (CTL) has been enabled (**Tools > Options > Language Settings > Languages**), then the Font page is divided into three parts for Western, Asian, and CTL text fonts allowing you to specify text fonts and their attributes for the majority of font families.

- **Font Effects** – apply special effects to the text, such as overlining and underlining, color, shadow, and so on. A sample of the text is displayed in the lower part of the dialog as a quick visual check of the effects applied. This page is also available when creating or modifying a graphics style.

- **Position** – sets the text position relative to the baseline when you need to insert subscripts or superscripts. This page is not available when creating or modifying a graphics style.

  - *Scaling* – specifies the percentage of the font width by which to compress or expand the *individual* characters of the selected text.

- *Spacing* – sets the spacing between the characters of the font, which can be defined in number of points.
- *Pair kerning* – automatically adjusts the spacing between certain pairs of characters to visually improve the appearance.

Paragraph formatting

Any individual paragraph formatting will override any formatting that has been applied using a drawing object style.

Note	If the text box has been selected, then any individual paragraph formatting to text will be applied to all of the text contained within the text box. For more information about selecting text, see "Selecting text" on page 175.

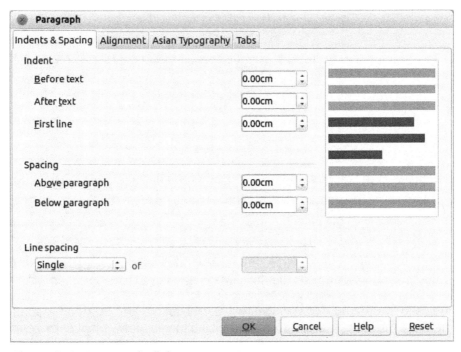

Figure 213: Paragraph dialog

1) Click on the **Text** icon then select the paragraph you want to format. See "Selecting text" on page 175 for information on how to select text.

2) Go to **Format** > **Paragraph** on the main menu bar, or click the **Paragraph** icon on the Text Formatting toolbar, or right-click on the selected text and select **Paragraph** to open the Paragraph dialog (Figure 213).

3) Make your changes to the paragraph formatting using the available options in the tabbed pages in the Paragraph dialog, then click **OK** to save your changes.

   To cancel any changes you have made to the paragraph format, click **Reset** and the text reverts back to its original formatting.

Alternatively, use the tools available on the **Paragraph** subsection (Figure 214) on the Sidebar to format the selected paragraphs.

Alternatively, right-click on the selected paragraphs and use the options available in the context menu (**Font**; **Size**, **Style**, **Alignment** and **Line Spacing**).

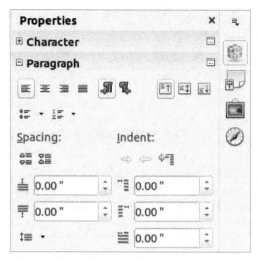

Figure 214: Sidebar Paragraph subsection

Note	Selecting **Format > Text** on the main menu bar, or right-clicking on selected text and then selecting **Text** from the context menu, opens the Text dialog. The Text dialog is used to format a text box or an object that contains text and any text animation applied to text within a text box or object.

Paragraph formatting options

The formatting options in the tabbed pages of the Paragraph dialog are used as follows:

- **Indents and Spacing** – determines the indents and spacing used in a paragraph.

    - *Indent* – modifies the indentation of the text (before and after) as well as the indentation of the first line.

    - *Spacing* – defines the space before and after each paragraph formatted with the style.

    - *Line spacing* – determines the spacing between two lines formatted with the style. Note that selecting *Proportional* spacing requires specifying the percentage of a line to be used as spacing; 100% single line, 200% double line, 50% half a line. If *Leading* is selected, specify the amount of line spacing in your default unit of measurement.

Tip	Setting line spacing to less than 100% is a good method to cram a lot of text into a text box, however care must be taken as too small a value will make the text hard to read.

Tip	You can change the default unit of measurement by going to **Tools > Options > LibreOffice Draw > General**.

- **Alignment** – determines the paragraph alignment: Left, Right, Center, or Justified. A preview shows the effects of the changes. The same alignment options can be accessed using the paragraph alignment icons on the Text Formatting toolbar.

Note	If you have *Complex Text Layout* enabled in **Tools > Options > Language Settings > Languages**, an extra selection — *Text Direction* — appears at the bottom of the dialog; you can choose Left-to-right or Right-to-left.

- **Tabs** – determines the tab stops. This page is also available in the graphics styles dialog.
- **Asian Typography** – sets the following properties relative to line changes and is only available if *Enabled for Asian Languages* is selected in **Tools > Options > Language Settings > Languages**.
    - Apply list of forbidden characters to the beginning and end of lines.
    - Allow hanging punctuation.
    - Apply spacing between Asian, Latin and Complex text.

Creating bulleted and numbered lists

Bulleted and numbered lists can be created in text boxes, shapes, and objects. However, when creating lists in shapes and objects, remember that shapes and objects are not dynamic and do not automatically expand as you create a list.

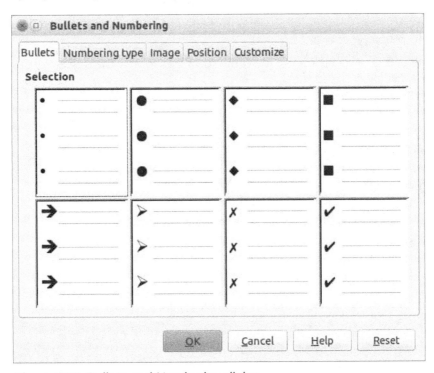

Figure 215: Bullets and Numbering dialog

Creating lists

1) Click on the **Text** icon, then select the text you want to use for a bulleted list.
2) Go to **Format** > **Bullets and Numbering** on the main menu bar, or right-click on the selected text and select **Bullets and Numbering** on the context menu to open the Bullets and Numbering dialog (Figure 215).
3) Select the list style from the *Bullets*, *Numbering*, or *Image* pages, then click **OK** to save your changes.

    To cancel any changes you have made, click **Reset**. The text reverts back to its original formatting.

Alternatively, click the **Bullets On/Off** icon ⦂⚌ on the Text Formatting toolbar. This quickly creates a list using the previously selected settings in the Bullets and Numbering dialog.

Alternatively, select a list style from the drop-down lists for the **Bullets** or **Numbering** icons on the **Paragraph** subsection on the Sidebar (Figure 214). Clicking on **More Options** at the bottom of these drop-down lists opens the Bullets and Numbering dialog.

Editing and customizing a list

You can edit and customize the appearance of a list by changing the bullet type or numbering for the entire list or a single entry or the outline level of a list item. All changes are made using the **Bullets and Numbering** dialog.

Editing lists

1) Click on the **Text** icon, then select the list or the items in the list that you want to edit and customize.

2) Go to **Format > Bullets and Numbering,** or right-click on the selected text and select **Bullets and Numbering** to open the **Bullets and Numbering** dialog (Figure 215).

3) Select a new list style from the *Bullets*, *Numbering* or *Image* pages.

4) Click **OK** to save your changes.

Alternatively, select a new list style from the drop-down lists for the **Bullets** or **Numbering** icons on the **Paragraph** subsection on the Sidebar (Figure 214). Clicking on **More Options** at the bottom of these drop-down lists opens the Bullets and Numbering dialog.

Changing position

Use the *Position* page (Figure 216) to adjust the outline level, indentation, and spacing of bullet points and the associated text. This page is particularly effective when used in combination with the *Customize* page.

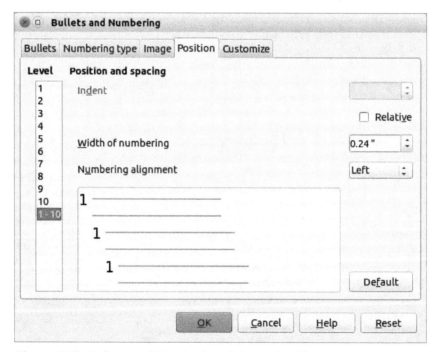

Figure 216: Bullets and Numbering dialog – Position page

To set up an outline level:

1) Select an outline level from the list on the left hand side of the page or select levels **1 – 10** to modify all levels simultaneously.

---

2) Set the **Indent**, which is the spacing between the bullet or number and the text. If you select the Relative option, the indent value will be measured relative to the previous level and not from the margin.

3) Set the measurement for **Width of numbering**. This is the space to leave between the numbering or bullet point and the text.

4) Set the **Numbering alignment**, which is normally only used on a numbered list. Setting this option does not set the alignment of the text.

   – Select *Left* to align the numbering at the left edge of the alignment space for numbering.

   – Select *Right* to align the numbering at the right edge of the alignment space for numbering.

   – Select *Centered* to align the numbering in the center of the alignment space for numbering.

5) Click **OK** to save your changes.

   To revert back to the default values of the list, click **Reset**.

Tip	To fully appreciate how **Numbering alignment** works, create a numbered list with more than ten elements, making sure there is enough room for two (or more) numerical characters using the *Width of numbering* field. Select *Right* alignment and the right edge of the numbers will form a neat, straight line before the text.

Customizing

Use the *Customize* page (Figure 217) to customize the style of all the outline levels. The options available on this page depend on the type of marker selected for the list.

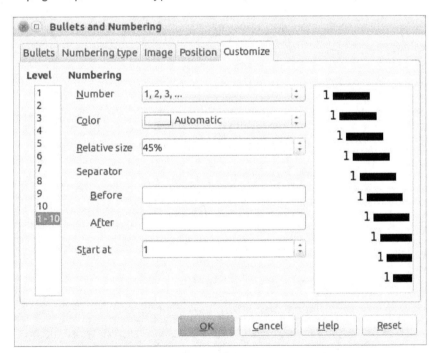

Figure 217: Bullets and Numbering dialog – Customize page

1) Select first the level you want to modify on the left hand side of the box. To modify all levels at once, select **1 – 10** as the level. With levels being arranged in a hierarchical structure, changing, for example, the font attribute of one of the levels ripples through all the lower levels.

2) Make your changes to the list using the options on this page. The preview on the right hand side of the dialog shows the effect of the changes.

3) Click **OK** to save your changes.

To revert back to the default values of the list, click **Reset**.

Depending on the bullet style selected (for example, bullet, native numbering, graphics), some of the following options may not be available on the *Customize* page:

- **Before** – enter any text to appear before the number (for example, *Step*).
- **After** – enter any text to appear after the number (for example, a punctuation mark).
- **Color** – pick the color for the list marker (number or bullet character).
- **Relative size** – specify the size of the number relative to the size of the characters in the paragraph of the list.
- **Start at** – enter the first value of the list (for example, you might want the list to start at 4 instead of 1).
- **Character button** – click this button to select the special character for the bullet.
- **Graphics** – opens a gallery of available graphics or allows the selection of a graphic file used as a marker.
- **Width** and **Height**: – specify the dimensions of the graphic marker.
- **Keep ratio checkbox** – if selected, the ratio between the width and the height of the graphic marker is fixed.

Using tables

Tables are useful when you want to show structured information in your drawing, for example a specification list or drawing title block. You can create tables directly in Draw, eliminating any need to embed a Calc spreadsheet or a Writer text table in your drawing. The tables provided by Draw do have a limited functionality.

Creating tables

When working with tables, it is useful to know the number of rows and columns required as well as the appearance. Tables are placed on a drawing in a text box and cannot be placed into objects or shapes. Also, unlike text boxes and other objects, tables cannot be rotated.

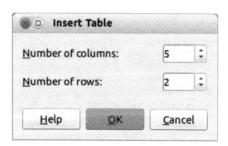

Figure 218: Insert Table dialog

1) Go to **Insert > Table** on the main menu bar to open the **Insert Table** dialog (Figure 218).

2) Select the number of columns and number of rows for the table.

3) Click **OK** and a table is placed in the center of your drawing inside its own text box.

4) Move the table into position by dragging it to its new position, see "Using text boxes" on page 168 for more information.

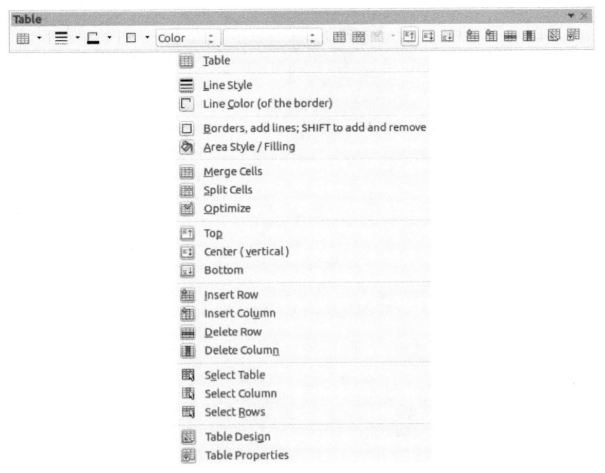

Figure 219: Table toolbar and table tools

Modifying tables

Once the table is added to your drawing, you can control its appearance, size, position, and so on using a combination of the tools on the Table toolbar (Figure 219) and the Format Cells dialog (Figure 223).

The Table toolbar is only active when a table has been selected. If the Table toolbar does not display when you select a table, go to **View > Toolbars > Table**. The default setting in LibreOffice is to append the Table toolbar to the Drawing toolbar. However, the Table toolbar can be detached from the Drawing toolbar, creating a floating toolbar.

The Table toolbar contains the majority of the tools you need to manipulate a table. These tools are shown in Figure 219 and described below.

- **Table** – creates a new table in a drawing. Opens the Insert Table dialog (Figure 218) where you can select the required number of rows and columns.

    Alternatively, click on the small triangle next to the **Table** icon to open a graphic representation for creating a table (Figure 220). To use this tool, move the mouse to the right and down in the grid until you have the columns and rows you require and click the left mouse button. Clicking on the **More** button opens the Insert Table dialog.

- **Line Style** – changes the line style of the borders of selected cells. Opens a new dialog where you can choose from a range of predefined styles.

- **Line color (of the border)** – opens a color selection dialog where you can choose the color of the borders around selected cells.

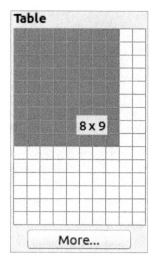

Figure 220: Table graphic tool

- **Borders** – selects predefined border configurations. The borders are applied to the selected cells. If the desired border pattern is not available, you will need to use the **Format Cells** dialog.

- **Area Style/Filling** – select the cells to be filled, then select the type of fill from the drop-down list: *Invisible* (no color), *Color*, *Gradient*, *Hatching*, or *Bitmap*. The fillings drop-down menu is populated with the available fillings for the fill type selected.

- **Merge Cells** – merges the selected cells into one cell. Note that the contents of the merged cells are also merged. You can also merge cells by right-clicking in the selected cells and using the context menu that opens.

- **Split Cells** – opposite operation of merging cells. Make sure that the cursor is positioned on the cell you want to split, then click to open the Split Cells dialog (Figure 221). Select the number of cells required from the split as well as whether the cell should be split horizontally or vertically. When splitting horizontally, you can select the *Into equal proportions* option to get all cells of equal size. The contents of the split cell remain in the original cell (the one on the left or top). You can also split cells by right-clicking in the cell and using the context menu that opens.

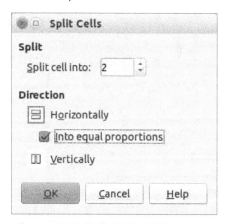

Figure 221: Split Cells dialog

- **Optimize** – evenly distributes the selected cells either horizontally or vertically. Select **Distribute Columns Evenly** for columns or select **Distribute Rows Equally** for rows.

- **Top, Center (vertical), Bottom** – you can select the vertical alignment of text in a cell by selecting the required cells and clicking on one of these tools.

- **Insert Row**, **Insert Column**, **Delete Row**, **Delete Column** – select a row or column and use these four tools to insert or delete rows and columns into or from your table. Rows and columns are inserted/deleted below and to the right of the selected cell. You can also select, insert, or delete rows and columns by right-clicking a cell and using the context menu that opens.

- **Select Table**, **Select Column**, **Select Row** – Use these tools to select a table, column, or row if you want to perform the same change to attributes for a table, column, or row.

- **Table Design** – opens the Table Design dialog (Figure 222) where you can select a table style and display options.

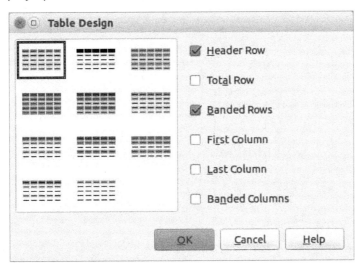

Figure 222: Table Design dialog

- **Table Properties** – opens the Format Cells dialog (Figure 223), which contains the following tabbed pages. You can also open this dialog by right-clicking on the table and selecting **Table** from the context menu.

  - *Font* – use to select the desired font type and family, style (*Italic*, **Bold**, etc.), size, and language. A sample of the font is displayed in the lower part of the dialog.

  - *Font Effects* – use to apply effects to the text: font color; relief; overlining; strikethrough; underlining; and emphasis mark.

  - *Borders* – use to set borders and border properties not available when using the **Borders** tool on the **Table** toolbar; line arrangement (default or user defined); line (style, width, and color); and spacing to contents (cell margins).

  - *Background* – changes the background of the selected cells and provides the same functions as the **Area Style/Filling** tool on the **Table** toolbar.

  - *Reset* – clicking this button resets the table back to default values.

Position and size

On a drawing, you can change position and size of a text box that contains a table. However, the text box containing a table cannot be rotated. See "Using text boxes" on page 168 for more information.

Deleting tables

1) Click and drag over the table to select it or select the table then click on the text box border around the table.

2) Press the *Delete* key.

Figure 223: Format Cells dialog

Using fields

Fields allow the automatic insertion of text into a drawing. You can think of a field as a kind of formula which is calculated when the drawing is loaded or printed and the result is written in the drawing.

Inserting fields

1) Move the cursor where the field will be positioned.
2) Go to **Insert > Fields** on the main menu bar. A text box is created when you insert a field and can be repositioned just like any other text box. See "Using text boxes" on page 168 for more information.
3) Select a field from the options shown in the context menu.

The fields available in Draw are as follows:

- **Date (fixed)** – inserts the current date when the field was inserted.
- **Date (variable)** – inserts a field that is updated with the date each time the file is opened.
- **Time (fixed)** – inserts a field displaying the current time when the field was inserted.
- **Time (variable)** – inserts a field which is updated with the time each time the file is opened.
- **Author** – inserts the author of the drawing. This information is derived from the value recorded in the general options. To modify this information go to **Tools > Options > LibreOffice > User Data**.
- **Page Number** – inserts a page number for each page in a drawing.
- **Page Count** – inserts the total number of pages in a drawing.
- **File Name** – inserts a field that contains the name of the file.

Customizing fields

The appearance of fields can be customized as follows. **Page Number**, **Page Count**, and **File Name** fields cannot be customized.

1) Place the cursor at the start of the field data and go to **Edit > Fields** on the main menu bar to open the Edit Field dialog (Figure 224) and select the desired format from the available options.
2) Click **OK**.
3) Alternatively, right-click on the field and select the required options from the context menu.

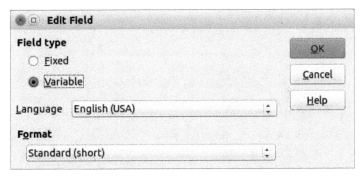

Figure 224: Edit Field dialog

Using hyperlinks

When inserting text (for example website address or URL) that can be used as a hyperlink, Draw formats it automatically, creating the hyperlink and applying color and underlining.

Inserting hyperlinks

1) Click in the text box at the position where you want to insert a hyperlink.

2) Go to **Insert > Hyperlink** on the main menu bar, or click on the **Hyperlink** icon on the **Standard** toolbar, or use the keyboard shortcut *Ctrl+K* to open Hyperlink dialog (Figure 225).

3) Select the type of hyperlink you want to insert and the options you want to use.

4) Click **Apply** to insert the hyperlink and save your selections. If you are creating several hyperlinks, click **Apply** after each one.

5) Click **Close** to close the Hyperlink dialog.

On the left side, select one of the four types of hyperlinks. The dialog changes according to the type of hyperlink selected.

- **Internet** – select whether the link is Web or FTP. Enter the required web address (URL).

- **Mail & News** – select whether the link is an E-mail or news link. Enter the receiver address and for email, also the subject.

- **Document** – creates a hyperlink to another document or to another place in the drawing, commonly referred to as a bookmark. Enter the document path, or click on the **Open File** icon to open a file browser; leave this blank if you want to link to a target in the same drawing. Optionally, you can specify a target (for example. a specific slide). Click on the **Target** icon to open the **Target in Document** dialog, where you can select the target; or, if you know the name of the target, you can type it into the box.

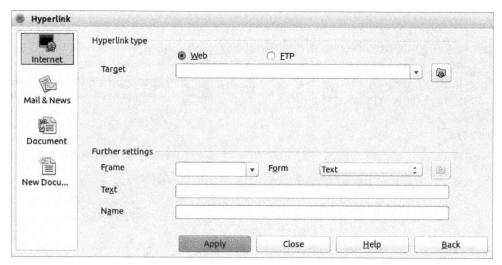

Figure 225: Hyperlink dialog

- **New Document** – creates a hyperlink to a new document. Choose whether to edit the newly created document immediately (**Edit now**) or just create it to edit later (**Edit later**). Choose the type of document to create (text, spreadsheet, etc.). The **Select path** button opens a file browser so that you can choose the directory for the new document.

Tips	To prevent LibreOffice from automatically turning website addresses (URLs) into hyperlinks, go to **Tools > AutoCorrect > Options** and deselect the **URL Recognition** checkbox.
	To change the color of hyperlinks, go to **Tools > Options > LibreOffice > Appearance**, scroll to *Unvisited links* and/or *Visited links*, select the checkboxes, pick the new colors and click **OK**. Caution: this will change the color for all hyperlinks in all components of LibreOffice which may not be what you want.

The *Further settings* section on the Hyperlink dialog is common to all the hyperlink types, although some choices are more relevant to some types of links.

- **Frame** – determines how the hyperlink will open. This applies to documents that open in a Web browser.
- **Form** – specifies if the link is to be presented as text or as a button. See "Working with hyperlink buttons" on page 191 for more information.
- **Text** – specifies the text that will be visible to the user.
- **Name** – applicable to HTML documents. It specifies text that will be added as a NAME attribute in the HTML code behind the hyperlink.

Editing text hyperlinks

1) Select the hyperlink by dragging across the text, not clicking on it.
2) Go to **Edit > Hyperlink** on the main menu bar to open the Hyperlink dialog (Figure 225).
3) Make your editing changes from the available options, then click **Apply** when done. If you need to edit several hyperlinks, click **Apply** after each one.
4) Click **Close** to close the Hyperlink dialog.

Working with hyperlink buttons

A hyperlink button is inserted in the center of the current drawing. In most cases, that is not where you want it to appear. To edit the text or size of a hyperlink button, or to move it to another place on the drawing:

1) Go to **View > Toolbars > Form Controls** on the main menu bar to open the **Form Controls** toolbar (Figure 226).

2) Select the **Design Mode On/Off** icon.

3) Now click on the hyperlink button and drag it to another position, or right-click to open a dialog where you can change the text on the button, the size of the button, and other properties.

4) When you have finished editing the button, click the **Design Mode On/Off** icon again to make the button inactive. For a more detailed description of the properties and how to work with Form Controls, refer to the *Writer Guide*.

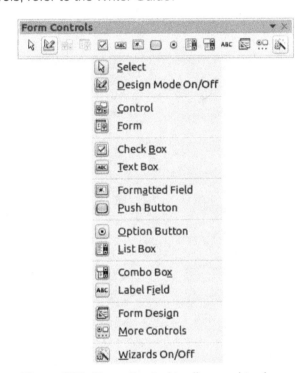

Figure 226: Form Control toolbar and tools

Chapter 10
Printing, Exporting, and
E-mailing

Quick printing

To quickly print a document or drawing, click on the **Print File Directly** icon 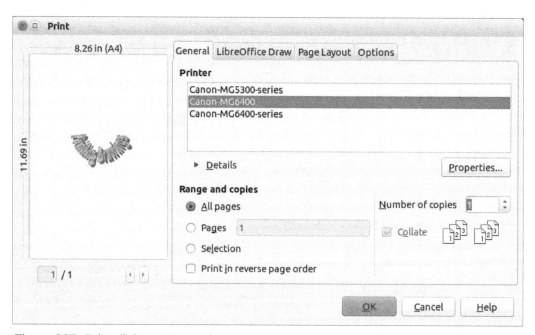 on the Standard toolbar to send the entire document to the default printer that is defined for your computer.

Note	You can change the action of the **Print File Directly** icon by sending a document to the printer defined for the document instead of the default printer for the computer. Go to **Tools > Options > Load/Save > General** and select the **Load printer settings with the document** option.

Controlling printing

For more control over printing, use the Print dialog by going to **File > Print** on the main menu bar, or by using *Ctrl+P*. The Print dialog (Figure 227) has four tabs where you can choose a range of options, which are described in the following sections.

Note	The options selected on the Print dialog only apply to the printing of the current document that is open in Draw. To specify default print settings for LibreOffice, go to **Tools > Options > LibreOffice > Print**.

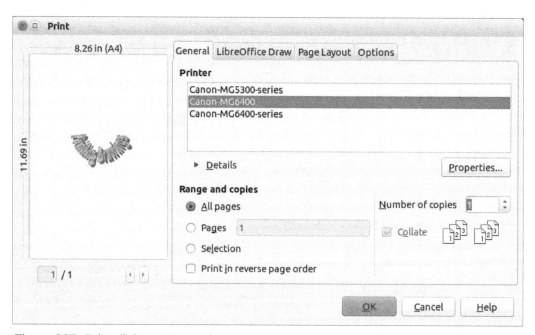

Figure 227. Print dialog – General page

General page

On the **General** page of the Print dialog (Figure 227), you can select:

- Which printer to use from the printers available in the *Printer* section.
- Which pages to print, number of copies to print, whether to collate multiple copies, and page order for printing in the *Range and copies* section.

LibreOffice Draw page

On the **LibreOffice Draw** page of the Print dialog (Figure 228), you can define settings that are specific to the current document type:

- In the *Contents* section, print the page name and/or the date and time on the drawing.

- In the *Colors* section, print the drawing in original colors, as a grayscale, or in black and white.

- In the *Size* section, print the drawing in its original size, fit the drawing to the printable area of the page, print the drawing on multiple sheets of paper if the drawing is too large for the paper size being used, or print the drawing as multiple tiles on a sheet of paper.

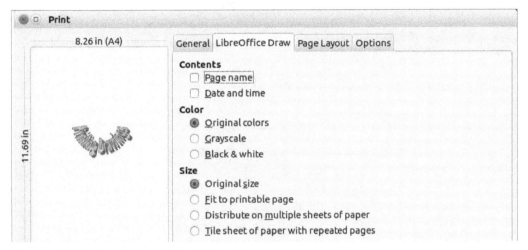

Figure 228. Print dialog – LibreOffice Draw page

Page Layout page

On the **Page Layout** page of the Print dialog (Figure 229), you can define the page layout when your drawing is printed.

- In the *Layout* section, select how many pages per sheet of paper are printed, the order in which the pages are printed on a sheet, whether a border is drawn around each page, or the drawing is printed as a brochure.

- In the *Page* sides section, select whether to print all the pages, the back sides/left pages only, or the front sides/right pages only. This option is useful when you want to print double-sided when your printer does not support duplex printing.

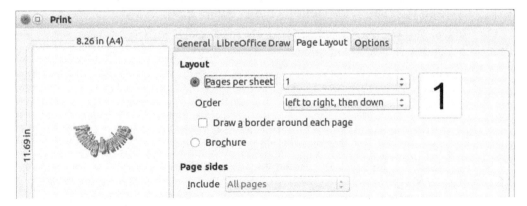

Figure 229. Print dialog – Page Layout page

Options page

On the **Options** page (Figure 230) you can select whether to print to file, create single print jobs when you want to use collated output, use only the printer tray specified in the printer preferences, or use the paper size specified in the printer preferences.

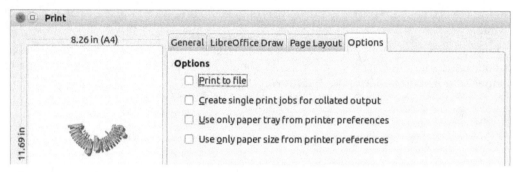

Figure 230. Print dialog – Options page

Printing multiple pages on a single sheet

To print multiple pages of a document on one sheet of paper:

1) Go to **File > Print** on the main menu bar or use the keyboard shortcut *Ctrl+P* to open the Print dialog and then select the **Page Layout** page (Figure 229).

2) In the *Layout* section, select from the *Pages per sheet* drop-down list the number of pages to print per sheet. The preview panel on the right shows how the pages will look in the printed document.

3) When printing more than two pages per sheet, select the order in which the pages are printed on a sheet from the *Order* drop down list.

4) To distinguish each page on a sheet, select the *Draw a border around each page* option.

5) Click **Print** to print the document.

Selecting pages to print

In addition to printing a full document, you can choose whether to print individual pages, a range of pages, or a highlighted selection within a document.

Individual page

1) Go to **File > Print** on the main menu bar or use the keyboard shortcut *Ctrl+P* to open the Print dialog and then select the **General** page (Figure 227).

2) In the *Ranges and copies* section, select the *Pages* option.

3) Enter the number of the page to print.

4) Click **Print** to print the document.

Range of pages

1) Go to **File > Print** on the main menu bar or use the keyboard shortcut *Ctrl+P* to open the Print dialog and then select the **General** page (Figure 227).

2) In the *Ranges and copies* section, select the *Pages* option.

3) Enter the number of the pages to print (for example 1-4 or 1,3,7,11), or any combination of the two (for example: 1-4,5-9,10).

4) Click **Print** to print the document.

To print a selection from a page or multiple pages:

1) In the document, highlight the section of the page or pages to print.
2) Go to **File > Print** on the main menu bar or use the keyboard shortcut *Ctrl+P* to open the Print dialog and then select the **General** page (Figure 227).
3) In the *Ranges and copies* section, select the *Selection* option.
4) Click **Print** to print the document.

Brochure or booklet printing

In Writer, Impress, and Draw, you can print a document with two pages on each side of a sheet of paper, arranged so that when the printed pages are folded in half, the pages are in the correct order to form a booklet or brochure.

Tip	Plan your document so it will look good when printed half size; choose appropriate margins, font sizes, and so on. You may need to experiment.

Single-sided printer

To print a brochure or booklet on a printer only capable of single-sided printing:

1) Go to **File > Print** on the main menu bar or use the keyboard shortcut *Ctrl+P* to open the Print dialog and then select the **General** page (Figure 227).
2) Select the printer you want to use if more than one printer is connected to your computer.
3) Click **Properties** to open the properties dialog for the selected printer (Figure 231).
4) Check the printer is set to the same orientation (portrait or landscape) as specified in the page setup for your document. Usually the orientation does not matter, but it does for brochures and booklets.
5) Click **OK** to return to the Print dialog.
6) Select the **Page layout** tab in the Print dialog (Figure 229).
7) Select the *Brochure* option (Figure 232).

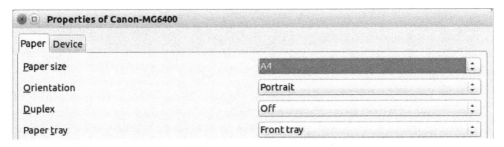

Figure 231: Printer Properties dialog

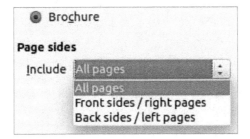

Figure 232: Brochure or booklet printing

8) In the *Page sides* section, select *Back sides/left pages* option from the drop-down list.
9) Click **Print**.
10) Take the printed pages out of the printer, turn the pages over, and put them back into the printer in the correct orientation to print on the blank side. You may need to experiment a bit to find out what the correct arrangement is for your printer.
11) In the *Page sides* section, select *Front sides/right pages* option from the drop down list.
12) Click **Print** to print the document.

Double-sided or duplex printer

To print a brochure or booklet on a printer that is capable of double-sided or duplex printing:

1) Go to **File > Print** on the main menu bar or use the keyboard shortcut *Ctrl+P* to open the Print dialog and then select the **General** page (Figure 227).
2) Select the printer you want to use if more than one printer is connected to your computer.
3) Click **Properties** to open the properties dialog for the selected printer (Figure 231).
4) Check the printer is set to the same orientation (portrait or landscape) as specified in the page setup for your document. Usually the orientation does not matter, but it does for brochures and booklets.
5) From the *Duplex* drop-down list, select *Long Edge* or *Long Side* printing. Actual options available for duplex printing depend on the printer model and the computer system being used.
6) Click **OK** to return to the Print dialog.
7) Select the **Page layout** tab in the Print dialog (Figure 229).
8) Select the *Brochure* option (Figure 232).
9) In the *Page sides* section, select *All pages* option from the drop-down list.
10) Click **Print** to print the document.

Printing in black and white or grayscale

You may wish to print documents in black and white or grayscale on a color printer. However, some color printers may only allow you to print in color regardless of the settings you choose. More details can be found in the information that came with your printer.

Printer settings

To change the printer settings to print in black and white or grayscale:

1) Go to **File > Print** on the main menu bar or use the keyboard shortcut *Ctrl+P* to open the Print dialog and then select the **General** page (Figure 227).
2) Click **Properties** to open the properties dialog for the printer, then click the **Device** tab. The available choices available depend on printer model and computer operating system, but you should easily find options for the *Color* settings. An example of what you may see is shown in Figure 233.
3) In *Color* and select either black and white or grayscale from the drop-down list.
4) Click **OK** and return to the Print dialog, then click **Print** to print the document.

Tip	Grayscale is the best option if you have any colored text or graphics in the document. Colors will print in shades of gray giving more detail. When printing color in black and white some of this detail maybe lost.

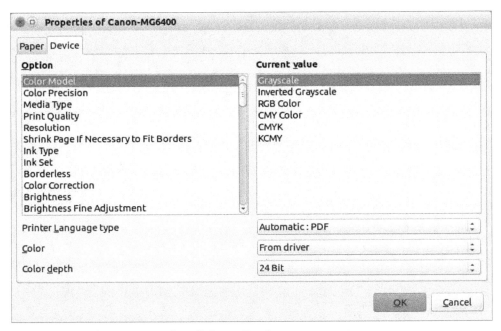

Figure 233: Printer Properties dialog – Device page

LibreOffice settings

To change the LibreOffice settings to print all color text and graphics as grayscale:

1) Go to **Tools > Options > LibreOffice > Print** on the main menu bar.

2) Select *Convert colors to grayscale* option then click **OK** to save the change.

3) Go to **File > Print** on the main menu bar or use the keyboard shortcut *Ctrl+P* to open the Print dialog and then select the **General** page (Figure 227).

4) Click **Print** to print the document.

Draw settings

To change the Draw settings to print all color text and graphics as either black and white or grayscale:

1) Go to **Tools > Options > LibreOffice Draw > Print** on the main menu bar.

2) In the *Quality* section, select either *Grayscale* or *Black & white* option, then click **OK** to save the change.

3) Go to **File > Print** on the main menu bar or use the keyboard shortcut *Ctrl+P* to open the Print dialog and then select the **General** page (Figure 227).

4) Click **Print** to print the document.

Exporting

LibreOffice can export documents to PDF (Portable Document Format). This industry-standard file format is ideal for sending a file for someone else to view using Adobe Reader or other PDF viewers. The process and dialogs are the same for Writer, Calc, Impress, and Draw, with a few minor differences mentioned in this section.

Directly as PDF

Click on the **Export Directly as PDF** icon ![PDF icon] on the Standard toolbar to export the entire document using your default PDF settings. You are asked to enter the file name and location for the PDF file, but you cannot choose page range, image compression, or other options.

Controlling PDF content and quality

For more control over the content and quality of the resulting PDF you have to use the option Export as PDF. For more information on the available options, see the *Getting Started* guide.

1) Go to **File > Export as PDF** on the main menu bar to open the PDF Options dialog (Figure 234). Use this dialog to select options in the *General*, *Initial View*, *User Interface*, *Links*, and *Security* pages.
2) When you have selected the appropriate options, click **Export**.
3) In the dialog that opens, enter the location and file name of the PDF to be created.
4) Click **Save** to export the file.

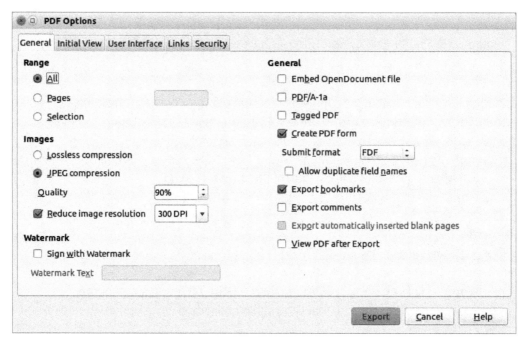

Figure 234: PDF Options dialog

Other formats

LibreOffice uses the term "export" for some file operations involving a change of file type. If you cannot find what you want in **File > Save As**, look in **File > Export**. LibreOffice can export files in various formats, which are listed in the drop-down list for *File format*.

To export a file in another format:

1) Go to **File > Export** on the main menu bar to open the Export dialog. An example of this dialog is shown in Figure 235.
2) Navigate to the directory where you want to export your drawing.
3) Specify a file name for the exported document in the *File name* text box.
4) Select the required format from the *File format* drop-down list.
5) Click **Export**.

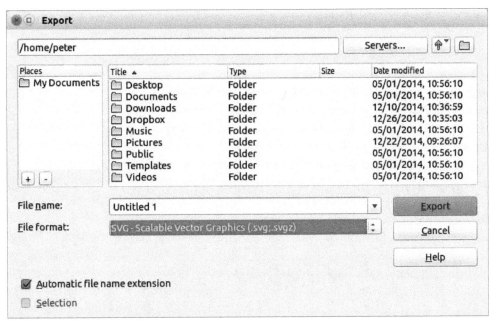

Figure 235: Export dialog

See *Chapter 6 Editing Pictures* in this guide for more information on exporting graphics.

Note	The content of the exported file will depend on the elements selected on the page. No selection results in the entire image being exported. For most export formats, only the image on the current page will be exported.

Web pages

To export a multi-page Draw document to a series of web pages, go to **File > Export** on the main menu bar and select **HTML Document** as the file type to open the HTML Export wizard. Follow the prompts to create the web pages. If required, the wizard can generate a navigation aid to help in moving from page to page. For more information, see *Chapter 12 Creating Web Pages* in the *Getting Started* guide.

E-mailing documents

LibreOffice provides several ways to send documents quickly and easily as an e-mail attachment in OpenDocument format (LibreOffice default format), or as a PDF. You can email a document to several recipients. For more information, see *Chapter 10 Printing, Exporting, and E-mailing* in the *Getting Started* guide.

Note	Documents can only be sent from the LibreOffice menu if a mail profile has been set up.

OpenDocument format

To email the current document in OpenDocument format:

1) Go to **File > Send > Document as E-mail** on the main menu bar. LibreOffice opens your default e-mail program with the document attached.

2) In your e-mail program, enter the recipient, subject, and any text you want to add, then send the e-mail.

PDF format

To email the current document as a PDF file:

1) Go to **File > Send >-E-mail as PDF** on the main menu bar. LibreOffice creates a PDF using the default PDF settings and then opens your email program with the PDF file attached.

2) In your e-mail program, enter the recipient, subject, and any text you want to add, then send the e-mail.

The Document Foundation

Chapter 11
Advanced Draw Techniques

Multi-page documents

Draw documents, like Impress presentation documents, can consist of multiple pages. This allows you to create a drawing that has several sections that are stored as one file on a computer.

When pages are inserted into a drawing, they are automatically named as *Slide 1*, *Slide 2*, and so on in the Navigator. As you change page order, the pages are automatically renumbered. However, if you want to easily identify each page, then it is recommended to give each page a memorable name.

Using the page pane

By default the **Page Pane** (Figure 236) appears docked on the left of the workspace when you open Draw and shows every page in the drawing as a thumbnail. If the Page Pane is not displayed, go to **View > Page Pane** on the main menu bar.

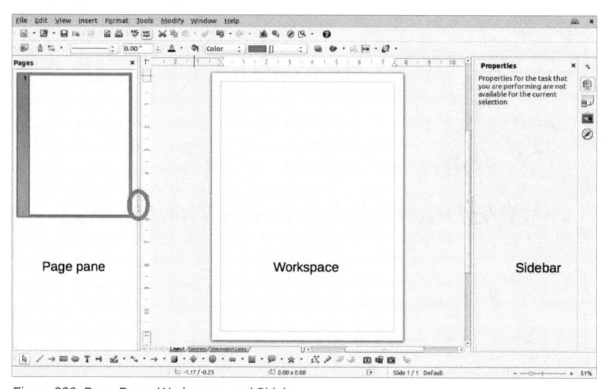

Figure 236: Page Pane, Workspace, and Sidebar

Note	The **Page Pane** is called **Pages** when it is in its docked position on the left of the workspace.

- Select a thumbnail in the Page Pane and the corresponding page is loaded in the workspace. Click on a page in the Workspace to activate it for editing.

- Alternatively, click on the **Navigator** icon ⊘ on the Standard toolbar or press the *F5* key or go to **View > Navigator** on the main menu bar to open the **Navigator** dialog (Figure 237) and select pages using this dialog.

- Alternatively, click on the **Navigator** icon ⊘ on the Sidebar to open the Navigator section (Figure 238) and select pages using the Sidebar.

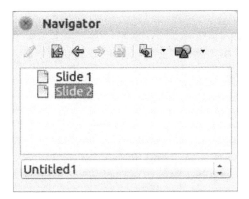

Figure 237: Navigator dialog

Figure 238: Navigator section on Sidebar

- Select a thumbnail in the Page pane, then drag and drop the thumbnail to change the order of pages in the document.
- Click and drag on the separator line between the Page pane and workspace to change the width of the Page pane.
- Click on the middle of this line to show or hide the Page pane (highlighted in Figure 236).
- Press and hold the *Ctrl* key, then double-click in the title bar of the Page pane to undock it and turn it into a floating window.
- Press and hold the *Ctrl* key, then double-click in the title bar of the undocked Page pane to dock it back into its default position on the left of the workspace.
- Right-click in the Page pane and, using options in the context menu, you can insert, delete or rename pages and cut, copy, and paste pages.
- Go to **Insert > Slide** on the main menu bar to insert a new page or **Insert > Duplicate Slide** to insert a duplicate page.

Master pages

A master page is a page that is used as the starting point for other pages in your drawing. It is similar to a page style in Writer and controls the basic formatting of all pages based upon it. A drawing can have more than one master page so that you can assign a different look to pages in your drawing, for example title page, contents page, and drawing pages.

A master page has a defined set of characteristics, including the background color, graphic, or gradient; objects (such as logos, decorative lines, and other graphics) in the background, the formatting of text, blocks of standard text, and insert fields such as page numbering, date, and filename.

Note	LibreOffice uses interchangeable terms for one concept: slide master, master slide, and master page. All refer to a page which is used to create other pages. When searching for information in Draw Help, it may be necessary to use alternative search terms.

Master page view

To add objects and fields to a master page, go to **View > Master** on the main menu bar to open the master page view. The **Master View** toolbar (Figure 239) also opens when you switch to master view. If this toolbar does not appear, go to **View > Toolbars > Master View** on the main menu bar.

To return to normal page mode, click on **Close Master View** in the Master View toolbar or go to **View > Normal** on the main menu bar.

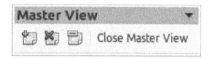

Figure 239: Master View toolbar

Creating master pages

Each drawing you create already has a default master page, but you can create extra master pages to change the look of some of the pages in your multi-page drawing.

1) Go to **View > Master** on the main menu bar to open the master page view.
2) Click on the **New Master** icon in the Master View toolbar to create a new master page. The new master page is automatically selected allowing you to add a new set of items to create a new look for your pages.

Renaming master pages

Each new master page created has the default name of Default 1, Default 2, and so on. It is recommended to rename your new master page with a more meaningful name. The default master page that was created when you first created your drawing can also be renamed.

1) Go to **View > Master** on the main menu bar to open the master page view.
2) Right-click on a master page in the Page pane and select **Rename Page** from the context menu or click on the **Rename Master** icon on the Master View toolbar. This opens a dialog where you can type a new name.
3) Click **OK** to save the master page with its new name.

Deleting master pages

1) Go to **View > Master** on the main menu bar to open the master page view.
2) Select the master page you want to delete.
3) Right-click on a master page that you created in the Page pane and select **Delete Page** from the context menu or click on the **Delete Master** icon on the Master View toolbar.

Note	The Delete option and Delete icon are only available when there is more than one master page in your drawing. You cannot delete the default master page that was created when you first created your drawing.

Inserting fields

You can insert fields on each master page by going to **Insert > Fields** on the main menu bar and selecting a field from the context menu. The following fields can be inserted into a master page.

- **Date (fixed)** – inserts the current date into the master page as a fixed field. The date is not automatically updated.

- **Date (variable)** – inserts the current date into the master page as a variable field. The date is automatically updated when you reload the file.

- **Time (fixed)** – inserts the current time into the master page as a fixed field. The time is not automatically updated.

- **Time (variable)** – inserts the current time into the master page as a variable field. The time is automatically updated when you reload the file.

- **Author** – inserts the first and last names listed in the LibreOffice user data into the active page.

- **Page Number** – inserts the page number into every page of the drawing. To change the number format, go to **Format > Page** on the main menu bar and select a format from the drop-down list in *Layout Settings*.

- **File name** – inserts the name of the active file. The name only appears after you save the file.

Assigning master pages

When your drawing has more than one master page, you can assign different master pages to different pages.

1) Make sure you are in normal page view by going to **View > Normal** on the main menu bar and select the page you want to assign a new master page to it.

2) Right-click on the page in the workspace area and select **Page > Slide Design** from the context menu to open the **Slide Design** dialog (Figure 240).

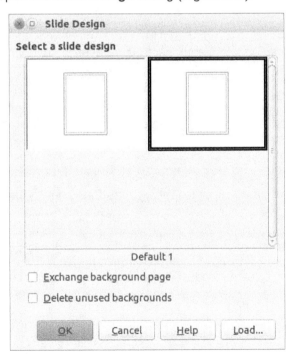

Figure 240: Slide Design dialog

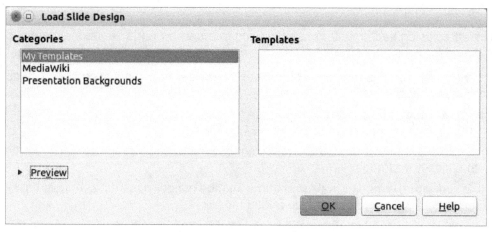

Figure 241: Load Slide Design dialog

3) If necessary, click **Load** to open the **Load Slide Design** dialog and use any predefined Draw master pages or templates (Figure 241).

4) If necessary, select the **Exchange background page** option to use the selected master page for all pages in the drawing.

5) If necessary, select the **Delete unused backgrounds** option to delete any master pages shown in the Slide Design dialog that have not been assigned to a page.

6) Click **OK** to assign the selected master page to your page.

Templates

A *template* is a special type of document that you use as a basis for creating other documents. For example, you can create a template for company drawings so that any new drawing has your company logo and name on the first page and any remaining pages in your drawing only show the company name.

Templates can contain anything that regular documents can contain, such as text, graphics, a set of styles, and user-specific setup information such as measurement units, language, the default printer, and toolbar and menu customization.

All documents created using LibreOffice are based on templates. You can create a specific template for any document type (text, spreadsheet, drawing, or presentation). If you do not specify a template when you start a new document, then the document is based on the default template for that type of document. If you have not specified a default template, LibreOffice uses the blank template for that type of document that is installed with LibreOffice. This default template can be changed, see "Setting default template" on page 210 for more information.

For more information on templates, see the *Getting Started Guide Chapter 3 Using Styles and Templates*.

Note	Draw does not have any predefined templates when it is installed on a computer. However, you can install templates from other sources or create your own templates; these methods are described in the following sections.

Templates from other sources

You can download templates for LibreOffice from many sources, including the official template repository at http://templates.libreoffice.org/, and install them on your computer. On other websites you may find collections of templates that have been created using OpenDocument format that Draw uses as its default format. These templates from other sources are installed using the Extension Manager, as described in "Importing template collections" on page 213.

Some of these templates are free of charge; others are available for a fee. Check the descriptions to see what licenses and fees apply to the ones that interest you. To import individual templates, see "Importing templates" on page 213 for more information and to import a template collection, see "Importing template collections" on page 213 for more information.

Creating templates

1) Open the drawing that you want to use for a template, or open a template that you want to use as a basis for your template.

2) Add any extra content and styles or edit the content and styles in your drawing.

3) Go to **File > Templates > Save As Template** on the main menu bar to open the Template Manager (Figure 242).

4) Open the *My Templates* folder as your destination folder to activate the **Save** icon , then click the **Save** icon.

Alternatively, click on the **New Folder** icon and create your own folder for your Draw templates, then open your own folder to activate the **Save** icon and click the **Save** icon.

5) Type a name for the new template in the *Enter template name* text box.

6) Click **OK** to save the new template in the destination folder.

7) Close the Template Manager.

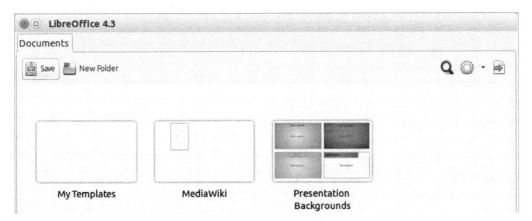

Figure 242: Template Manager as it appears when saving a template

Note	When you are saving a new template, the Template Manager shows only one tab, Documents, as shown in Figure 242. However, when you are creating a document from a template, as described in "Using templates" below, four tabs are shown in the Template Manager (see Figure 243). The new template is automatically displayed on the tabbed page corresponding to that type of template. For example, Draw templates are located on the **Drawings** page.

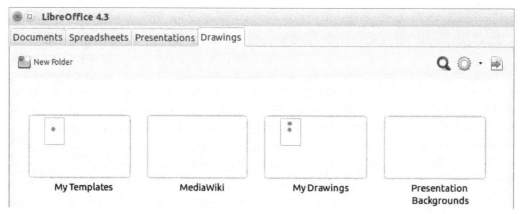

Figure 243: Template Manager when creating a document from a template, showing Drawing templates located in two folders, one of which is user-created. See note below.

Note	The **Drawings tab** shows all Drawing templates, regardless of their location in folders. In Figure 243, the user has created a separate folder for *My Drawings* and has saved one Drawing template in it. If you have not created a separate folder for drawings and saved or moved a template into it, all of your templates will be displayed in the *My Templates* folder; the example shows one Drawing template there.

Using templates

1) Click on **Templates** in the LibreOffice Start Center, or go to **File > New > Templates** on the main menu bar, to open the Template Manager (Figure 243).

2) Click on the **Drawings** tab to open the page containing all the templates for use in Draw.

3) Navigate to the folder that contains the selection of drawing templates you want to use.

4) Select the template you want to use.

5) Click on the **Open** icon on the Template Manager toolbar or double-click on the template. A new drawing will be created using the selected template and the Template Manager dialog will close.

Setting default template

If you create a presentation by using **File > New > Drawing** on the main menu bar and do not select a template, LibreOffice creates the drawing from the default Draw template, which is normally a blank template. However, you can set any drawing template to be the default template, even a template that you have created, so long as it is located in a folder displayed in the Template Manager dialog. You can always reset the default template back to the blank template later if you so choose.

Setting a custom template as default

To set a template that you have created or imported as default instead of using the Draw default template:

1) Click on **Templates** in the LibreOffice Start Center or go to **File > New > Templates** to open the Template Manager and select the **Drawing** tab (Figure 243).

2) Double-click on the *My Templates* folder or the folder that contains the template you want to use to open the folder.

3) Select the template you want to use as the default template.

4) Click the **Set as default** icon ⬚ and your selected template becomes the default template. The next time that you create a new drawing using Draw, the drawing will be created from the default template you have just set.

Resetting default template

To reset the default template for a new drawing to use the Draw default template:

1) Click on **Templates** in the LibreOffice Start Center or go to **File > New > Templates** to open the Template Manager (Figure 243).

2) Select the **Action Menu** icon ⚙ and choose **Reset Default Template** from the drop-down menu. This command does not appear unless the default template has been previously changed to a template of your choosing.

3) Select **Drawing** from the drop-down list to reset the default template. If other modules in LibreOffice have had their default template changed, then these modules will also appear in this drop-down list.

4) The next time that you create a new drawing using Draw, the drawing will be created from the default Draw template.

Editing templates

You can edit template styles and content, and then, if you wish, you can reapply the template styles to drawings that were created from that template.

Note	You can only reapply styles. You cannot reapply content.

Editing

1) Click on **Templates** in the LibreOffice Start Center or go to **File > New > Templates** to open the Template Manager (Figure 243).

2) Navigate to the folder where the template you want to edit is located and click once on it to activate the file handling controls.

3) Select the **Edit** icon ⬚ and the template opens in Draw. Edit the template just as you would any other drawing.

4) To save your changes, go to **File > Save** on the main menu bar.

Updating documents from a modified template

The next time that you open a drawing that was created from the changed template, you will be asked to confirm whether you want to update the styles in your drawing to the formatting used in the modified template.

Click **Update Styles** to update any styles in the template that have been changed in the document. Click **Keep Old Styles** if you do not want to update any styles in the template that have been changed in the document. Whichever option you choose, the message box closes and the drawing opens in Draw.

Note	If you select **Keep Old Styles**, then this message will not appear again the next time you open the document after changing the template it is based on. You will not get another chance to update the styles from the template.

Organizing templates

LibreOffice can only use templates that are in LibreOffice template folders. You can create new LibreOffice template folders and use them to organize your templates. For example, separate template folders for different projects or clients. You can also import and export templates.

Tip	The location of LibreOffice template folders varies with your computer operating system. To learn where the template folders are stored on your computer, go to **Tools > Options > LibreOffice > Paths**.

Creating template folders

To create a template folder:

1) Go to **File > New > Templates** on the main menu bar to open the Template Manager.
2) Select the **Drawings** tab to open the tab for drawings (Figure 243).
3) Click the **New Folder** icon and enter a name for the new folder in the *Enter folder name* box, then click **OK**.
4) Alternatively, click on the template you want to move to a new folder and the file handling controls are displayed.
5) Click the **Move to folder** icon and select **New folder** from the drop list that appears.
6) Type a name for the new folder in the *Enter folder name* box, then click **OK**. The selected template is then moved to the new folder you have just created.

Deleting template folders

You cannot delete the template folders supplied with LibreOffice or installed using the Extension Manager. You can only delete folders that you have created.

To delete a template folder that you have created:

1) Go to **File > New > Templates** on the main menu bar to open the Template Manager.
2) Select the **Drawings** tab to open the tab for drawings (Figure 243).
3) In the Template Management dialog select the folder that you want to delete.
4) Select the **Delete** icon and a message box appears asking you to confirm the deletion. Click **Yes**.

Moving templates

To move a template from one template folder to another template folder:

1) Go to **File > New > Templates** on the main menu bar to open the Template Manager.
2) Select the **Drawings** tab to open the tab for drawings (Figure 243).
3) Navigate to the template that you want to move and then select it.
4) Click the **Move to folder** icon and select the folder from the drop-down list to move your selected template.

Deleting templates

You cannot delete the templates supplied with LibreOffice or installed using the Extension Manager. You can only delete templates that you have created or imported.

To delete a template:

1) Go to **File > New > Templates** on the main menu bar to open the Template Manager.
2) Select the **Drawings** tab to open the tab for drawings (Figure 243).
3) Navigate to the template that you want to delete and then select it.
4) Click the **Delete** icon ⊗ and a message box appears and asks you to confirm the deletion. Click **Yes**.

Importing templates

If the template that you want to use is in a different location, you must import it into an LibreOffice template folder.

To import a template into a template folder:

1) In the Template Manager (Figure 243), navigate to and select the folder into which you want to import the template.
2) Click the **Import** icon and a standard file browser dialog opens.
3) Navigate to the template on your computer that you want to import, select it and click **Open.** The file browser window closes and the template appears in the selected folder.
4) Alternatively, click the **Get more templates from LibreOffice** icon on the right of the Template Manager toolbar to open your web browser at the LibreOffice template page.
5) Locate the template you want to import and select it.
6) Download the template to your computer, then repeat Steps 1 to 3 above to import the template into LibreOffice.

Importing template collections

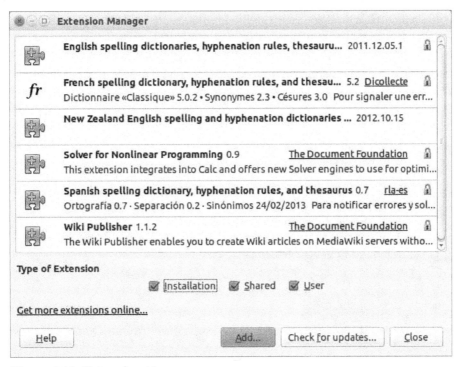

Figure 244: Extension Manager

The Extension Manager (Figure 244) provides an easy way to install collections of templates that have been packaged as extensions. For more about the Extension Manager, see the *Getting Started Guide*.

1) Download the extension package (.OXT file) and save it anywhere on your computer. You can find several templates at http://templates.libreoffice.org/template-center that have been developed for use with LibreOffice.

2) Go to **Tools > Extension Manager** on the main menu bar to open the Extension Manager dialog (Figure 244).

3) Click **Add** to open a file browser window.

4) Find and select the template package you want to install and click **Open**. The package begins installing. You may be asked to accept a license agreement.

5) When the package installation is complete, the templates are available for use through **File > New > Templates** and the extension is listed in the Extension Manager.

Exporting templates

To export a template from a template folder to another location:

1) Go to **File > New > Templates** on the main menu bar to open the Template Management dialog.

2) Select the **Drawings** tab to open the tab for drawings (Figure 243).

3) Navigate to the template that you want to export and then select it.

4) Click the **Export** icon and a standard file browser dialog opens.

5) Navigate to the folder into which you want to export the template and click **OK**.

Multiple layers

Layers in LibreOffice Draw allow you to assemble elements on a drawing page that are related. Think of layers as individual workspaces that you can hide from view, hide from printing, or lock. Any layers that do not contain any objects are transparent.

Layers do not determine the stacking order of objects on your drawing page, except for the **Controls** layer which is always in front of all other layers. The stacking order of objects on your drawing page is determined by the sequence in which you add the objects. You can rearrange the stacking order by going to **Modify > Arrange** on the main menu bar.

Note	You can lock a layer to protect its contents, or hide a layer and its contents from view or from printing. When you add a new layer, the layer is added to all of the pages in your drawing. However, when you add an object to a layer, it is only added to the current drawing page.
	If you want the object to appear on all of the pages (for example, a company logo), add the object to the master page by going to **View > Master**. To return to your drawing, go to **View > Normal**.

Default layers

LibreOffice Draw provides three default layers and these default layers cannot be deleted or renamed.

- **Layout** – is the default workspace and determines the location of title, text and object placeholders on your drawing page.

- **Controls** – used for buttons that have been assigned an action, but should not be printed and the layer properties are set to not printable. Objects on this layer are always in front of objects on other layers.
- **Dimension Lines** – is where the dimension lines are drawn. By switching the layer to show or hide, you can easily switch dimension lines on and off.

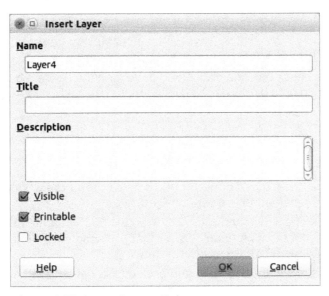

Figure 245: Insert Layer dialog

Inserting layers

1) Right-click the layer tab area at the bottom left of the Workspace area and select **Insert Layer** from the context menu, or go to **Insert > Layer** on the main menu bar to open the **Insert Layer** dialog (Figure 245).
2) Type meaningful names for the layer in the *Name* and *Title* text boxes.
3) If necessary, type a description for the layer in the *Description* text box.
4) Select *Visible* if you want the layer to be visible in your drawing. When *Visible* is not selected, a layer is hidden and the title in the layer tab changes color to blue.
5) Select *Printable* if you want the layer to print when you print your drawing. Not printing is useful if you want use a draft layer for guides or annotations that you use in making the drawing, but do not want to appear in the final output.
6) Select *Locked* to prevent any objects on this layer from deletion, editing, or moving. No additional objects can be added to a locked layer. Locking a layer is useful, for example, when a base plan is to be protected while adding a new layer with other details.
7) Click **OK** and the new layer automatically becomes active.

Modifying layers

1) Right-click on the name tab of the layer and select **Modify Layer** from the context menu or double-click on the name tab to open the **Modify Layer** dialog. This dialog is similar to the Insert Layer dialog in Figure 245.
2) Make your changes to the layer, then click **OK** to save the changes and close the dialog.

Working with layers

Selecting a layer

To select a layer, click on the name tab of the layer at the bottom of the drawing workspace.

Hiding layers

1) Right-click on the name tab of the layer and select **Modify Layer** from the context menu or double-click on the name tab to open the **Modify Layer** dialog.
2) Clear the *Visible* check box and click **OK**. The text on the name tab changes color to blue. Any objects placed on a hidden layer will no longer be visible on the other layers in your drawing.
3) Alternatively, hold down the *Shift* key and click on the name tab to hide the layer.

Showing hidden layers

1) Right-click on the name tab of the layer and select **Modify Layer** from the context menu or double-click on the name tab to open the **Modify Layer** dialog.
2) Check the *Visible* check box and click **OK**. The text for the name tab changes to the default color for text for your computer setup. Any objects placed on a hidden layer will now become visible on the other layers in your drawing.
3) Alternatively, hold down the *Shift* key and click on the name tab to make the layer visible.

Locking layers

1) Right-click on the name tab of the layer and select **Modify Layer** from the context menu or double-click on the name tab to open the **Modify Layer** dialog.
2) Check the *Locked* check box and click **OK** to prevent any modification of the layer.

Unlocking layers

1) Right-click on the name tab of the layer and select **Modify Layer** from the context menu or double-click on the name tab to open the **Modify Layer** dialog.
2) Uncheck the *Locked* check box and click **OK** to allow modification of the layer.

Renaming layers

1) Right-click on the name tab of the layer and select **Rename Layer** from the context menu.
2) Type a new name for the layer and click outside the tab area to save the change.
3) Alternatively, follow the procedure in "Modifying layers" above to rename the layer.

Deleting layers

1) Right-click on the name tab of the layer and select **Delete Layer** from the context menu.
2) Confirm the deletion and the layer and all its objects are deleted.

Note	You can only delete layers that you have added to a drawing. The default layers, Layout, Controls, and Dimensioning, cannot be deleted.

Dimensioning

Draw allows you to dimension objects and display these dimensions to make your drawing look more like an engineering drawing. When you create dimensions, they are automatically placed on the **Dimension Lines** layer (see "Default layers" on page 214 for more information).

Configuring dimensioning

Two ways are available to access the options to configure dimensioning. Both methods use a similar dialog where you can change the length, measurement, and guide properties of a dimension line.

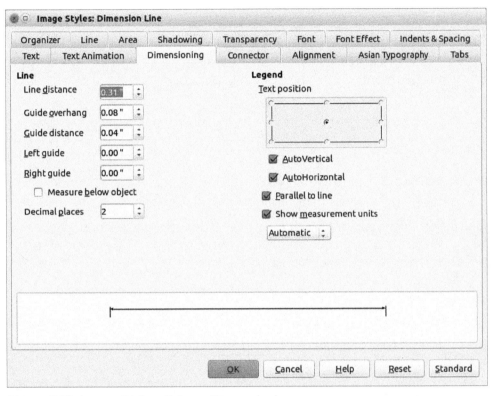

Figure 246: Image Styles dialog – Dimensioning page

Drawing object styles

1) Go to **Format >Styles and Formatting** on the main menu bar, or click on the **Styles and Formatting** icon on the Line and Filling toolbar, or press the *F11* key on your keyboard to open the **Styles and Formatting** dialog.

2) Alternatively, click on the **Styles and Formatting** icon on the Sidebar to open the **Styles and Formatting** section.

3) Right-click on *Dimension Line* in the list of styles and select *Modify* from the context menu to open the **Image Styles** dialog (Figure 246).

4) Click on the **Dimensioning** tab to open the **Dimensioning** options page.

5) Make the changes you want to use for dimensioning using the various options on this page.

6) Click **OK** to save your changes and close the dialog.

7) To reset the dimensioning options to the default properties of the template, click **Standard.**

1) Draw a dimension line. See "Dimensioning objects" on page 219 for more information.
2) Right-click on the dimension line and select **Dimensions** from the context menu to open the **Dimensioning** dialog (Figure 247).

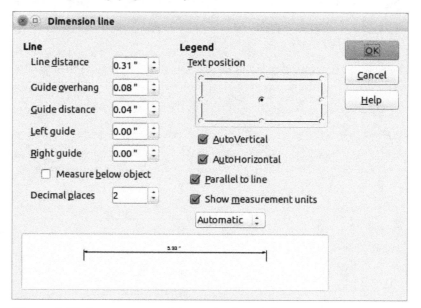

Figure 247: Context menu Dimensioning dialog

3) Make the changes you want to use for dimensioning using the various options on this dialog.
4) Click **OK** to save your changes and close the dialog.

Dimensioning dialog

With reference to Figure 246 and Figure 247, the dimensioning options are as follows.

- **Line** – sets the distance properties of the dimension line and the guides with respect to each other and to the baseline.
  - *Line distance* – specifies the distance between the dimension line and the baseline (line distance = 0).
  - *Guide overhang* – specifies the length of the left and right guides starting at the baseline (line distance = 0). Positive values extend the guides above the baseline and negative values extend the guides below the baseline.
  - *Guide distance* – specifies the length of the right and left guides starting at the dimension line. Positive values extend the guides above the dimension line and negative values extend the guides below the dimension line.
  - *Left guide* – specifies the length of the left guide starting at the dimension line. Positive values extend the guide below the dimension line and negative values extend the guide above the dimension line.
  - *Right guide* – specifies the length of the right guide starting at the dimension line. Positive values extend the guide below the dimension line and negative values extend the guide above the dimension line.
  - *Measure below object* – reverses the properties set in the Line options.
  - *Decimal places* – specifies the number of decimal places used for the display of line properties.

- **Legend** – sets the properties of the dimension text.
    - – *Text position* – determines the position of the dimension text with respect to the dimension line and the guides. The *AutoVertical* and *AutoHorizontal* checkboxes must be cleared before you can assign a text position.
    - – *AutoVertical* – determines the optimal vertical position for the dimension text.
    - – *AutoHorizontal* – determines the optimal horizontal position for the dimension text.
    - – *Parallel to line* – displays the text parallel to or at 90 degrees to the dimension line.
    - – *Show measurement units* – shows or hides the dimension measurement units. You can also select a measurement unit you want to display from the list.

Note	The dimensioning style *Dimension Line* is always linked and stored with the current work page. All the changes that you make apply only to this page. New drawings are started with the standard properties of Draw. If you want to use the amended style for future drawings, save your drawing as a template.

Tip	When dimensioning objects, it is recommended to use the zoom function, guide lines and snap functions so that you can accurately place dimension lines on an object. See *Chapter 3 Working with Objects and Object Points* for more information.

Dimensioning objects

1) Click on the small triangle next to the **Lines and Arrows** icon ⇒ on the Drawing toolbar to open the **Arrows** pop-up toolbar. Note that this icon changes depending on the last **Lines and Arrows** tool used. Also, this toolbar can become a floating toolbar by clicking on the bottom of the pop-up toolbar and dragging it into the workspace.

2) Click on the **Dimension Line** icon ⊢⊣ on the **Arrows** toolbar and the cursor normally changes to a cross. This depends on your computer setup.

3) Position the cursor at one corner of the object, then click and drag the cursor to the other corner of the object to draw the dimension line. To restrict drawing the dimension line in the horizontal or vertical direction, press and hold the *Shift* key while dragging the cursor.

4) Release the mouse button when you reach the other corner of the object and the dimension line is drawn with the dimension automatically added (Figure 248). The dimension line is also placed automatically on the **Dimension Lines** layer; see "Default layers" on page 214 for more information.

5) To edit the text of the dimension, double-click on an unselected dimension line to enter text edit mode and make your changes. Click outside the dimension line to save the changes.

6) To configure the dimension line, see "Configuring dimensioning" on page 217.

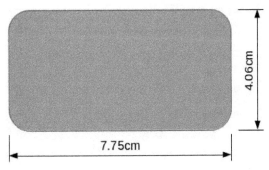

Figure 248: Dimensioning objects

Drawing to scale

In Draw a drawing is made on a predefined drawing area. This is normally Letter or A4 page size depending on your locale, computer setup, and the default printer connected to your computer. However, depending on the actual size of the drawn objects, it is often convenient to reduce or enlarge the drawing by scaling (for example 1:10 or 2:1).

You can specify a scale value by going to **Tools > Options > LibreOffice Draw > General** (Figure 249) and selecting a value from the *Drawing scale* drop-down list. The default setting for this option is 1:1. When you make a change to the drawing scale, it is reflected in the rulers at the top and left side of your drawing.

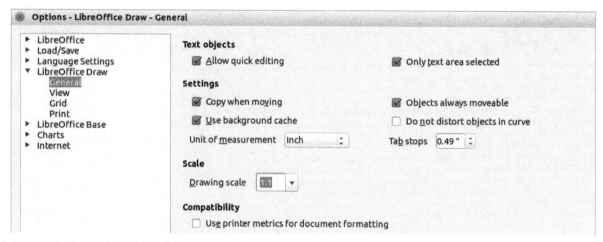

Figure 249: Options LibreOffice Draw dialog -- General page

Any change in the drawing scale has no effect on the basic drawing operations. Draw automatically calculates the necessary values (for example, dimension lines). The spacing of the grid points is independent of drawing scale as the grid is an optical drawing aid and not a drawing element.

An increase in scale (for example 1:4) allows you to draw objects that would not fit into the paper size for your drawing. A decrease in drawing scale (for example 4:1) allows you to draw small objects accurately at an increased size to make them easier to understand. An example of drawing to scale is shown in Figure 250. All three rectangles are the same size.

- The left rectangle was drawn at the default 1:1 scale and dimensioned.
- The drawing scale was then changed to 1:4 and the dimensions were automatically increased by Draw to reflect the decrease in scale for the center rectangle.
- The drawing scale was then changed to 4:1 and the dimensions were automatically decreased by Draw to reflect the increase in scale for the right rectangle.

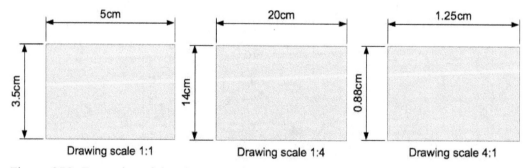

Figure 250: Examples of drawing to scale

Gallery images

Draw includes several images in a **Gallery**. These images are grouped into themes: *Bullets*; *Rulers*; *Homepage*; *Rulers*; *Sounds* and so on. The left pane of the gallery window lists the available themes. Click on a theme to see its images displayed in the right pane of the **Gallery** dialog (Figure 251).

The default themes are read only; no images can be added to or deleted from these themes. The default themes are easily recognizable by right-clicking on each category and the only available option in the pop-up menu is **Properties**.

Any themes that you create are the only themes that are customizable allowing you delete or rename themes and add or delete your own graphics. For more information on creating themes, see "Creating themes and adding images" on page 221.

Figure 251. Gallery dialog

Using the Gallery

1) Click on the **Gallery** icon ![icon] on the Drawing toolbar or go to **Tools > Gallery** on the main menu bar to open the **Gallery** dialog (Figure 251).

2) Alternatively, click on the **Gallery** icon ![icon] on the Sidebar to open the **Gallery** section (Figure 252).

3) Choose a theme in the Gallery dialog or Sidebar Gallery section.

4) Click on an image in the Gallery dialog or Sidebar Gallery section and drag the image into your drawing.

    Alternatively, right-click on a gallery image and select **Insert** from the context menu. The gallery image is pasted into your drawing.

5) Use the tools available in the Picture toolbar to edit the gallery image to your preferences. For more information on editing pictures, see *Chapter 6 Editing Pictures*.

Creating themes and adding images

1) Open the Gallery dialog (Figure 251) or the Sidebar Gallery section (Figure 252) and click New Theme to open the Properties of New Theme dialog (Figure 253).

2) Type a memorable name for your theme in the text box and click **OK**.

3) Right-click on the new theme name that you have created and select **Properties** from the context menu to open the Properties of New Theme dialog (Figure 254) and click on the **Files** tab.

4) Click on **Find Files** to open the Select Path dialog (Figure 255).

5) Browse to the folder that contains the images you want to use.

Figure 252: Sidebar Gallery section

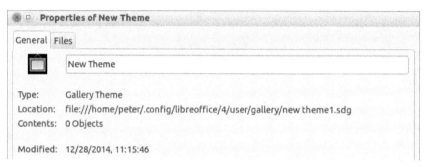

Figure 253. Properties of New Theme dialog – General page

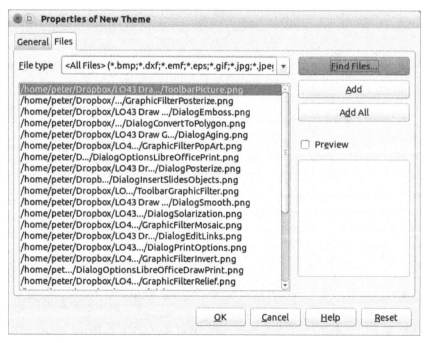

Figure 254. Properties of New Theme dialog – Files page

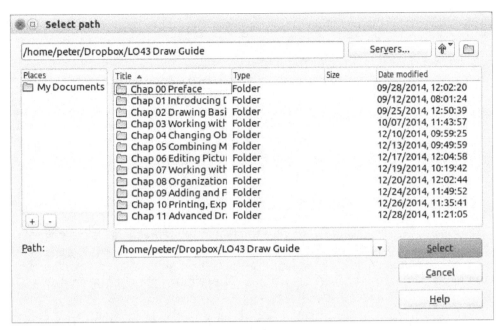

Figure 255. Selecting path for new images in themes

6) Click **Select** to select the files contained in the folder and the Select Path dialog closes. The list of files contained in the folder now appear in the Properties of New Theme dialog.

7) Select the files you want to use in for your new theme and click **Add**. The added files will disappear from the file list and the images will appear in the Gallery.

8) If you want to add all the files in the list, click **Add All**. All the files will disappear from the list and the images will appear in the Gallery.

9) Click **OK** when finished and the Properties of New Theme dialog will close.

Deleting gallery themes and images

You can only delete new themes that you have created and any images that you have added to a new theme.

1) Right-click on on a theme you have created or an image you have added to the Gallery.

2) Select **Delete** from the context menu.

3) A confirmation message appears, asking if you want to delete this object. Click **Yes.**

Note	The image is a linked file and is deleted from the Gallery only. The original image file is not deleted.

Updating the Gallery

All the images in a gallery are linked files. From time to time it is beneficial to update a theme you have created to make sure that all the files are still there. To do so, right-click on a theme you have created and you have added at least one file and then select **Update** from the context menu.

Note	If you wish, you can rename this new theme by manually by right-clicking the theme name and selecting **Rename** from the context menu.

Colors and color palettes

Draw (like all LibreOffice components) uses color palettes for the representation of colors. You can customize the color palette to suit your own needs by modifying colors in a palette, adding other colors, or creating new color palettes.

Note	LibreOffice uses the RGB color model internally for printing in all of its software modules. The CMYK controls are provided only to ease the input of color values using CMYK notation.

Using colors

Two color dialogs are available where you can select, add, modify, edit, or delete colors. Go to **Tools > Options > LibreOffice > Colors** (Figure 256) or **Format > Area > Colors** (Figure 257) on the main menu bar to open these color dialogs. You can also right-click on a selected object and choose **Area** in the context menu, then click on the **Colors** tab to open the **Area** dialog (Figure 257).

Each color value has a numeric value, which can be input directly as numbers. The color values for the RGB color model (Red, Green, and Blue) can be any integer value between 0 and 255. The color values for the CMYK color model (Cyan, Magenta, Yellow, and Black (K)) are percentages. When selecting between the RGB and CMYK color models in both dialogs, the value boxes automatically change to show RGB or CMYK.

When using CMYK values, the conversion to RGB values used in LibreOffice is made automatically. Any modifications made to colors apply only to the active palette in your drawing unless you save the modified color palette for future use.

Tip	More information on color models can be found at http://en.wikipedia.org/wiki/Color_model

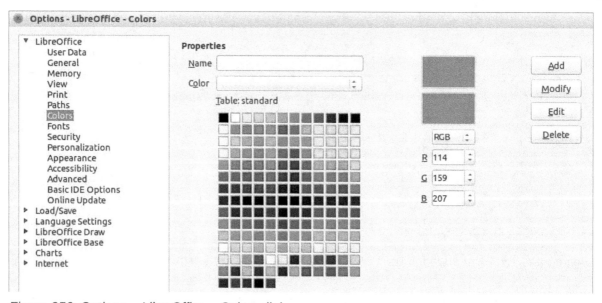

Figure 256: Options – LibreOffice – Colors dialog

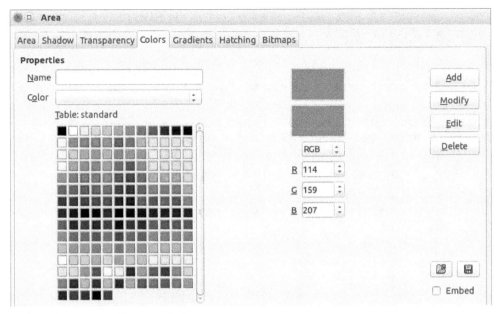

Figure 257: Area dialog – Colors page

Selecting colors

1) Go to **Tools > Options > LibreOffice > Colors** (Figure 256) or **Format > Area > Colors** (Figure 257) on the main menu bar to open a color dialog.

   Alternatively, right-click on a selected object and select **Area** from the context menu, then click on the **Colors** tab to open the color dialog (Figure 257).

2) Select a color from the *Color* drop-down list, or select a color from the color table, or enter the RGB or CMYK values for the color you want to use.

3) Click **OK** to use the selected color and close the dialog.

Color palettes

Use the **Colors** page in the Area dialog (Figure 257) to load color palettes or create and save color palettes for future use.

- Click on the **Load Color List** icon 📁 to open a dialog where you can select a color palette to use in Draw.

- If you have made any changes to the color palette, click on the **Save Color List** icon 💾 to open a dialog where you can save your color palette for future use in Draw. The file format used in LibreOffice for color palettes is .soc.

Note	The **Load Color List** and **Save Color List** icons are only available if you select the color dialog using the **Format > Area > Colors** command or right-click on a selected object and select **Area** from the context menu.

Creating colors

Using color values

1) Select either RGB or CMYK from the drop-down options on the color dialog.

2) Enter integer values or percentage values in each of the RGB or CMYK boxes or use the spinners at the right of each box.

3) The original color is shown the top color sample and the new color is shown in the lower color sample.

4) Click **Modify** to apply and store the new setting in the color palette without changing the color name.

   Or, click **Add** and you will be prompted to give the color a new name. Enter a new name and click **OK** to add the new color to the end of the color list and store it in the currently active palette.

5) Click **OK** to use the modified or new color and close the dialog.

Note	To store your new color in a color palette for future use in Draw, see "Color palettes" on page 225.

Using the Color Picker

You can define colors using the Color Picker dialog (Figure 258).

1) Go to **Format > Area > Colors** on the main menu bar, or right-click on a selected object and go to **Area** in the context menu to open the **Area** dialog and then click on the **Colors** tab to open the **Colors** page of the Area dialog (Figure 257).

2) Click **Edit** to open the Color Picker dialog, where you have three ways to select a color to create and use.

   - Click on the colored bar to the right of the color sample area to select a color. The values in the RGB, HSB (Hue, Saturation, and Brightness) and CMYK boxes will change.

   - Or, enter values in either the RGB, HSB, or CMYK boxes to create the color. Entering values in one set of value boxes will change the values in the other two sets of boxes.

   - Or, click on the small circle in the color sample area and drag it to a new position to create a new color.

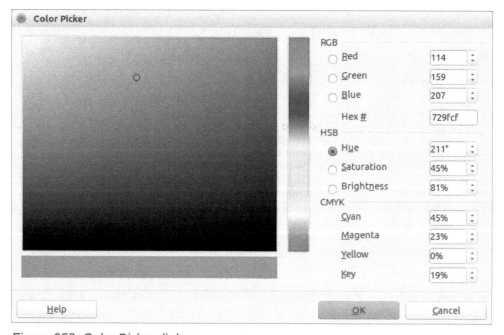

Figure 258: Color Picker dialog

3) The color bar below the sample color area will show the new color on the left half of the bar so that you can compare it with the original color on the right half of the bar.

4) If you are satisfied with the color created, click **OK** to use the color.

5) See "Using color values" on page 225 to save the color.

Deleting colors

1) To delete a color from a color palette, open the color dialog (Figure 256 or Figure 257).

2) Select the color from the **Color** drop-down list or the color table and click **Delete**.

3) Click **Yes** to confirm the deletion of the color.

4) Click **OK** to close the color dialog.

Bézier curves

In LibreOffice you can use Bézier curves in your drawing. A curve is defined by means of a start point P_0, an end point P_3, and two control points P_1 and P_2 (Figure 259). For points on the curve the terms *nodes* or *anchors* are often used. For the mathematical background of Bézier curves, see http://en.wikipedia.org/wiki/Bezier_curve.

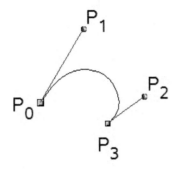

Figure 259: Points in Bézier curves

Bézier curves are very useful for experimenting with the shape and form of curves. In point mode you can change the curve alignment by dragging the points with the mouse. The curve leaves the start point P_0 in the direction of the control point P_1 and arrives at the end point P_3 from the direction of the control point P_2. The more distant a control is from its start or end point the smaller the curvature at that point. If a control point lies directly on one of these points, it has no influence on the curve.

Drawing Bézier curves

1) Click on the small triangle to the right of the **Curve** icon on the Drawing toolbar to open the Lines toolbar (Figure 260). The **Curve** icon on the Lines toolbar is the last tool selected on the Lines toolbar. To make this toolbar a floating toolbar, click at the bottom of the pop-up toolbar and drag it onto the workspace.

2) Click on the **Curve** icon on the Lines toolbar.

Figure 260: Lines toolbar

3) Click at the start point where you want to draw the curve and, keeping the mouse button pressed, drag the cursor to the approximate the position of the end point for the curve.

4) Release the mouse button, then drag the end point of the curve to its end position.

5) Double-click when you have reached the end position of the curve and a curve is drawn. The arc of the curve is determined by the distance you have dragged to create the end point.

6) Click on the **Points** icon 💡 on the Drawing toolbar or press the *F8* key to open the **Edit Points** toolbar (Figure 261).

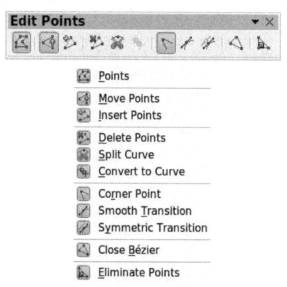

Figure 261: Edit Points toolbar and tools

7) Click once on the curve to display the start and end points. The start point of the curve is larger than the end point.

8) Move the cursor over the start or end point and drag the control point to its correct position, if necessary. As you drag a start or end point, a control point appears at the end of a dashed line connected to the point you have selected (Figure 262).

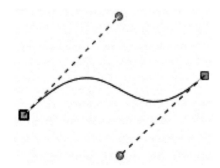

Figure 262: Control points on a curve

9) When you have the position for your start or end point, release the cursor and the control point remains active.

10) Click on the control point and drag it to change the shape of the curve.

11) When you have finished editing the curve, click anywhere on the workspace to deselect the curve and stop editing points.

Edit Points tools

With reference to Figure 261, the tools available on the **Edit Points** toolbar allow you to edit and change the shape of a Bézier curve and are explained as follows:

- **Points** – allows you to activate or deactivate the edit mode for Bézier objects. In the edit mode, individual points of the drawing object can be selected.

- **Move Points** – activates a mode in which you can move points. The mouse pointer displays a small empty square when resting on a point. Drag that point to another location. The curve on both sides of the point follows the movement; the section of the curve between points changes shape. Point at the curve between two points or within a closed curve and drag the mouse to shift the entire curve without distorting the form.

- **Insert Points** – activates the insert mode and allows you to insert points. You can also move points, just as in the move mode. If, however, you click at the curve between two points and move the mouse a little while holding down the mouse button you insert a new point. The point is a smooth point, and the lines to the control points are parallel and remain so when moved. If you wish to create a corner point you must first insert either a smooth or a symmetrical point which is then converted to a corner point by using **Corner Point**.

- **Delete Points** – deletes one or several selected points. If you wish to select several points, click the appropriate points while holding down the *Shift* key. First select the points to be deleted, and then click this icon or press *Delete* key.

- **Split Curve** – splits a curve into two or more curves. Select the point or points where you want to split the curve, then click.

- **Convert To Curve** – converts a curve into a straight line or converts a straight line into a curve. If you select a single point, the curve before the point will be converted. If two points are selected, the curve between both points will be converted. If you select more than two points, each time you click this icon, a different portion of the curve will be converted. If necessary, round points are converted into corner points and corner points are converted into round points. If a section of the curve is straight, the end points of the line have a maximum of one control point each. They cannot be modified to control points unless the straight line is converted back to a curve.

- **Corner Point** – converts the selected point or points into corner points (Figure 263). Corner points have two movable control points, which are independent from each other. A curved line, therefore, does not go straight through a corner point, but forms a corner.

Figure 263: Corner point

- **Smooth Transition** – converts a corner point or symmetrical point into a smooth point (Figure 264). Both control points of the corner point are aligned in parallel and can only be moved simultaneously. The control points may differ in length, allowing you to vary the degree of curvature.

*Figure 264: Smooth transition
point*

- **Symmetric Transition** – converts a corner point or a smooth point into a symmetrical point (Figure 265). Both control points of the corner point are aligned in parallel and have the same length. They can only be moved simultaneously and the degree of curvature is the same in both directions.

*Figure 265: Symmetric transition
point*

- **Close Bézier** – closes a line or a curve. A line is closed by connecting the last point with the first point, indicated by an enlarged square.
- **Eliminate Points** – marks the current point or the selected points for deletion. This happens when the point is located on a straight line. If you convert a curve or a polygon with the **Convert to Curve** tool into a straight line or you change a curve with the mouse so that a point lies on the straight line, it is removed. The angle from which the point reduction is to take place can be set by going to **Tools > Options > LibreOffice Draw > Grid**.

Adding comments to a drawing

Draw supports comments similar to those in Writer and Calc.

1) Go to **Insert > Comment** the main menu bar. A comment box appears with a small marker box containing your initials in the upper left-hand corner of your drawing. Draw automatically adds your name and the date at the bottom of the comment (Figure 266).
2) Type or paste your comment into the text box.
3) To apply basic formatting to the text, right-click and select the formatting option from the context menu.
4) To delete a comment, right-click on the comment or marker box and select an option from the context menu or click on the small triangle in the bottom right of the comment and select an option from the context menu.
5) To move a comment, click on the small marker box and drag it to a new position.
6) To show or hide the comments, go to **View > Comments**.

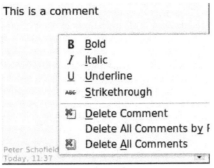

Figure 266: Comment in a drawing

Note	For your initials and name to appear in a comment, you have to enter your user data. Go to **Tools > Options > LibreOffice > User Data** and enter all the necessary data. If more than one person edits the document, each author is automatically allocated a different background color.

Connecting and breaking lines

It is possible in Draw to connect separate line elements together to make one line, or to break a line that is composed of separate elements.

To connect lines, select them and go to **Modify > Connect** on the main menu bar. The lines are converted to curves and adjacent end points are joined together. The resulting shape is a poly line, not a closed shape.

To break a line that is composed of separate elements, select it and go to **Modify > Break**. Each separate element is now indicated with start and end points. Click on an element and drag it to a new position.

Appendix A
Keyboard Shortcuts

Introduction

You can use LibreOffice without requiring a pointing device, such as a mouse or trackball, by using its built-in keyboard shortcuts. Tasks as varied and complex as docking and un-docking toolbars and windows, or changing the size or position of objects can all be accomplished with only a keyboard. Although LibreOffice has its own extensive set of keyboard shortcuts, each component provides others which are specific to its work.

For help with LibreOffice keyboard shortcuts, or using LibreOffice with a keyboard only, search the LibreOffice Help using the "shortcut" or "accessibility" keywords.

In addition to using the built-in keyboard shortcuts (listed in this Appendix), you can also define your own. You can assign shortcuts to standard Draw functions or your own macros and save them for use with Draw only, or with the entire LibreOffice suite.

To adapt shortcut keys to your needs, use the Customize dialog as described in this section.

Tips for Macintosh users

Some keystrokes are different on a Mac from those used in Windows and Linux. The following table gives some common substitutions for the instructions in this book. For a more detailed list, see the application Help.

Windows or Linux	Mac equivalent	Effect
Tools > Options menu selection	**LibreOffice > Preferences**	Accesses setup options.
Right-click	Control+click and/or right-click depending on computer setup	Opens a context menu.
Ctrl (Control)	⌘ (Command)	Used with other keys.
F5	Shift+⌘+F5	Opens the Navigator.
F11	⌘+T	Opens the Styles and Formatting dialog.

Note	Some of the shortcut keys in this appendix may be assigned to your desktop system. Keys that are assigned to the desktop system are not available to LibreOffice. Try to assign different keys either for LibreOffice in **Tools > Customize > Keyboard**, or in your computer system. For more information on customizing LibreOffice, see the *Getting Started Guide*.

Draw-specific function keys and keyboard shortcuts

Function keys

Shortcut Keys	Effect
F1	Opens LibreOffice Draw Help.
F2	Enters text mode, to add or edit text.
F3	Enters group to edit individual objects.
Shift+F3	Opens the Duplicate dialog.
Ctrl+F3	Exits a group.
F4	Opens the Position and Size dialog.
F5	Opens the Navigator.
F7	Check spelling.
Ctrl+F7	Opens the thesaurus.
F8	Turns Edit points on/off.
Ctrl+Shift+F8	Fits text to frame.
Shift+F10	Opens context menu of a selected object.
F11	Opens the Styles and Formatting dialog.

Shortcut keys for drawings

Shortcut Keys	Effect
Plus (+) key	Zooms in.
Minus (-) key	Zooms out.
Multiple (×) Key (number pad)	Zooms to fit entire page in screen.
Divide (÷) Key (number pad)	Zooms in on the current selection.
Ctrl+Shift+G	Groups selected objects.
Shift+Ctrl+Alt+A	Ungroups selected group.
Ctrl+Shift+K	Combines selected objects.
Ctrl+Alt+Shift+K	Un-combines selected objects.
Ctrl+Shift+Plus (+) key	Brings current selection to front.
Ctrl+Plus (+) key	Brings current selection forward.
Ctrl+Minus (-) key	Sends current selection backward.
Ctrl+Shift+Minus (-) key	Sends current selection to back.
Page Up	Switches to previous page.

Shortcut Keys	Effect
Page Down	Switches to next page.
Ctrl+Page Up	Switches to previous layer.
Ctrl+Page Down	Switches to next layer.
Arrow Key	Moves the selected object in the direction of the arrow key.
Ctrl+Arrow Key	Moves the page view in the direction of the arrow key.
Ctrl+click while dragging an object.	Creates a copy of the object being dragged when mouse button is released. Note that this shortcut key works only when the **Copy when moving** option in **LibreOffice > Preferences > LibreOffice Draw > General** is enabled (this option is enabled by default).
Ctrl+Enter with keyboard focus (F6) on a drawing object icon on Tools bar.	Inserts a drawing object of default size into the center of the current view.
Shift+F10	Opens the context menu for the selected object.
F2	Enters text mode.
Enter	Enters text mode if a text object is selected.
Ctrl+Enter	Enters text mode if a text object is selected. If there are no text objects or if you have cycled through all of the text objects on the page, a new page is inserted.
Alt	Press the Alt key and drag with the mouse to draw or resize an object from the center of the object outward.
Alt + click on an object	Selects the object behind the currently selected object.
Alt+Shift + click on an object	Selects the object in front of the currently selected object.
Shift key while selecting an object	Adds or removes object to or from the selection.
Shift key while moving an object	Constrains the movement of the selected object by multiples of 45 degrees.
Shift key while dragging to create or resize an object	Constrains the size to keep the object aspect ratio.
Tab	Cycles through the objects on the page in the order in which they were created.
Shift+Tab	Cycles through the objects on the page in the reverse-order in which they were created.
Esc	Exits current mode.

Page Pane navigation

Shortcut Keys	Effect
Home/End	Sets the focus to the first/last page.
Left/Right arrow keys or Page Up/Page Down	Sets the focus to the next/previous page.
Enter	Creates a new page.

General function keys and keyboard shortcuts

Opening menus and menu items

Shortcut Keys	Result
Alt+<?>	Opens a menu where <?> is the underlined character of the menu you want to open. For example, Alt+F opens the File menu.
	With the menu open, menu items have underlined characters. To access these menu items directly, press the underlined character key. Where two menu items have the same underlined character, press the character key again to move to the next item.
	If an item in a menu has no underlined character, you need to click it directly.
Esc	Closes an open menu.
F6	Repeatedly pressing F6 switches the focus and circles through the following objects:
	• Menu bar
	• Every toolbar from top to bottom and from left to right
	• Every free window from left to right
	• Document
Shift+F6	Switches through objects in the opposite direction.
Ctrl+F6	Switches the focus to the document.
F10 or Alt	Switches to the Menu bar and back.
Esc	Closes an open menu.

Accessing menu commands

Press *Alt* or *F6* or *F10* to select the first item on the menu bar (the **File** menu). With the *right-arrow*, the next menu to the right is selected; with the *left-arrow*, the previous menu. The *Home* and *End* keys select the first and the last item on the Menu bar.

The *down-arrow* opens a selected menu. An additional *down-arrow* or *up-arrow* moves the selection through the menu commands. The *right-arrow* opens any existing submenus.

Press *Enter* to execute the selected menu command.

Accessing toolbar commands

Press *F6* repeatedly until the first icon on the toolbar is selected. Use the right and left arrows to select an icon on a horizontal toolbar. Similarly, use the up and down arrows to select an icon on a vertical toolbar. The *Home* key selects the first icon on a toolbar and the *End* key, the last.

Press *Enter* to activate the selected icon. If the selected icon normally requires a consecutive mouse action, such as inserting a rectangle, then pressing the *Enter* key is not sufficient; in these cases, press *Ctrl+Enter*.

- Press *Ctrl+Enter* on an icon to create a draw object. The draw object will be placed into the middle of the view, with a predefined size.

- Press *Ctrl+Enter* on the Selection tool to select the first draw object in the document. If you want to edit, size, or move the selected draw object, first use *Ctrl+F6* to move the focus into the document.

Navigating and selecting with the keyboard

You can navigate through a document and make selections with the keyboard.

- To move the cursor, press the key or key combination given in the following table.

- To select the characters under the moving cursor, additionally hold down the *Shift* key when you move the cursor.

Key	Function	Plus Ctrl key
Right, left arrow keys	Moves the cursor one character to the left or to the right.	Moves the cursor one word to the left or to the right.
Up, down arrow keys	Moves the cursor up or down one line.	(*Ctrl+Alt*) Moves the current paragraph up or down.
Home	Moves the cursor to the beginning of the current line.	Moves the cursor to the beginning of the document.
End	Moves the cursor to the end of the current line.	Moves the cursor to the end of the document.
PgUp	Scrolls up one page.	Moves the cursor to the header.
PgDn	Scroll down one page.	Moves the cursor to the footer.

Controlling dialogs

When you open any dialog, one element (such as a button, an option field, an entry in a list box, or a checkbox) is highlighted or indicated by a dotted box around the field or button name. This element is said to have the focus on it.

Shortcut Keys	Result
Enter	Activates selected button. In most cases where no button is selected, *Enter* is equivalent to clicking **OK**.
Esc	Closes dialog without saving any changes made while it was open. In most cases, *Esc* is equivalent to clicking **Cancel**. When an open drop-down list is selected, *Esc* closes the list.
Spacebar	Checks an empty checkbox. Clears a checked checkbox.

Shortcut Keys	Result
Up, down arrow keys	Moves focus up and down a list. Increases or decreases value of a variable. Moves focus vertically within a section of dialog.
Left, right arrow keys	Moves focus horizontally within a section of a dialog.
Tab	Advances focus to the next section or element of a dialog.
Shift+Tab	Returns focus to the previous section or element in a dialog.
Alt+Down Arrow	Shows items in a drop-down list.

Getting help

Shortcut Keys	Result
F1	Opens the LibreOffice Help dialog. In LibreOffice Help: jumps to the first help page of the selected tab.
Shift+F1	Turns the cursor into the *What's This?* question mark. Shows the tip for an item underneath the cursor.
Shift+F2	Shows tip for a selected item.
Esc	In LibreOffice Help: goes up one level.

Managing documents

Shortcut Keys	Result
Ctrl+F4 or Alt+F4	Closes the current document. Closes LibreOffice when the last open document is closed.
Ctrl+O	Launches the Open dialog to open a document.
Ctrl+S	Saves the current document. If you are working on a previously unsaved file, the shortcut launches the Save As dialog.
Ctrl+N	Creates a new document.
Shift+Ctrl+N	Opens the Templates and Documents dialog.
Ctrl+P	Opens the Print dialog to print the document.
Ctrl+Q	Closes the application.
Del	In the Save and Open dialogs, deletes the selected files or folders. Items can be retrieved from the Recycle Bin (Trash).
Shift+Del	In the Save and Open dialogs, deletes the selected files or folders. Items are permanently deleted: they can not be retrieved from the Recycle Bin.
Backspace	In the Save and Open dialogs, shows contents of the current directory's parent folder.

Editing

Shortcut Keys	Result
Ctrl+X	Cuts selected items.
Ctrl+C	Copies selected items to the clipboard.
Ctrl+V	Pastes copied or cut items from the clipboard.
Ctrl+Shift+V	Opens the Paste Special dialog.
Ctrl+A	Selects all.
Ctrl+Z	Undoes last action.
Ctrl+Y	Redoes last action.
Ctrl+Shift+Y	Repeats last command.
Ctrl+F	Opens the Find dialog
Ctrl+H	Opens the Find & Replace dialog.
Ctrl+Shift+F	Searches for the last entered search term.
Ctrl+Shift+R	Refreshes (redraws) the document view.
Ctrl+Shift+I	Shows or hides the cursor in read-only text.

Selecting rows and columns in tables

Shortcut keys	Result
Spacebar	Toggles row selection, except when the row is in edit mode.
Ctrl+Spacebar	Toggles row selection.
Shift+Spacebar	Selects the current column.
Ctrl+Page Up	Moves pointer to the first row.
Ctrl+Page Down	Moves pointer to the last row.

Defining keyboard shortcuts

In addition to using the built-in keyboard shortcuts listed in this Appendix, you can define your own keyboard shortcuts. See the *Getting Started Guide* for more information on defining keyboard shortcuts.

Further reading

For help with LibreOffice keyboard shortcuts, or using LibreOffice with a keyboard only, search the LibreOffice Help using the key words "shortcut keys" or "accessibility".

Index

Our apologies that this book has no index. It is produced by volunteers from the LibreOffice community, and no one among the volunteers has updated the index. Our choices were to have no index or to delay publication for so long that it would be very out of date. We decided that "no index" was the best choice.